Sommerset County, Maryland
Orphans Court Proceedings
Volume 2
1823-1838

David V. Heise

HERITAGE BOOKS
2009

HERITAGE BOOKS
AN IMPRINT OF HERITAGE BOOKS, INC.

Books, CDs, and more—Worldwide

For our listing of thousands of titles see our website
at
www.HeritageBooks.com

Published 2009 by
HERITAGE BOOKS, INC.
Publishing Division
100 Railroad Ave. #104
Westminster, Maryland 21157

Copyright © 1997 David V. Heise

Other books by the author:

Somerset County, Maryland Orphans Court Proceedings, Volume 1: 1777-1792 and 1811-1823
Somerset County, Maryland, Orphans Court Proceedings, Volume 3: 1838-1852
Worcester County, Maryland, Orphans Court Proceedings Volume 1, 1777-1800
Worcester County, Maryland, Orphans Court Proceedings Volume 2, 1800-1816
Worcester County, Maryland, Orphans Court Proceedings, MH23, Volume 3, 1816-1832

All rights reserved. No part of this book may be reproduced or transmitted in any form or by any means, electronic or mechanical, including photocopying, recording or by any information storage and retrieval system without written permission from the author, except for the inclusion of brief quotations in a review.

International Standard Book Numbers
Paperbound: 978-1-58549-433-0
Clothbound: 978-0-7884-7622-8

INTRODUCTION

This book, Vol. 2 of the Somerset County, Maryland, Orphans Court Proceedings, covers the period 1823-38. Two libers are abstracted; Book 3, 1823-29, and Book 4, 1829-38.

The original liber covering 1823-29 disappeared from the court house in Princess Anne sometime after it was microfilmed in the 1950's. While I don't like to publish from microfilm, I decided, after seeing that the film was in very good shape, that it would be better to include it, and complete the series. Researchers should make every effort to verify the information in this book from other sources, which should be the rule whenever using published works.

While actual testimony was seldom recorded, there are two cases in Book 3 where it was, and more family information than usual is given. The first is the will of John Austin, and the caveat filed against it, starting on p. 1; the second is the will of Thomas Williams beginning on p. 34. In all cases I have only abstracted the testimony where it gives names and relationships. You will want to go the microfilm to get the full testimony. (A note on the index; the surnames Bennett and Rowe appear on page 97, having been left out at their proper place.)

Book 4, covering 1829-38, is at the Hall of Records, in Annapolis. Also there is a portion of the original minutes covering the period from Jan. 12, 1830 to April 5, 1836. The minutes were the notes actually taken in court, and are in several handwritings. These were later copied into the libers that became the Court Proceedings. Any differences between the two have been noted.

As in Book 3, there are several cases giving actual testimony and more family relationships than usual. These include the will of Elizabeth Dixon, starting on p. 17; the heirs of Revolutionary War veteran James Broadwater, p. 24; the administration of the estate of Gowan White, p. 33; the petition of Hetty Disharoon, p. 34; the will of John Jones (of Benjamin), p. 54; the administration of the estate of Ann Handy, p. 65; the will of Henry Crawford, p. 78; the heirs of veterans Benjamin & John Marshall, p. 88, giving a genealogy to several generations (names include Marshall, Hayman, Morris, Bounds, Banks, White, Smith, Fitzgerald, Riggin, Hall, Swift, Lankford & Ritcher); the heirs of veteran Ezekiel Haynie, p. 109.

Everything in this book has been checked several times to make it as accurate as possible. I hope it will be a help to those who, like myself, have several branches of their family tree that have defied tracing before the early 1800's.

TABLE OF CONTENTS

Book 3, 1823 - 1829..........................1

Index to Book 3............................75

Index to free Negroes without surnames.....97

Index to free Negroes with surnames........97

Index to slaves............................98

Book 4, 1829 - 1838........................101

Index to Book 4............................215

Index to free Negroes without surnames....245

Index to free Negroes with surnames.......245

Index to slaves............................246

SOMERSET COUNTY, MARYLAND

ORPHANS COURT PROCEEDINGS

BOOK 3

Sept. 23, 1823 - June 9, 1829

SOMERSET COUNTY REGISTER OF WILLS

(Orphans Court Proceedings)   MSA C 1794

Somerset County Orphans Court Proceedings, 1823-29

Justices; William Williams, George Jones (of Robt.), Francis H. Waters

Crier; Samuel Heath   Register of Wills; James Polk

Tues., Sept. 23, 1823   William Williams, George Jones (of Robt.)

Orphan; Betsy Jane Aires (of George)
Appointed Guardian; Jane Bennett
Sureties; George A. Dashiell, George Dashiell (of John)

Elijah Lawson, guardian to Mary, Kesandy & Emeline Lawson

Orphan; Alexander S. Evans
Appointed Guardian; Levin Crockett
Sureties; John S. Evans, Robert Jones (of Robert)

William Miles & George B. R. Costen to view estate of Matthias C. T. Beauchamp, in care of John Beauchamp, guardian

William Whayland & Jonathan Huffington to view estate of Alexander & Wilhelmina Waller, in care of William L. Waller, guardian

F. 2   Joshua Jones(?) & Eleanor, his wife, & Harriet Christopher, caveators, vs. William Austin, devisee

William Austin offers for probate writing purporting to be will of John Austin;

1) To son William land, 'Georges Lot', 5 head of nigroes; woman Leah, boy Saul, girl Grace, boy York, boy Benjamin
2) To son Purnell's children, to daughter Harriet Christopher's children, to daughter Ellender Jones' children

F. 3   13 June, 1823   John Austin

Witnesses; Isaac Morris, Benjn. Vincent, John Lawes

Joshua Jones & Elenna, his wife, & Harriet Christopher, by Robert N. Martin, their attorney, enter caveat against will

Harriet Christopher & Ellena, wife of Joshua Jones, are lawful
         children of John Austin. State John Austin was not of a
F. 4   sound mind, will gotten by fraud and not free & voluntary

Replication filed by William Austin, by Thomas Bayly, his attorney; denies caveat. Sworn before William Whayland

F. 5   John Lawes, aged 43, testifies; I wrote will, it was executed at Wm. Vincent's, at Fork Town; I know John Austin 14-15 years; he was little changed, more childish & in his dotage;
F. 6   I recopied will at home

Isaac Morris, aged 35, testifies; states John Austin in right mind; Mr. Vincent's wife & John Richardson were present, & other witnesses

F. 7   Benjamin Vincent, aged 38, testifies; did not sign original
F. 8   will, but signed copy; not sure if John Austin of right mind; contents of copy very different from original; John Austin
F. 9   not a sober man since death of his son George, in Jan. last; John Lawes stated to me that will not of John Austin

Wed., Sept. 24, 1823   William Williams, George Jones (of Robt)

F. 10 John Lawes testifies; states he never said will was not John Austin's; he was sober at will writing; Harriet Christopher,
F. 11 a widow, has three children, the oldest 12-13, the youngest 8-9

F. 12 Benjamin Vincent testifies; states John Lawes & Isaac Morris to receive negro for signing will

William H. Lankford testifies; have known John Austin for 20 years; he was given to intoxication

F. 14 Isaac Morris testifies; denies being offered negro

Tues., Sept. 30, 1823   All Justices present

Adm. cwa of George Aires to pay over to Henry Hyland & Samuel Robertson all property of deceased

Apprentice; Sally Dashiell
Bound to; Joseph Harper(?)

       Elijah Ennis testifies in case of John Austin;
F. 15 states John given to intoxication in latter part of his life; not capable of transacting business I had with him concerning estate of James Toadvine; claims John Lawes told him will was not John Austin's, but that of Billy Austin & Isaac Morris; had
F. 16 conversation with Mr. Lawes at mill belonging to him, & the heirs of Kirk Gunby; John Lawes & his wife, Mary, thought John Austin would be killed by Billy Austin & Isaac Morris once will was written; black woman Vilet brought news of John Austin's
F. 17 death; John Austin left 3 children; Harriet Christopher, a widow, indigent, with 3 or 4 children; Eleanor Jones, wife of Joshua, 3 or 4 children, indigent; William Austin, single; son Purnell, dec., left children in Baltimore; Mr. Austin was
F. 18 around 70 when he died; told me his son William had a child by a Miss Prior; I am a Justice of the Peace in Worcester
F. 19 Co., & had not issued a warrant for Miss Prior, as she lived in Somerset Co.; he said she lived in Worcester Co., at
F. 20 Sally Sturgis'; only his son William lived with him; Mrs. Christopher lives in a house rented from widow of James Toadvine; Priscilla Toadvine had mill near Harriet's house

F. 21   Levin Hitch testifies; William Austin & Isaac Morris came to
F. 22   my shop to get John Austin to sign all his negroes over to
        William; he refused; they went across street to Tilghman's
store to get him some grog, to try to change his mind

F. 23   Polly Morris testifies;
F. 24   I am the wife of Isaac Morris

F. 26   Wed., Oct. 1, 1823   All Justices present

William Pollitt, aged 66, testifies in case of John Austin; I have
known John Austin 40 years; mentions Levi Stevens

F. 27   Isaac Toadvine testifies; heard John Lawes, at Elijah Ennis',
        state will not that of John Austin

F. 29   William Williams, f.n.(?), Tony Tank(?) testifies; states
        John Austin drunk on day of death; mentions Wooden-legged
Levin

F. 30   William Taylor testifies;
F. 31   John Austin lived off his plantation; I was his blacksmith

F. 32   John Richardson testifies

F. 35   Samuel Vincent testifies; heard John Austin state he would
        not leave any property to daughters; I am brother of Benjamin
F. 36   Vincent; was sitting with Capt. Hooper, at his store; he said
        to Benjamin Vincent, 'your whiskey has killed John Austin'

Mon., Oct. 13, 1823   All Justices present

Apprentice; John Dixon
Bound to; Jesse Bozman

F. 37   Benjamin Vincent testifies in case of John Austin ; says
        actual contents of will were, to Harriet Christopher, one
negro; to Joshua Jones' children, one negro; rest to son Billy; Mr
Austin had will and asked me to sign it; Mr. Lawes brought different
will

F. 40   Arthur Burroughs testifies; first time I saw John Austin, the
        day after I was married, 4th of Apr.

F. 41   Isaiah Toadvine testifies; John Austin told me he would cut
        off Harriet Christopher without shilling, and Jones would not
get one cent

F. 42   Benjamin Vincent testifies

Tues., Oct. 14, 1823   All Justices present

Thomas Humphreys, exe. of Betty Nicholson

F. 43   Orphan; Charlotte James, Esther A. C. Nelson
            Appointed Guardian; Charlotte Nelson
            Sureties; Levin Crockett, Charles Venables

James Donoho, adm. of John Donoho

Jesse Hughes & Shiles Crockett to view estate of Charlotte & Esther Nelson (of James T.), in care of Charlotte Nelson, guardian

Joseph Leonard, adm. cwa of Mary Smith

Citation issued for James Holland, guardian to Stephen Dryden, to deliver to ward estate of Peggy Dryden

F. 44   Orphan; Joseph Leonard (of John)
            Appointed Guardian; Elihu Jackson
            Sureties; Jesse Walter, Levin Crockett

Orphan; Henrietta, George P., Maria Jones (of Levin)
Appointed Guardian; Mary Jones
Sureties; Charles Jones, Geo. Jones (of Robert)

Settlement in guardian account of William Hilly(?) against James Goslee, for building a mill in 1816, to be stricken out

Sarah Tilghman, guardian to Esther E. W. Tilghman

Francis Waters, former guardian to Levin & Arnold Waters

Jane Bennett, adm. of Edmond

Mon., Oct. 20, 1823   Francis H. Waters, William Williams present

F. 45   Benjamin Fooks testifies in case of John Austin; John Lawes told me will was not Captain Austin's

Jonathan Huffington testifies

F. 46   John Lawes testifies

F. 47   Isaac Morris testifies; John Austin said he would not leave
F. 48   anything to Harriet, because she said he wanted Billy to
            marry, so he could have her while Billy was at sea; and
nothing to Jones, because he tried to get his property when his son
George died; he did plan to give $50 to each of his grandchildren,
            including those of his deceased son Purnell; I have written
F. 49   three wills for John Austin; one in Jan., after the death of
            his son George; one in March, when his son William was
reported drowned at Norfolk

James Wilson, adm. of Elizabeth Waters

Tues., Oct. 21, 1823   William Williams, George Jones (of Robt.)

James Goslee & William Twilley to view estate of George P., Maria & Henrietta Jones (of Levin D.), in care of Mary Jones, guardian

F. 50   James Goslee & William Twilley to divide negroes from estate of Levin D. Jones, among widow & children

Tues., Nov. 4, 1823   William Williams, George Jones (of Robt.)

James Wilson, guardian to Arnold Waters, to sell negroes to pay debt due adms. of William G. Waters, said negroes given to said orphan are more than his share of his father's estate

Mrs. Jane Bennett, guardian to Samuel G. W. & Martha Jane Bennett

F. 51   Tues., Nov. 18, 1823   William Williams, George Jones (of Robt.) present

Molly Cox, guardian to Sally Marshall

Sally U. Adams, guardian to Edward & Louisa(?) Adams

Sally Powell, guardian to Mary A. P. Smulling

Wed., Nov. 19, 1823   All Justices present

Orphan; John B. Slemons, Mary E. McBryde
Appointed Guardian; Elizabeth McBryde
Sureties; Samuel McBryde, William Done

Court declares will of John Austin good & valid

F. 53   Nov. 25, 1823   William Williams, George Jones (of Robt.)

Nancy Cottingham, adm. of Thomas Cottingham

Orphan; Henry W., Eliza A. C., Elizabeth R. Dashiell
Appointed Guardian; Chapman Dashiell
Sureties; James W. Dashiell, Doughty Bounds

Robert Stewart & James C. Dashiell to view estate of above children

F. 54   Ann Lowes, adm. of Tubman Lowes

Eleanor Collier, adm. of Esme Collier

James Holland, guardian to Stephen Dryden, to sell negroes Tom, Maria & Sam, to pay over to estate of Peggy Dryden

Eleanor Collier, adm. of Esme Collier, to sell negro Charlotte

Wed., Nov. 26 [1823]   All Justices present

Benjamin I. Jones & Geo. D. Atkinson to liquidate accounts between Doughty Bounds, & heirs of Samuel Acworth

Thomas Goslee & John S. Evans to divide negroes from estate of Esme Collier

F. 55   James Wilson, adm. of Elizabeth Waters

William Done & George Handy to divide negroes from estate of Elizabeth Waters

Apprentice; John (negro)
Bound to; Jesse Bosman, revoked
Bound to; William Scofield

Division of negroes from estate of Richardson Donoho annulled; Littleton Aires & Matthias Dashiell to redivide

Ordered that all legacies of heirs of Matthias Miles abate(?) in proportion, except a bond of Benjamin Simpson, given to Mary Ann Jones & Nancy Irving

Adm. of John C. Stewart to seek counsel as to whether or not Henry Riggin & wife entitled to part of estate

F. 56   Thurs., Nov. 27, 1823   All Justices present

Levin Tyler, guardian to Elizabeth, Sally N., William T. & Henry White

Tues., Dec. 16, 1823   Francis H. Waters, William Williams present

John Rider, exe. of Mary Townsend

F. 57   Arthur W. Burroughs, adm. cwa of John Austin

John H. Bell & Obediah Stanford to adjust accounts between exes. of Joseph Cottman, & Daniel Whitney

Dec. 30, 1823   Francis H. Waters, William Williams present

George D. Atkinson & Benjamin Jones to adjust accounts of William Harris, exe. of Samuel Acworth, & Doughty Bounds

F. 58   Matthias Dashiell, guardian to L. F. Dashiell

George Hopkins, guardian to Margaret & Eleanor Wailes

Sally U. Adams, guardian to Edward & Louisa Adams

William Whayland, adm. of James Hughes

William Crockett, guardian to Jesse H. Wainright

James Donoho, adm. of John Donoho

F. 59   James Donoho, adm. of John Donoho, to sell negro Jacob

Tues., Jan. 13, 1824   Francis W. Waters, William Williams present

Orphan; Elizabeth W. Hurley (of Dorchester Co.)
Appointed Guardian; John Hurley (of same)
Sureties; James Bounds, William Bounds

Wm. W. Moore, adm. cwa of Mary Cottingham

James Tyler, adm. of William Croswell

F. 60   William Pollitt, adm. of William Bell

Josiah Furnace, guardian to William & Henry J. C. Furnace

R. Sampson, guardian to Jos. Heath's heirs

Gideon Bradley, guardian to Mary Dean

Henry Gale, adm. of James Weatherly

William Sudler & Isaac Beauchamp to view estate of William Turpin's heirs, in care of Henry Maddux

Henry Maddux, guardian to John & E. L. Turpin

Rosanna A. Wainright, guardian to E. J. C., Ann F. D. & R. E.(?) M. J. Wainwright

Levin Morris, guardian to William & Alex.(?) Waller

F. 61   Exe. of Matthias Miles to sell legacies left to widow, & at death, to Matthias & Levin Miles

John W. King, exe. of Whittington King

James Stewart, adm. of John C. Stewart, to sell negroes to pay claim of Bank of Salisbury on estate

F. 62   Wed., Jan. 14, 1824   Francis H. Waters, William Williams

James Dashiell & Robert Stewart to view estate of Henry W. & Eliza A. C. Dashiell, in care of Chapman Dashiell

Isaac Denson & wife, guardian to Henry J. W. Dashiell

Leah Irving, guardian to Levin Irving

Priscilla Traverse, guardian to Matthew, Alce & Edwd. Traverse

John Insley, guardian to Priscilla Dunn

Jesse Hughes & George D. Atkinson to view estate of Priscilla Dunn, in care of John Insley

William Matthews & David Jones to report on work on the dwelling house, kitchen & c., on farm of Samuel T. Bounds, orphan, in care of Geo. Jones (of Geo.)

Tues., Jan. 27, 1824   Francis H. Waters, William Williams present

F. 63   Hancock Shrieves, adm. of Joseph Stevenson

Beauchamp D. Adams, guardian to E. R. & Julia Moore

Orphan; E. R. Moore
Guardian; B. D. Adams, revoked
Appointed Guardian; William Aikman

Charles Jones & Robert Leatherbury to divide negroes from estate of Levin King

F. 64   Tues., 9 Mar., 1824   William Williams, George Jones (of
                                Robt.) present

Anna Beauchamp, guardian to Isaac Beauchamp

Noah Holland, guardian to Samuel & Smith Holland

Orphan; Sophia A. M., Henry A. P.(?), Berry T. T., Alexander W. W. Webster (of Michael)
Appointed Guardian; Elizabeth Webster
Sureties; John Webster, Jun., Bennett Gibson

Willin Wright, guardian to Henry Wright

F. 65   William Evans & Traverse Daniel to view estate of Sophia A.
         M., Henry A. P., Berry T. T. & Alexander W. W. Webster (of Michael), in care of Elizabeth Webster, guardian

William Whayland, guardian to Joseph, Eleanor, Isaac, George, John & Robert Price

James T. Bennett, adm. of Joshua Bennett

Samuel Handy, adm. of Simon Horsey

F. 66   Admx. of William Kelly to sell negro Ann

John Goslee, 2nd adm. of Asa Leatherbury

Isaac M. Adams & Whittington Polk to view estate of heirs of Joseph Stevenson, in care of Handcock Shreves

James Herron, guardian to Ann C. J. Dashiell

Ann Beauchamp, guardian to Aliceana Beauchamp

Thomas Marshall, guardian to Isaac T. & Josias Marshall

Thomas Robinson, guardian to Jacob Marshall

F. 67   William Boggs, guardian to [Isaac crossed out] Thomas Gibbons

James Wilson, adm. cwa of Jesse Long

Stephen Ward & wife, guardian to Thomas M. & George F. Ward

John S. Evans, guardian to James W., Robert & John Dougherty

Wed., Mar. 10, 1824   William Williams, George Jones (of Robt.)

William Whayland, adm. of James Hughes

F. 68   Betsy Coulbourn, exe. of John Coulbourn

Elizabeth Kelly, adm. of William Kelly

Henry K. Long & wife allowed same commission as Henry Curtis, former exe. of Thomas Curtis

Henry K. Long & wife, surviving exe. of Thomas Curtis, to pay to John C. Wilson, Jun., & Arnold E. Jones, adms. cwa of said dec.

Tues., Mar. 23, 1824   William Williams, George Jones (of Robt.)

Henry Moore, guardian to William H. Moore

F. 69   John Walter, adm. cwa of John Jones (of James)

James Wilson, adm. cwa of Jesse Long, to sell negroes; James, Jesse, Zadock & Matilda Long

Tues., Apr. 13, 1824   All Justices present

Mary Curtis, guardian to Edward W., Henry James, Susan A., Elizabeth W. & Sarah T. Curtis

Betsy Broughton, guardian to William Broughton

F. 70   James Donoho, adm. of John Donoho, to sell negro man Jacob

Priscilla Dashiell, guardian to Robert, Edward, Anne, John, Isabella, Priscilla & Sarah Dashiell (of Peter)

John Hopkins, guardian to Kitturah H. Acworth

Stephen Collins, guardian to William S. Broughton

James Wilson, one of exes. of George S. Wilson, to proceed to Baltimore &, if necessary, to Washington, at expense of estate, to attend to business of U.S. against dec.

Amelia Bedsworth, guardian to Arnold H. & Edward J. Ballard

Adm. cwa of estate of Thomas Curtis, by Arnold E. Jones & John C. Wilson, Jun., revoked; Henry K. Long & wife reinstated

F. 71   Orphan; John, Henrietta F. King (of Levin)
Appointed Guardian; Margaret King
Sureties; Littleton Pollitt, Planner H. King

Wm. R. Moore, guardian to Elizabeth R. Moore

Citation issued for Levin Tull to answer interrogations regarding estate of Whittington King

Tues., Apr. 20, 1824   All Justices present

James C. Coulbourn, guardian to Emeline B. Parker

Orphan; Elizabeth E. Nelson
Appointed Guardian; Henry Crawford
Sureties; William Harris (of Wm.), John Bounds

Robert Bell, guardian to Robert Bell

James Goslee, adm. cwa of Thomas Goslee

F. 72   Esther H. Cottman, guardian to Joseph [& Sarah, crossed out] Cottman

John Beauchamp, guardian to Matthias C. T. Beauchamp

William Harris, guardian to Thomas D. Evans

Henry Hyland, guardian to James C. H. Hyland

Samuel G. Holbrook, guardian to Edward H., Rebecca A. & Sarah Jane Holbrook

Citation issued for Sarah Hyland, former adm. of Lambert Hyland, to shew cause why she doesn't return account of negro hire for 1822

John P. Langford, guardian to Aaron C. Langford

Elizabeth Acworth, guardian to John L.(?) Moore

William Boggs & Joseph Handy to view estate of Thomas M. & George F. Ward (heirs of John H.), in care of Stephen Ward, guardian

F. 73   Wed., Apr. 21, 1824   All Justices present

Peregrine Weatherly & Samuel Walter to view estate of Beauchamp, Rachael, James & Sarah Ann Rhodes, in care of Wm. Wilson, guardian

Orphan; John A. H., Joseph Cottman
Appointed Guardian; Sally Cottman
Sureties; Esther H. Cottman, George Jones (of Robt.)

Adm. of Daniel Maddux

John W. King, exe. of Whittington King

John S.(?) Dunn, adm. of Peggy Dunn

F. 74   Elijah Dougherty, guardian to Benjamin H. & Henry Matthews

Thomas K. Carroll, Daniel Ballard & William Boggs to adjust accounts between William Roach, & Betsy Coulbourn, exe. of John Coulbourn

Robert Leatherbury & Samuel Polk to view estate of John A. H. & Joseph Cottman, in care of Sally Cottman, guardian

James Holland, guardian to Stephen Dryden

Thomas Humphreys, exe. of Betty Nicholson

George Hopkins, guardian to Jane, Leah & Margaret Dashiell

Amelia Bell, guardian to Nathaniel Bell

Orphan; Teresa Ann Jones
        Appointed Guardian; George J. (?) Jones
F. 75   Sureties; Levin D. Jones, William M. Jones

William Wilson, guardian to Beauchamp, Rachael, James & Sarah Ann Rhodes

William Wilson, guardian to James Rhodes, to sell negro Sam

Thurs., Apr. 22, 1824   All Justices present

Betsy Coulbourn, exe. of John Coulbourn, to sell vessel on the stocks

F. 76   Tues., Apr. 27, 1824   All Justices present

Matthias C. Taylor, exe. of Margaret Fitchett

George B. R. Costen, exe. of Matthias C. Taylor

George Jones (of George), guardian to Samuel T. Bounds

William Reddish, guardian to Noah, James & Joseph Handy

Isaac M. Adams, adm. of Samuel Adams

Isaac M. Adams, exe. of Thomas M. Jones

George B. R. Costen, adm. dbn of Margaret Fitchett

F. 77   John P. Langford, guardian to Nathan J. & Benjamin Langford

Tues., May 11, 1824   All Justices present

Citation issued for John L.(?) Dunn, adm. of Margaret Dunn, at instance of John Insley

William W. Moore, guardian to Thomas P. Adams

Philip M. Donoho, guardian to John L. W. Stanford

Leah H. Stanford, adm. of William Stanford; mentions children

F. 78   Littleton Tyler, adm. cwa of Ann Tyler

Elizabeth Kelly, adm. of William Kelly

George B. R. Costen, adm. dbn of Margaret Fitchett

F. 79   Tues., 25 May, 1824   All Justices present

John Mason, guardian to Henry, Hamilton, Eleanor & Benjamin Evans

Francis D. Nelson, guardian to Hamilton, Francis & Amelia Mitchell

Eleanor Collier, adm. of Esme Collier

William Miles, guardian to Mary Ann, James K., William, Amelia & John Gunby

James Powell, guardian to Henry Smulling

James Russell, guardian to Nelly, Robert & Levin Russell

Apprentice; Josiah Bayly
Bound to; James McGee, on 19 Feb., 1822, revoked
Bound to; John Johnston

F. 80   Tues., 8 June, 1824   William Williams, George Jones (of Robt.) present

Thomas Humphreys, guardian to Eleanor McCree

John S.(?) Dunn, adm. of Peggy Dunn

Henry Crawford, adm. of John Crawford

Royston Weatherly, adm. of John Weatherly

[crossed out] John Dryden, guardian to Littleton Dryden

[crossed out] Lucretia Harris, guardian to John Harris

[crossed out] Henry Crawford, guardian to Elizabeth E. Nelson

[crossed out] Wm. Humphriss(?), guardian to Charles E. M. Collier(?)

Henry Gale, adm. of James Weatherly

F. 81   Tues., 22 [Mar.], 1824   Francis H. Waters, George Jones (of Robt.) present

Sale of negroes by Elizabeth Kelly, adm. of William Kelly, disapproved

Isaac Nicols, adm. of Joseph B. Russom

F. 82   Chapman Dashiell, guardian to Henry W., Eliza Ann C. & Elizabeth R. Dashiell

Tues., Aug. 10, 1824   All Justices present

Seth Wilkins, adm. of John Wilkins

F. 83   John Insley, adm. of Philiss Nutter (free negro)

George Jones (of Geo.), guardian to Tubman Bounds, to give counter security to John Insley & Charles Jones, his sureties

Thomas Walker, adm. of George Ansley

F. 84   Joshua Brattan & Charles Venables to view estate of William & Robert Russum, in care of Isaac Nichols, adm. of William Russum

Moses C. Smith, adm. cwa of William Hilman

John Rider, exe. of Mary Townsend

Citation issued against John Adams (of John), to answer interrogations regarding his father's estate

Attachment issued against James W. Dashiell, for contempt, & to shew cause why he does not deliver to the adm. of John Adams, papers belonging to estate

Citation issued for all interested in will of Matthias Costen Taylor, to wit; George B. R. Costen, exe. & legatee; Matthias C.
F. 85   Beauchamp, Margaret T. Boston, Thomas H.(?) Newton, Samuel Smith Costin (of Wm.) & Isaac Harris Costin (of Wm.)

Jonathan Huffington, guardian to George & Sally Wallis

Jacob Cullin, guardian to Walter Cullin

Orphan; William D., Theodore, Eleanor, Margaret Phillips
Appointed Guardian; Elijah Phillips
Sureties; Francis D. Nelson, Asa Phillips

Orphan; Hetty, William, Asbury, Elizabeth Ansley (of George)
Appointed Guardian; Thomas Walker
Sureties; Charles Venables, Levin Crockett

Charles Venables & Levin Crockett to view estate of heirs of George
Ansley

Betsy Broughton, adm. of James Broughton

F. 86   Arnold E. Jones & Robert Leatherbury to adjust accounts
between Dr. John King, & adm. of Wm. Bell

Orphan; Josiah S.(?) W. Heath
Appointed Guardian; William Fleming
Sureties; Charles Jones, Joseph Richards

Tues., 17th   All Justices present

Orphan; John, Mary, Severn T. Croswell
Appointed Guardian; Zipporah Croswell
Sureties; John Mason, Charles Parks

Orphan; Samuel Collins, Patty Ann, Rebecca Mary Broughton
Appointed Guardian; Stephen Collins
Sureties; L.(?) R. King, John H. Cohoon

Maria Twilley, adm. of William Twilley

F. 87   Jehu Parsons, guardian to Henry A. Smith

William Twilley & James Goslee to view estate of children of Levin D.
Jones

James Donoho, exe. of Richardson Donoho

Charles Elzey, guardian to William Hillman(?)

Henry Crawford & wife, guardian to E. E. Nelson

William Hopkins, guardian to Charles E. M. Collier

Lucretia Harris, guardian to John Harris

Tues., 24th   Francis H. Waters, George Jones (of Robt.) present

Exe. of George S.(?) Wilson to pay debt due U.S.; mentions Littleton
D. Teackle

F. 88   Elizabeth Taylor, by Thomas Bayly, her attorney, files
petition for half of the personal estate of her dec. husband

Job Moore, adm. of Stephen Moore, to sell negro Frank

'15'

Tues., 7 Sept., 1824   All Justices present

Isaac Atkinson, exe. of Sarah Ann Leatherbury

F. 89   Henry Newman & George Wallace, exes. of Henry Walston Miles

William Costin, exe. of Isaac Harris

Sept. 21, 1824   All Justices present

F. 90   Littleton D. Maddux, guardian to Henry D. & Sarah S.(?) Maddux

John Dryden, guardian to Littleton Dryden

Horsey Summers, exe. of Isaac Summers

John H. Anderson to adjust accounts between George H. Gale, dec., & George D. Atkinson, in their partnership capacitys

Thomas Walston & Thomas Slocomb to view estate of Esther E. W. Tilghman (of William), in care of Sarah Tilghman, guardian

Apprentice; Arnold H. Ballard
Bound to; James Polk
Trade; business of Register of Wills

Tues., 28 Sept., 1824   All Justices present

Col. Levin Pollitt allowed interest for account against Jesse Wainright, dec.

F. 91   Louisa James, exe. of Francis U. James, to give counter security to Wm. T. Polk & James Anderson

Esther Broughton, adm. of Josiah Broughton

Orphan; William E. Waters
Guardian; Col. W. Jones, revoked
Appointed Guardian; Elizabeth A. W. Waters
Sureties; Col. Wm. Jones, George Jones (of Robt.)

James Stewart & William Costen to view estate of Levin & Arnold Waters (of William G.), in care of James Wilson, guardian

James Stewart & William Costen to view estate of Levin, Arnold & William E. Waters (of William G.), in care of James Wilson & Elizabeth A. W. Waters [William Jones, Sen., crossed out] , guardians

F. 92   Esther Broughton, adm. of Josiah, to sell negroes; Hamilton, Robert, Isaac, Ebben. Ned(?) & Flora

[folio numbers only appear sporadically from this point on, and when they do, they are sometimes wrong, which I will note as needed]

Tues., 12 Oct., 1826[4]   Francis H. Waters, William Williams present

Daniel Dakes, adm. cwa of Stephen Dakes

Louisa Fack(?), alias Louisa James, exe. of Francis U. James, revoked, for refusal to give counter security to William T.(?) Polk & James Anderson; James Barkly appointed adm. cwa

F. 93   Tues., 2 Nov., 1824   William Williams, George Jones (of Robt.) present

Turner(?) Davis, adm. cwa of Samson Davis

Abraham Wilson, adm. of Sally Cottingham

Elihu Jackson, guardian to Joseph Leonard

Isaac Nicols, adm. dbn of William Russum, to sell negro Levin

F. 94   Orphan; Henry, Henrietta, Ann Eliza, Patty, Alexgean(?) & Jane Amelia Davis (of Samson)
Appointed Guardian; Nancy Davis
Sureties; Turner(?) Davis, Charles Hammond

Orphan; Winder Cannon (of Burton, dec.)
Appointed Guardian; Burton Cannon
Sureties; Joseph Richards, John W. B. Parsons

James Wilson, adm. of Elizabeth E. Waters

William Costen, Sen., & William Miles to view estate of Winder Cannon (of Burton), in care of Burton Cannon, guardian

Elijah Parsons & David Howard to view estate of Henry, Henrietta, Ann Eliza, Patty, Alexgean(?) & Jane Amelia Davis, in care of Nancy Davis, guardian

F. 95   Tues., 23 Nov., 1824   Francis H. Waters, William Williams

Joseph Leonard, exe. of Joseph Leonard

Robert Stewart, adm. of George D. Atkinson

Joseph Barkley, adm. cwa of Francis W. James

F. 96   Handcock Shreves, adm. of Joseph Stevenson

Orphan; Maria Gale, William W., George W., Eleanor A., Benjamin, Stephen Mills (of Benjamin)
Appointed Guardian; Mary Mills
Sureties; Jonathan Waller, Isaac Mills

'17'

Edward Fowler & Jonathan Waller to view estate of Maria G., William W., George W., Eleanor A., Benjamin & Stephen Mills, in care of Mary Mills, guardian

Charles Venables & Levin Crockett to view estate of Hetty, William, Asbury & Elizabeth Ansley, in care of Thomas Walker, guardian

Wed., 24 Nov., 1824   All Justices present

F. 97   Lucretia Dickerson, adm. of William Dickerson

William Wilson, guardian to children of Charles Rhodes, to survey land

Apprentice; John Price
Bound to; William Crockett
Trade; Taylor

Tues., 30 Nov., 1824   Francis H. Waters, William Williams present

Chapman Dashiell, guardian to Henry W., Eliza A. C. & Elizabeth R. Dashiell

F. 98   Tues., 14 Dec., 1824   All Justices present

Josiah Johnson, adm. of Josiah Johnson

Elijah Gunby, adm. of Esther Gunby

James Ward, adm. of Eleanor Ward

F. 99   William Harris, exe. of Samuel Acworth

John H. Anderson & John Woolford to adjust accounts between Josiah Broughton, dec., & Samuel Heath

Littleton Aires & Benjamin I. Jones to divide negroes from estate of Samuel Acworth, between widow & representatives

William Costen & William Miles to view estate of Winder Cannon, in care of Burton Cannon, guardian

Molly Cox, guardian to Sally Marshall

F. 100   Levin Tyler, guardian to Henry, William T., Sally N. & Elizabeth White

Elijah Lawson, guardian to Emeline Lawson

Priscilla Traverse, guardian to Matthew Traverse

Sally Powell, guardian to Mary Ann Smulling

Peregrine Weatherly & Samuel Walter to view estate of Beauchamp, Rachael, James & Sarah Ann Rhodes, in care of William Wilson, guardian

James Vincent, adm. cwa of Eli Vincent

William Costen, exe. of Isaac Harris

F. 101   William Aikman, guardian to Elizabeth Moore, offers George M. Willing & Hope Adams as counter security to indemnify Thomas Gillis

William Whayland, adm. of James Hughes

Tues., 28 Dec., 1824   William Williams, George Jones (of Robt.)

Isaac Denson & wife, guardian to Henry J.(?) W. Dashiell

Samuel G. Holbrook, adm. of Jane S.(?) Holbrook

Tues., 11 Jan., 1825   All Justices present

James Stewart, adm. of John Adams (of Stephen)

F. 102   Thomas Walston & Thomas Slocomb to view estate of Esther E. W. Tilghman, in care of Sarah Hayward, guardian

Elizabeth Webster, guardian to Sophia A. M., Henry A. P., Alexander & Benjamin T. T. Webster

Robert Leatherbury, guardian to John T. Riggin

William Crockett, guardian to Jesse H. Wainright

John Dashiell, exe. of John Dashiell, to give counter security to Robert Dashiell

James Donoho, adm. of John Donoho

[crossed out] Peregrine Weatherly & Tubman Bedsworth to view estate of James & Robert Dougherty, in care of John S. Evans, guardian

F. 103   Tues., 22 Feb., 1825   All Justices present

Charlotte Nelson, guardian to Esther A. U. & Charlotte J. Nelson

James Stewart & William Costin, Sen., to view estate of Levin L. & Arnold E. Waters, in care of James Wilson, guardian

F. 104   James Stewart & William Costen, Sen., to view estate of William E. Waters, in care of Elizabeth A. W. Waters, guardian

Thomas Robertson, guardian to Jacob Marshall

William S.(?) Aikman, guardian to Elizabeth R. Moore

Rosanna A. W. Wainright, guardian to Rosanna E. M. J., Nancy F. D. & Edward J. C. Wainright

Willing Wright, guardian to Henry Wright

James Holland, guardian to Stephen Dryden

James Herron, guardian to Ann C. J. Dashiell

Levin Hitch & George Maddux to adjust accounts between Noah Tilghman & Turner Davis, adm. of Samson Davis

Peggy King, guardian to Henrietta, John U.(?) & William F. King

Littleton Aires & James Walter to divide negroes from estate of Isaac Winsor

Turner Davis, adm. cwa of Samson Davis

F. 105   Charles Venables, exe. of James T. Nelson, to sell negroes; Bob, Ned, Mary & William

James Ward, adm. of Eleanor Ward

Robert Leatherbury, guardian to John T. Riggin, to sell negro Leah

George Jones (of George), guardian to William T. W. & Matilda C. Holbrook

John H. Anderson & John H. Bell to view estate of John T. Riggin, in care of Robert Leatherbury, guardian

Thomas Bayly to adjust accounts between Samuel T. Bounds, & George Jones (of George), his late guardian

Citation against James Ward, adm. of Eleanor Ward, to answer allegations of Louther Riggin as to property not in inventory

Summons for Stephen Bounds & Louther Riggin to testify about property alleged to belong to estate of Eleanor Ward & kept back by adms.

Tues., 1 Mar., 1825   Francis H. Waters, George Jones (of Robt.)

F. 106   Levin Hall, adm. of Robert N. Marshall

Exe. of Mary Townsend

John H. Anderson, Esq., to adjust accounts between Robert Stewart, adm. of George D. Atkinson, & Jesse Hughes, exe. of George H. Gale

Orphan; William Leatherbury (of Asa)
Appointed Guardian; John Harskins
Sureties; Jonathan Huffington, John Goslee

Samuel T. Bounds, indebted to his guardian, George Jones (of George), for repairs done on farm

F. 107   Turner Davis, adm. cwa of Samson Davis

Stephen Collins, adm. of Ann Broughton, to sell negroes Durham & Grace

Thomas Marshall, guardian to Isaac & Josias Marshall

Apprentice; John Dashiell
Bound to; Peter McGee
Trade; farming

Jonathan Huffington & William Whayland to divide negroes from estate of Gamaliel Banks

Guardians of children of William G. Waters to ditch farm on Pokomoke, and pay all expenses, except 1/6 to be paid by widow

F. 108   Tues., 15 Mar., 1825   All Justices present

Elisha Gunby, adm. of Esther Gunby; mentions Roach's store

John Beauchamp, guardian to Matthias T. C. Beauchamp

Samuel G. Holbrook, adm. of William T. Holbrook

Stephen Ward & wife, guardian to Thomas M. & George F. Ward

William Boggs & Joseph Handy to view estate of George F. & Thomas M. Ward, in care of Stephen Ward & wife, guardian

F. 109   Sarah Hayward, guardian to Esther E. W. Tilghman

Orphan; Samuel T. Bounds
Guardian; George Jones (of George), revoked
Appointed Guardian; John Newman
Sureties; Henry James Carroll, George W. Jackson

George Jones (of George) to deliver estate of Samuel T. Bounds (of James) to John Newman, guardian

Sarah Ballard, adm. of Jarvis Ballard

Henry Banks & Levin Morris to view estate of Samuel T. Bounds (of James), in care of John Newman, guardian

Henry Banks, adm. of Gamaliel Banks

F. 110   Henry Lankford, exe. of Benjamin Lankford

Orphan; Samuel S., Isaac T. Costin (of William)
Appointed Guardian; James Polk
Sureties; Robert J. H. King, Elizabeth Taylor

Levin Morris, guardian to Alexander & Williamina Waller

Samuel McBryde, adm. cwa dbn of Josiah W. Heath

James Polk, guardian to Isaac T. & Samuel S. Costin, to sell legacies left them by Matthias C. Taylor

F. 111   Tues., 22 Mar., 1825   William Williams, George Jones (of Robt.) present

Noah Holland, guardian to Smith Horsey Holland & Samuel Holland

Henry Moore, guardian to William H. Moore

John Insley, guardian to Priscilla Dunn

Robert Stewart, adm. of George D. Atkinson

Posthumous account of Isaac Harris, guardian to Josiah S. W. Heath, exhibited by William Costin, exe. of Isaac

Elijah Williams, adm. of Rencher Roberts; mentions Underwood Roberts

F. 112   Adam Hitch, guardian to his children, to give counter security to adm. of William Collins

Benjamin Puzey to deliver to Isaiah Hayman, exe. of Randal Hayman, a gun

Tues., 29 Mar., 1825   William Williams, George Jones (of Robt.)

John S. Evans, guardian to Robert & James W. Dougherty

Lee P. Harcum & wife, guardian to Henrietta Maria & George P. Jones

John S. Evans, adm. of James Evans

Elizabeth Hopkins, adm. of George Hopkins (of Stephen)

F. 113   Samuel Brown, exe. of Stephen Disharoon

Priscilla Dashiell, guardian to Robert, Edward, Ann, John, Isabella, Priscilla & Sarah Dashiell

Leah Irving, guardian to Levin Irving

Philip M. Donoho, guardian to John L. W. Stanford

John Insley, guardian to Priscilla Dunn, to shew cause why he should not be removed as guardian

Levin Hall, adm. of Robert M. Marshall

F. 114   Tues., 12 Apr., 1825   All Justices present

Ann Beauchamp, guardian to Alissanna & Isaac Beauchamp

On petition of Ephraim K. Wilson, ordered that Dr. Samuel Ker be appointed trustee to convey real estate of James Wilson, dec., in place of John Stewart, dec., former trustee, who sold it to James Murray, by virtue of act of Assembly passed Dec., 1812, entitled 'Act for the benefit of heirs of James Wilson'

Littleton Dennis, Sen., & Robert J. Henry to adjust accounts between adm of Stephen Dakes, & adm. of Stephen Collins

Exes. of James Ritchie to give indulgence to Richard Waller

Charles Jones, adm. of Mary Roberts

F. 115   Exe. of Joseph Cottman allowed for loss of a claim against Don Carlos Barrett(?) & Peter Guillett

Elizabeth Byrd, guardian to John & Benjamin H. Byrd

Samuel McBryde, adm. dbn of Josiah W. Heath

Jonathan Moore, 2nd adm. of Jonathan Hickman, gives counter security to James Donoho, exe. of Richardson Donoho. Sureties; Joseph Barkley, Isaiah Hayman

Henry Banks, adm. dbn of Henry Banks

F. 116   Tues., 19 Apr., 1825   All Justices present

Apprentice; John Dashiell
Bound to; Littleton Sturgis
Trade; farming

Betsy Broughton, guardian to William Broughton

John Mason & wife, guardian to Henry, Hamilton, Eleanor & Benjamin Evans

Wed., 20 Apr., 1825   Francis H. Waters, William Williams present

Samuel McBryde, guardian to Elizabeth & Matilda Wainright

Betsy Acworth, guardian to John L. Moore

Richard Samson, guardian to Rebecca, Matilda & Parthena Heath, to get 5,000 staves off land

Thurs., 21 Apr., 1825   William Williams, George Jones (of Robt.)

F. 117   Amelia Bell, guardian to Nathaniel & Betsy Bell

William Wailes, guardian to _?_elia E. Dashiell

Tues., 26 [Apr.], 1825   All Justices present

Robert Bell, guardian to Robert Bell

William Hopkins, guardian to Charles E. M. Collier

Francis D. Nelson & Jonathan Waller to view estate of Maria G., William W., George W., Eleanor A., Benjamin & Stephen Mills, in care of Mary Mills, guardian

Exes. of James Ritchie to give indulgence to James Rider

Zacheus Lloyd, guardian to Maria & Thomas Lloyd

Lucretia Harris, guardian to John Harris

Elijah Dougherty, guardian to Benjamin & Henry Matthews

Leah H. Stanford, temporary guardian to Levin & Isaac Stanford

F. 118   William Boggs, guardian to Thomas Gibbons

Sally Cottman, guardian to John & Joseph Cottman, to cut timber, under direction of George Jones (of Robert)

Wed., 27 Apr., 1825   William Williams, George Jones (of Robt.)

William Wilson, guardian to Beauchamp Rhodes & others

Apprentice; Adam Dutton(?), free negro
Bound to; John Powell
Trade; farming

Tues., 10 May, 1825   All Justices present

John Walter, adm. cwa of John Jones

F. 119   William Wilson, adm. of Jesse Wilson

Samuel G. Holbrook, guardian to Edward, Rebecca & Sarah Jane Holbrook

John Hopkins, guardian to Kittura Acworth

George Hopkins, guardian to Leah, Jane & Margaret Dashiell

George Hopkins (of Stephen), guardian to Eleanor & Margaret Wailes

Roiston Weatherly, adm. dbn of Polly Weatherly

William Whayland, guardian to Robert, George, James, Joseph & Eleanor Price

F. 120   Charles Rhodes, dec., one surety of Thomas Bedsworth, on bond
         for purchase of lands; he & Henry Wilson, other surety,
responsible for debt; William Wilson, guardian to heirs of Charles
Rhodes, to pay to Philip Greyham, present holder of claim, 1/2 amount
due, as full payment

William & John Mathews to value repairs on estate of Nathaniel H. J.
Smulling, by James Powell, guardian

Apprentice; Mary A. Done
Bound to; Mary Ann Dutton
Trade; House work

May 17, 1825   William Williams, George Jones (of Robt.) present

Jacob Cullin, guardian to Walter Cullin

William W. Moore, guardian to Thomas P. Adams

F. 121   Tues., 14 June, 1825   All Justices present

William Harris, exe. of Samuel Acworth, to produce books of dec., to
adjust accounts between himself, & Doubty Bounds

Gideon Badly, guardian to Mary Dean

John Rumbolt & John Stephens, both of Caroline Co., to view estate of
children of George D. Atkinson, in that county, in care of Robert
Stewart, adm.

James Goslee & Robert Jones to divide negroes from estate of Esme
Collier, between widow (adm.) & children

Jane Bennett, guardian to Betsy(?) Jane Aires

F. 122   William W. Handy, agent for James Handy, exe. of Sophia L.(?)
         Davis, to put notices to creditors in papers in Washington,
D.C., & Delaware

William Wilson, adm. of Jesse Wilson, to sell negro Ginny(?)

John H. Cohoon & William Coulbourn to view estate of children of Jesse
Wilson, in care of William Wilson, temporary guardian

Apprentice; John Done (free negro)
Bound to; Freeborn Allan
Trade; shoemaker

F. 123   Handcock Shreves allowed 10% commission on inventory of
         Joseph Stevenson

Susan Benson, adm. of Thomas Roberts

Royston Weatherly, adm. dbn of Polly Weatherly

Tues., 28, June, 1825   Francis H. Waters, William Williams present

Roiston Weatherly, adm. dbn of Polly Weatherly

James Murray, adm. of John H. Rackliffe

James C. Coulbourn & wife, guardian to Emeline B. Parker

F. 124   Tues., 12 July, 1825   All Justices present

Isaac Nicols, adm. dbn of Wm. Russum, to sell 11 negroes; 2 women & 9 children

Roiston Weatherly, adm. dbn of Polly Weatherly

Elizabeth Kelly, adm. of William Kelly, sold negro William too cheaply

Train Acworth, adm. dbn of Edward Hull(?)

F. 125   John Dryden, guardian to Littleton Dryden

Amelia Bedsworth, guardian to Arnold H. & Edward Ballard

Jesse Hughes & Marcellus Jones to divide negroes from estate of George Aires

William Pollitt, adm. of William Bell

Isaiah Hayman, exe. of Randal Hayman, to put notice to creditors in paper in Washington, D.C.

Henry Maddux, guardian to John & Elizabeth L.(?) Turpin

F. 126   Tues., 19 July, 1825   All Justices present

George Jones & William Crockett, exes. of Joseph Cottman

John Rumbold & John Stephens to view estate of George Sydinham(?), Mary E., Eliza Ann, Isaac & William Atkinson (of George D.), in care of Robert Stewart, temporary guardian

Tues., 2 Aug., 1825   William Williams, George Jones present

Elizabeth Bounds to testify in behalf of James Ward, adm. of Eleanor Ward, concerning property alleged by Louther Riggin to be held back by adm.

F. 127   Thurs., 25 Aug., 1825   William Williams, George Jones (of R.) present

Orphan; Elizabeth H. Leatherbury
Guardian; Thomas Humphreys, revoked
Appointed Guardian; James J. Rowan
Sureties; Jehu Parsons, John W. B. Parsons

'26'

F. 128   Thomas Humphreys, late guardian to Elizabeth H. Leatherbury (of Peregrine), to deliver estate to James J. Rowan, guardian

Henry Crawford, guardian to Elizabeth E. Nelson

James Wilson, guardian to Levin L. & Arnold E. Waters

Henry Gale & James Goslee to view estate of William Leatherbury, in care of John Harskins, guardian

Henry Banks & Levin Morris to view estate of Samuel T. Bounds, in care of John Newman, guardian

John H. Cohoon & William Coulbourn to view estate of heirs of Jesse Wilson, in care of William Wilson, temporary guardian

Joshua Brattan & Charles Venables to view estate of William & Robert Russum (of William), in care of Isaac Nicols, guardian

Elijah Parsons & David Howard to view estate of Henrietta(?), Henry, Patty Alexgean(?) & Jane Emeline Davis (of Samson)

Sally U.(?) Adams, guardian to Louisa & Edward H. Adams

Elihu Jackson, guardian to Joseph Leonard

F. 129   Tues., 30 Aug., 1825   William Williams, George Jones

William S. Dashiell, guardian to Algernon S. Dashiell

William Harris, guardian to Thomas D. Evans

William Harris, exe. of Samuel Acworth

William Wilson, adm. of Jesse Wilson

Matthias Dashiell & Littleton Aires to adjust accounts between William Harris, exe.(?) of Samuel Acworth, & Doubty Bounds

Joshua Brattan & James Goslee to view estate of heirs of William Twilley, in care of George Twilley & wife, adms.

F. 130   William Miles, guardian to William John & James K. Gunby (of Kirk)

Tues., 20 Sept., 1825   William Williams, George Jones (of Robt.)

Exes. of James Ritchie to give indulgence to James Rider

Mary Dashiell, adm. of John Dashiell

F. 131   Elizabeth S. J. Evans, adm. of James Evans

Richard Waller & Levin Wilson to view estate of Solomon F. & Patty A. Vincent (of Solomon), in care of Theophilus Nicholson, who this day was appointed guardian. Sureties; Ralph Loe, Jonathan Waller

Orphan; George Johnson
Appointed Guardian; John Miles
Sureties; William Roach, Samuel Tull

Orphan; Littleton Johnson
Appointed Guardian; William Roach, Jun.
Sureties; William Roach, Sen., John Miles

F. 132   Wed., 21 Sept., 1826 [5]   William Williams, George Jones

Horsey Somers [Summers crossed out], exe. of Isaac Somers

William Coulbourn & Robert Bell to view estate of George Johnson, in care of John Miles, guardian

Orphan; Susan J. Jones (of Levin(?), Sen.)
Appointed Guardian; Susan L. Austin
Sureties; Charles Jones, George J. Jones

Fryday (sic), 23 Sept., 1825   William Williams, George Jones (of Robt.) present

Moses C. Smith, adm cwa of William Hilman

Mary Dashiell, adm. of John Dashiell

F. 133   Tues., 11 Oct., 1825   William Williams, George Jones (of Robt.) present

John P. Langford, guardian to Nathan J. & Benjamin Lankford

Elizabeth McBryde, guardian to John B. Slemons & Mary E. McBryde

William Johnston, guardian to Henrietta & Ellen Johnston

Margaret Long, adm. of William Long

F. 134   Hester Ann Twilley, adm. of Thomas Twilley

Henry Gale, adm. of Isaac Anderson

Estate of Littleton Johnson to be delivered to William Roach, guardian

Levin Wilson & Lanta(?) Dickerson, adms. of Isaac Dickerson

F. 135   Littleton D. Maddux, guardian to Henry D. & Sarah Maddux

Peregrine Weatherly & Joshua Brattan to divide negroes from estate of Edward Hull

'28'

Joseph Leonard, exe. of Joseph Leonard

Thomas Morris, exe. of Jacob Morris

Adm. of Isaac Dickerson

Thomas Morris, exe. of Jacob Morris

John A. Lankford, exe. of Stephen A. Lankford

F. 136   Tues., 25 Oct., 1825   William Williams, George Jones (of Robt.) present

William Collins, adm. of Stephen Collins

Robert Stewart, adm. of George D. Atkinson

Nancy Wilson, exe. of Thomas Cottingham

Jacob Henderson to shew cause why he doesn't deliver to William Costin, Jun., adm. of Betsy Ann Taylor, property in his possession

R. 137   Orphan; Patty(?) Ann, Rebecca M., Samuel C., William S. Broughton
Appointed Guardian; Samuel Milbourn
Sureties; William Boggs, Levin Tyler

Tues., 1 Nov., 1825   All Justices present

Margaret Long, adm. cwa of William Long

George Hopkins, adm. of Matthias D. Hopkins, to sell negroes John & Ann

James Handy, exe. of Sophia L. Davis

William Radish, guardian to Noah, James & Joseph Handy

F. 134b   [page numbers reappear at this point, but are off by four]

Tues., 22 Nov., 1825   All Justices present

Horsey Somers, exe. of Isaac Somers

James Tyler, adm. of Robert Dougherty

Littleton Tyler, adm. cwa of Ann Tyler, to sell negroes Henry, Joe & Isaac

William Roach & Samuel Tull to divide negroes from estate of Thomas Tull

F. 135b   Orphan; Samuel James, Ann Maria Twilley
          Appointed Guardian; George Twilley
          Sureties; Henry Crawford, Robert Twilley

Littleton Dennis, Sen.(?), & Robert J. Henry to adjust accounts between adm. cwa of Stephen Dakes, & adm. of Stephen Collins

James Wilson, guardian to Arnold E. & Levin L. Waters

James Powell, guardian to Nathaniel H. J. Smulling

William A. Schoolfield & William Coulbourn to view estate of Isaac T., Washington & Catherine Miles

Mary Cox, guardian to Sally Marshall

William Wilson, guardian to Rachael, James & Sarah Ann Rhodes

Wed., 23 Nov., 1825   All Justices present

William Coulbourn (of Wm.) & Thomas Handy to divide negroes from estate of Josiah Johnson

Thomas Walker, guardian to Hetty, William, Asbury & Elizabeth Ansley

George J. Jones, guardian to E__?__ A. E. Jones

F. 136b   George Jones (of George), late guardian to Samuel T. Bounds

William W. Moore & wife to shew cause why they do not enter into bond for guardianship of children of Isaac Green, deceased

John H. Anderson to adjust accounts between Charles Jones, & Margaret Long, adm. of Wm. Long

Tues., 29 Nov., 1825   All Justices present

Henry Lankford, adm. cwa of Pearce Riggin

Richard E. Waters, adm. of Mary Curtis

Marcellus Jones, adm. of William U.(?) Waters

F. 137b   Levin Tyler, guardian to Henry, William T., Sally N.(?) & Elizabeth White

William Costin, Sen., & Daniel Dakes to view estate of heirs of Pearce Riggin, in care of Henry Lankford, guardian

Henry Lankford, adm. cwa of Pearce Riggin, to deduct from inventory two horses, Figure & Rainbow, property of Henry J. Riggin

Tues., _?_ Dec., 1825   Francis H. Waters, William Williams present

John T. Fontain, guardian to Eleanor A. E. & John E. Fontain

Elizabeth [W. W. crossed out] Webster, guardian to Alexander W. W., Henry A. P., Berry T. T. & Sophia A. M. Webster

F. 138   Tues., 20 Dec., 1825   All Justices present

Robert Stewart, adm. of George D. Atkinson, to sell shares of Nantikoke Bridge stock

William Hopkins, guardian to Charles E. M. Collier, to exchange negro girl Rose, with Eleanor Collier, for negro girl Araminta

James Russel, guardian to Robert, Thomas, Elizabeth, Susan, Eleanor & Levin Russel

William Costin, adm. of Betsy Ann Taylor

George Todd, adm. of Spencer Todd

F. 139   George Twilley & wife, adm. of William Twilley

Sarah Ballard, adm. of Jarvis Ballard

James Donoho, adm. of John Donoho

Rosanna A. W. Wainright, guardian to Edward J. C., Rosanna E. M. J. & Nancy T. D. Wainright

Robert Leatherbury & Alexander Jones to view estate of Edward, Sarah Jane & Rebecca Holbrook (of Samuel), in care of Samuel G. Holbrook, guardian

Samuel Milbourn, adm. dbn of Isaac M. Broughton

Samuel Milbourn, adm. dbn of Ann Broughton

F. 140   Tues., 3 Jan., 1826   All Justices present

John H. Anderson & Robert Leatherbury to divide negroes from estate of William Bell

Charles Venables, exe. of James T. Nelson, to sell negro Hannah

William Costin, exe. of Isaac Harris

Orphan; John A. H., Joseph B. Cottman (of Joseph)
          Appointed Guardian; Joseph S.(?) Cottman
F. 141   Sureties; George Jones (of Robert), John Cottman

Josiah Furniss, guardian to William & Henry H. Furniss

James Tyler, adm. of Peter Dougherty

Tues., 10 Jan., 1826   All Justices present

Zadock Long, adm. of Levin R. King

John Cottman, exe. of John Chapman

F. 142   John Cottman, exe. of John Chapman

Orphan; George W., Mary A. Humphreys (of Thomas)
Appointed Guardian; Humphrey Humphreys
Sureties; Elizabeth McBryde, Francis Humphreys

Orphan; Leah M., Elizabeth McBryde Humphreys
Appointed Guardian; Francis Humphreys
Sureties; Elizabeth McBryde, Humphrey Humphreys

Joseph S. Cottman, adm. of Sally Cottman

Humphrey Humphreys, one of exes. of Thomas Humphreys

F. 143   Humphrey Humphreys, one of the exes. of Thomas Humphreys, to sell schooner out of county

Isaac Denson & wife, guardian to Henry J. W. Dashiell

Thomas Marshall, guardian to Josias Marshall

Orphan; [Noah crossed out] James & Joseph Handy
Guardian; William Radish, revoked
Appointed Guardian; Noah Handy
Sureties; James Anderson, Thomas Goddard

William Radish, late guardian to James & Joseph Handy (of James), to deliver estate to Noah Handy, guardian

Esther Broughton, adm. of Josiah Broughton, to sell negro Levin

F. 143b   [numbers reappear, off by one]

Robert Leatherbury, appointed to view estate of Edward, Rebecca & Sarah Jane Holbrook (of Samuel), refuses to serve; Joseph Whitney to view estate

Samuel Polk & Benjamin Bayly to view estate of Joseph & John A. H. Cottman (of Joseph), in care of Joseph S. Cottman, guardian

Tues., 24 Jan., 1826   William Williams, George Jones (of Robt.)

Noah Carsley, adm. of George Mathews

Jane Miles, guardian to Washington, Catherine & Isaac J. Miles

Esther Broughton, adm. of Josiah Broughton

F. 144   Thomas Holland, who intermarried with Betsy Lankford, adm. of William Lankford, to cut timber for support of children

Tues., 14, Feb., 1826   All Justices present

Henry Moore, guardian to William H. Moore

Jemima Moore, widow of Stephen Moore, to cut timber for support of children

Sarah Eleanor Robertson to shew cause why will of Thomas Robertson should not be admitted for probate

Stephen Ward & wife, guardian to Thomas M. & George F. Ward

F. 145   James Goslee & John J. Davis to adjust accounts between James Anderson, & Henry Calc, adm. of Isaac Anderson

James Holland, guardian to Stephen Dryden

Willing Wright, guardian to Henry Wright

Robert Bell, guardian to Robert Bell

James Herron, guardian to Ann C. J. Dashiell

Joshua Brattan & James Goslee to view estate of Samuel James & Ann Maria Twilley (of William), in care of George Twilley

Samuel Gordon, exe. of William Willing

F. 146   Daniel Dakes, adm. cwa of Stephen Dakes

Jonathan Huffington, guardian to Sally & George Willis

Isaac Gibons to shew cause why indenture of John Ballard should not be annulled, as permission was not obtained from his mother

Littleton Aires & George D. Walter to divide negroes from estate of Matthias D. Hopkins

Robert Venables, adm. of John Bargland(?)

William Aikman, guardian to Elizabeth R. Moore

Henry Lankford, adm. of Pearce Riggin

F. 147   Tues., 7 Mar., 1826   Francis H. Waters, George Jones (of Robt.) present

Esther Broughton, adm. of Josiah Broughton

F. 148   Samuel Milbourn, adm. dbn of Isaac M. Broughton

Samuel Milbourn, adm. dbn of Ann Broughton

Henry Newman, surviving exe. of Henry W. Miles

Estate of Samuel C., Patty Ann, Rebecca M. & William S. Broughton (of Isaac M.) to be delivered to Samuel Milbourn, guardian

F. 149   Elizabeth Byrd, guardian to John & Benjamin H. Byrd

Apprentice; Elizabeth Wallas(?)
Bound to: Sarah D. Waters
Trade; House & needle work

William Collins, adm. of Stephen Collins

Tues., 21 Mar., 1826   All Justices present

Noah Holland, guardian to Samuel & Smith Holland

Robert Stewart, exe. of Thomas Robertson

F. 150   Widow of David Vance wasting estate; Jacob W. Bailey granted letters of collection. Sureties; William Williams (of Saml.), Thomas D. Bailey

Levin Morris, guardian to Williamina & Alexander Waller

Daniel Benson, adm. of Alexander Coulbourn

Eleanor Philips, adm. of Noah Philips

Benjamin I. Jones & James Polk to settle dispute between George E. R. J. Collier, & Isaac Atkinson, his late guardian

F. 151   John Harskins, guardian to William Leatherbury

William Hopkins, guardian to William H. D. & John F. Collier

Levin Tyler, adm. of Asa A. Ross

George Jones (of Robert) & Samuel Polk to divide negroes belonging to representatives of James Ballard

George Jones (of Robert) & Saml. Polk to divide negroes which fell to the children of James Ballard out of estates of Tubman Walston(?) & Henry Ballard, among children now alive, & representatives of those that are dead

Peregrine Weatherly & James Goslee to divide negroes from estate of Francis Collins

Samuel Heath, exe. of Mary Milaway

F. 152   Tues., 4 Apr., 1826   All Justices present

Elizabeth McBryde, guardian to John B. Slemons & Mary E. McBryde

Thomas Robertson, guardian to Jacob Marshall

Orphan; Thomas Willing
Appointed Guardian; George Walter (of Benjamin)
Sureties; Charles Venables, Joshua Brattan

Samuel Gordon, exe. of William Willing

Winder Cannon, adm. dbn of Sally Cannon

F. 153   Winder Cannon, adm. cwa of George B. R. Costen

John Beauchamp, guardian to Matthias C. T. Beauchamp

William Coulbourn & Peggy, his wife, caveators to will of Thomas Williams, by Ephraim K. Wilson, their attorney, ask for subpoena for William Williams, to shew cause why instrument of writing filed Jan. 9, 1826, purporting to be will of Thomas Williams, should be admitted to probate

Tues., Apr. 11, 1826   William Williams, George Jones (of Robt.)

John Hopkins, guardian to Kitturah H. Acworth

George Twilley & wife, adms. of William Twilley

F. 154   George Hopkins, adm. of Matthias D. Hopkins

Sarah Hayward, guardian to Esther E. W. Tilghman

Negroes Ibby, Levin, Jenny & Arthur, from estate of Josiah Broughton, sold by adm for much less than actual value

Tues., Apr. 18, 1826   All Justices present

Thomas Hooper & Jehu Parsons to view estate of George W., Mary Ann, Leah McB. & Elizabeth McB. Humphreys, in care of Francis & Humphrey Humphreys, guardians

Gideon Badley, guardian to Mary Dean

Jane & Isaac Harris, adms. of William Harris

F. 155   Elihu Jackson, guardian to Joseph Leonard

Orphan; Gertrude, Sarah Ann, Almira Jones (of James)
Appointed Guardian; Joseph Whitney
Sureties; Robert Jones, John Leatherbury

Elizabeth Acworth, guardian to John L. Moore

Priscilla Dashiell, guardian to Robert Dashiell & others

Gideon Badley, guardian to Mary Dean

William Costen, exe. of Isaac Harris

Priscilla Donoho, adm. of Philip M. Donoho, to give additional security

F. 156   Wed., Apr. 19, 1826   All Justices present

Robert Leatherbury, guardian to John T. Riggin

William Whayland, guardian to Joseph Price & others

Chapman Dashiell, guardian to Henry W. Dashiell & others

Elizabeth Broughton, guardian to William Broughton

Amelia Bell, guardian to Nathaniel & Betsy Bell

William Collins, adm. of Stephen Collins (late guardian to William S. Broughton & others)

John Mason & wife, guardian to Henry Evans & others

Elijah S. Lawson, guardian to Emeline Lawson

Zipporah Croswell, guardian to John Croswell & others

John Waters & Littleton D. Maddux to view estate of John, Mary & Severn Croswell, in care of Zipporah Croswell, guardian

James Powell, guardian to Henry James Smulling

Orphan; Henry, William S. H., Levin J.(?) M. W., Isaac H. W. Stanford (of William)
Appointed Guardian; Aaron Driskell
Sureties; Thomas Morris, William Mezick

F. 157   William Coulbourn & Robert Bell to view estate of George Johnson, in care of John Miles, guardian

Winder Cannon, adm. cwa of George B. R. Costen, & Littleton Long, one of the representatives of Sally Cannon, ask court to appoint William Miles (of Saml.) & Levin Pollitt to settle dispute between them

Thurs., Apr. 20, 1826   William Williams, George Jones (of Robert.)

Francis Phillips, adm. of Day G.(?) Phillips

George Hopkins, guardian to Jane, Leah & Margaret E. Dashiell

F. 158   Tues., Apr. 25, 1826   All Justices present

Henry Maddux, guardian to John Turpin & others

Francis D. Nelson, guardian to Francis Mitchel & others

Esther Ballard, adm. of James Ballard

Esther Ballard, adm. of William Ballard

Jacob W. Bayley, adm. of David Vance

Priscilla Donoho, adm. of Philip M. Donoho

F. 159   Peregrine Weatherly & James Goslee to divide negroes belonging to William Hopkins & wife, William H. D. & John F. Collier, representatives of Francis Collier

Admx. of William Ballard to sell 1/2 interest in vessel

William Wilson, guardian to Beauchamp Rhodes & others

Theophilus Nicholson, guardian to Patty Ann Vincent & others

Robert Venables, adm. of Jonas Barglund

Priscilla Donoho, adm. of Richardson Donoho, gives additional security to John Austin

F. 160   Tues., May 16, 1826   All Justices present

Joseph Handy, adm. of William Tull

Elizabeth A. W. Waters, widow of William G.(?), to pay 1/3 of repairs done on house & outhouses on Pocomoke farm, & 1/3 cost of ditching, except on large ditch dug by James Anderson

Ann Davis, guardian to children of Samson Davis

F. 161   Thomas Hooper & Jehu Parsons to view estate of Thomas Humphreys

John Waters & Littleton D. Maddux to view estate of heirs of William Croswell

Benjamin I. Jones, adm. of Robert Morton(?)

Robert Leatherbury & Alexander Jones to divide negroes from estate of James Jones

Thomas Robertson, in his will, left 10 acres of land to Robert Stewart, if said Stewart would pay value to Thomas Robertson (of Benjamin), or his guardian; Littleton Aires & Benjamin I. Jones to appraise land

Robert Stewart, exe. of Thomas Robertson, to sell negroes Littleton & Belinda

James Lewis, adm. of Edward Gibbons

F. 162   Leah Jones, now Leah Ruckle, adm. of James Jones, to receive, for her children, cost of raising two negro children, born since death of James, from Robert Leatherbury & Alexander Jones, who divided negroes from estate

George Jones, one of exes. of Charles Jones

Tues., May 30, 1826   George Jones (of Robt.), William Williams

Jonathan Huffington, exe. of Gabriel Banks

F. 163   Levin Ballard, exe. of Sarah Ballard

James Goslee & Benjamin Moore to view estate of William H. D. & John F. Collier, in care of William Hopkins, guardian

Alexander Donoho, adm of James Donoho

Tues., 11 June, 1826   George Jones, William Williams present

Henry Hyland, guardian to James C. Hyland

Lucretia Harris, guardian to John L. Harris

James C. Coulbourn & wife, guardian to Emeline B. Parker

William Hopkins, guardian to Charles E. M. Collier

F. 163b   [page number appears, 1 off]

George Twilley & wife, temporary guardian to heirs of William Twilley

Royston C. Weatherly, adm. dbn of Polly Weatherly, & adm. of John L. Weatherly

James Goslee & Tubman Bedsworth to divide negroes from estates of Polly & John L. Weatherly

George Mason, guardian to Juliet Mason

Register of Wills appointed to adjust accounts between Chapman Dashiell & wife, adms. of Joseph Dashiell, & George Hopkins, adm. of Matthew(?)

Marcellus Jones, adm. of William U.(?) Waters

Orphan; Milcah Ann, Betsy Wallace
Appointed Guardian; Peter Evans
Sureties; Daniel Ballard, John Mason

William Miles (of Saml.), exe. of Bridget Johnston

Lee P. Harcum & wife, guardian to Henrietta, Perry & Maria Jones Orphan; William, Ware, Mary Willing (of William)
Appointed Guardian; Samuel Gordon
Sureties; Charles Venables, Joshua Brattan

Charles Venables, exe. of James T. Nelson

F. 164   Tues., June 20, 1826   William Williams, George Jones (of Robt.) present

Crop in ground of Littleton Pollitt, dec., to be sold by adm.

William Costen, adm. of Betsy Ann Taylor

Nathaniel Dixon(?), adm. cwa of Thomas Jenkins

Marcellus Jones, adm. of Samuel Shreves

F. 165   Register of Wills to adjust accounts between John Walter, adm. of Asa Walter, & James Donoho, adm. of John Donoho

William Costen, Sen., exe. of Isaac Harris

Isaac Atkinson, exe. of Sarah A. Leatherbury

James Donoho, exe. of Richardson Donoho

Tues., July 11, 1826   William Williams, George Jones (of Robt.)

Peregrine Weatherly & wife, exe. of Edward Austin

Stephen Collins, dec.

F. 166   John N. Whittington, adm. of John Milbourn

James Holland, adm. cwa of Stephen Dryden

Littleton Dennis & Thomas Adams to view estate of Sarah A. & Margaret E. Chapman (of John), in care of John Cottman, temporary guardian

Tues., July 18, 1826   William Williams, George Jones (of Robt.)

Milcah G. Jones, exe. of Matthias Jones

F. 167   Benjamin Bailey, adm. of William Crockett

Milcah G. Jones, exe. of Matthias Jones

John S. Evans & Tubman Bedsworth to view estate of Ann M. Austin, in care of Peregrine Weatherly & wife, temporary guardian

James Goslee & Benjamin Moore to view estate of William H. D. & John F. Collier, in care of William Hopkins, guardian

Esther Broughton, adm. of John H. Broughton

F. 168   John H. Bell, adm. of Littleton Pollitt

James Stewart & John King to divide negroes from estate of Thomas H. Bell

Alexander Jones & Joseph Whitney to view estate of Edward Holbrook & others

Tues., 8 Aug., 1826   George Jones (of R.), Thomas K. Carroll

Thomas K. Carroll appointed Justice
Witness; Theodorick Bland, Esq., Chancellor

F. 169   William Harris, dec., late adm. of Samuel Acworth

Robert Stewart, exe. of Thomas Robertson (of Geo.)

John Walter, adm. cwa of John Jones

Estate of Patty Ann & Solomon F. Vincent to be delivered to Theophilus Nicholson, guardian

Lucretia Handy, adm. of Richard H. Handy

F. 170   John Dryden, guardian to Littleton Dryden

John S. Crockett & Matthias Dashiell, adms. of Josiah Dashiell (one of the representatives of Thomas Dashiell, dec., & entitled to a share of his negroes); James Goslee & Isaac Nicols to divide negroes

John S. Crockett & Matthias Dashiell, adms. of Josiah Dashiell

Nancy Wilson, adm. of Thomas Cottingham

Joseph Handy, adm. of William Tull

F. 171   John S. Evans & Tubman Bedsworth to view estate of Ann Maria Austin, in care of Peregrine Weatherly & wife, temporary guardians

George A. Dashiell, guardian to Levin & George Gilliss

Tues., Aug. 15, 1826   All Justices present

Peregrine Weatherly, who intermarried with Susan Austin, exe. of Edward Austin

Daniel Benson, adm. of Alexander Coulbourn

Benjamin Bailey, adm. of William Crockett, to sell negroes Sally & Rhoda

F. 172   John Insley, guardian to Priscilla Dunn

John H. Anderson appointed to adjust accounts between George Jones & Robert Jones, exes. of Charles Jones, & Esther Broughton, adm. of Josiah Broughton

Tues., Aug. 29, 1826   All Justices present

James Goslee & Tubman Bedsworth to divide negroes among representatives of John L. & Polly Weatherly

Jehu Parsons, guardian to Henry A. Smyth

Orphan; Elizabeth Collins (of Stephen)
Appointed Guardian; Daniel Ballard
Sureties; Robert Stewart, Samuel Miles

Robert J. Henry & Levin Tyler to view estate of Elizabeth Collins, in care of Daniel Ballard, guardian

James F. Kelly, one adm. of Thomas Walston

F. 173   George Jones, acting exe. of Charles Jones

Orphan; William R., Sophia R. Donoho (of James)
Appointed Guardian; Alexander Donoho
Sureties; William Donoho, Asa Phillips

Joshua Brattan & Charles Venables to view estate of William R. & Sophia R. Donoho (of James)

Sept. 13, 1826   All Justices present

On 9 Jan., 1826, William Williams exhibited paper purporting to be will of Thomas Williams;
F. 174   1) To brother William Williams, all lands devised to me by my father, Thomas Williams
2) To brother William, bank stock in Bank of Baltimore, & all negroes
3) To brother William, residue of estate
4) Brother William appointed exe.

Witnesses; Jno.(?) Handy   3 July, 1803
          Edward Broughton
          Polly W. Schoolfield   Thomas Williams

On 28, Feb., 1826, caveat filed by William Coulbourn & Peggy, his wife, by Ephraim K. Wilson, their attorney;

F. 175   William Coulbourn (of Wm.) & Peggy, his wife; Peggy is heir
         at law & sister of Thomas Williams (Physician), who died
childless; Thomas not of sound mind, will not free & voluntary

William Williams, by L. P. Dennis, his attorney, files answer;

F. 176   Thomas died 6 Oct., 1825; will found among his valuable
F. 177   papers, never revoked

13 Sept., 1826   Sworn before W. H. Curtis

Edward Broughton testifies;

F. 179   Other witnesses were John S. Handy & Polly W. Schoolfield,
         now Polly Horsey; my signature in my handwriting; will was
F. 180   voluntary; Thomas had severe attack of fever in summer of
F. 181   of 1803; Drs. Ker & Jones attended him at his mother's house;
         Thomas was a candidate for MD legislature in 1803; led
Democratic party

F. 182   Tues., Sept. 19, 1826   William Williams, George Jones (of
                                 R.) present

William H. Curtis, adm. of Henry T. Mitchell

James Donoho, exe. of Richardson Donoho

F. 183   Mare(?) claimed by Sarah Slocomb, exe. of Thomas Slocomb, is
         property of Thomas Slocomb, Jun.

Tues., Oct. 3, 1826   William Williams, Thomas K. Carroll present

Littleton D. Maddux, guardian to Sarah S. & Henry D. Maddux

Sally U. Adams, guardian to Edward & Louisa Adams

Elizabeth A. W. Waters, guardian to William E. Waters

Caleb Hughes & wife, guardian to Esther A. & Charlotte E. Nelson

Littleton Aires, adm. of Jesse McIntire

F. 184   Shiles Crockett & Isaac Atkinson to view estate of heirs of
         James T. Nelson

Tues., 10 Oct., 1826   All Justices present

James Holland, adm. of Stephen Dryden

Orphan; Levin, Elizabeth Goslee
Appointed Guardian; Edmond R. Goslee
Sureties; John Bounds, John Mitchell

John Cottman, exe. of John Chapman, to sell negroes Rachael, Nelson, Alfred, Matthias, Mida(?), Charlotte & James

Robert J. Henry & Levin Tyler to view estate of heirs of John Milbourn

John N. Whittington, adm. of John Milbourn, to sell corn & fodder

F. 185   Tues., Oct. 24, 1826   All Justices present

Robert J. Henry & Levin Tyler to view estate of Elizabeth Collins, in care of Daniel Ballard, guardian

James Walter, adm. of William Walter

Estate of Levin & Elizabeth Goslee to be delivered to Edmond R. Goslee, guardian

Joshua & John U. Humphriss, exes. of Elijah Humphriss

F. 186   Priscilla Donoho, guardian to John L. W. Stanford

Alexander Donoho, adm. of James Donoho, to sell corn & fodder

Daniel Benson, adm. of Adrian Marshall

Orphan; William S. Broughton (of Isaac M.)
Appointed Guardian; John Howard, Sen.
Sureties; Henry Lankford, Daniel Benson

Estate of William S. Broughton to be delivered to John Howard, guardian

Francis Waters, exe. of Francis H. Waters

F. 187   William H. Curtis, adm. of Henry T. Mitchell

Littleton Dennis, Sen., & Thomas Adams to view estate of heirs of John Chapman

Property of others appraised in inventory of Josiah Broughton

Tues., Nov. 7, 1826   All Justices present

Note of George M. Willing, held by exes. of Charles Jones, having been satisfied, to be delivered to said Willing

Robert J. Henry & Daniel Dakes to view real estate of Pearce Riggin, whereon John Riggin formerly lived

John King, adm. of Nancy Stewart

F. 188   Dr. Samuel Ker testifies in case of will of Thomas Williams;
         I am 56; met Thomas at Washington Academy; was with him in
         Philadelphia; he had illness at his mother's house; was
F. 189   removed to his brother William's house; was deranged; had
F. 190   haepatic affection, or liver complaint; after illness he was
         in his right mind

Wed., Nov. 8, 1826   All Justices present

F. 191   Francis Waters, exe. of Francis H. Waters

Lazarus Adams testifies in case of will of Thomas Williams;

F. 192   I married Elizabeth Schoolfield & have two children living;
         Elizabeth, 18, & Amelia, 15; my wife, Elizabeth, is niece of
Thomas Williams; he left no kin except brothers & sisters; Jesse Adams
(father of grand nieces of Dr. Williams) & I agreed to pay part of
expenses of this suit, so that our children should not go without
rightful share of estate

Court declares Lazarus Adams not a competent witness

F. 194   Suit transferred to Worcester County Court

F. 195   Tues., Nov. 21, 1826   All Justices present

Molly Cox, guardian to Sally Marshall

10% commission allowed on estate of Betty Nicholson, to estate of
Thomas Humphreys, exe., dec.

F. 196   John H. Anderson appointed to adjust accounts between
         Benjamin Bailey, adm. of William Crockett, & George Jones (of
Robt.)

Orphans Court to arbitrate & award on accounts existing between estate
of William Crockett, & Benjamin Bailey

Covington Cordray & James Denson to divide negroes from estate of
William Walter

Apprentice; John Fleming
Bound to; David Jones
Trade; housejoiner

Wed., Nov. 22, 1826   William Williams, George Jones (of R.) present

James Goslee & Isaac Nicols to divide negroes from estate of Thomas
Dashiell

Covington Cordray & George D. Walter to view estate of William Willing
& others (of William), in care of Samuel Gordon, guardian

Amy Graham, adm. of Peter Graham

F. 197   John H. Ellegood, who intermarried with Elizabeth Bell, one heir of Hamilton Bell, who was one representative of Thomas H. Bell; James Stewart & Dr. John King to divide negroes which fell to said Elligood & Mary E. Bell, the other representative of Hamilton Bell, out of estate of Thomas Bell

Henry Lankford, adm. of Pearce Riggin, to use lawful means to collect from Henry J. Riggin money due dec.; an account of sundry executions in favor of John Rider, Cutter(?) Townsend & William R. Warwick, & paid by him as surety for the said Henry J. Riggin; also a debt against John Fontain & John Swift

William Roach, guardian to Littleton Johnston

Orphan; John Curtis
Guardian; Elizabeth Curtis, through Dr. Thomas Robertson, wished to be released; revoked
Appointed Guardian; Dr. Thomas Robertson

Elizabeth Curtis to deliver estate of John Curtis to Dr. Thomas Robertson, guardian

F. 198   Thurs., Nov. 23, 1826   William Williams, George Jones (of Robt.) present

William S. Dashiell, guardian to Algernon S. Dashiell

John N. Whittington, adm. of John Milbourn, to sell negroes Sarah, Arthur, George, Mary, Leah & Jacob

Levin Tyler, guardian to Sally N. White

Tues., Nov. 28, 1826   George Jones, William Williams present

Nathan Gordy, adm. of Thomas Connelly

F. 199   Tues., 12 Dec., 1826   George Jones (of R.), Thomas K. Carroll present

Benjamin I. Jones & Matthias Dashiell to divide negroes from estate of Samuel Acworth, reserving negro Levin, if necessary, for payment of debts

Isaac Denson & wife, guardian to Henry J. W. Dashiell

Elizabeth Webster, guardian to Berry T. T., Henry A. P., Alexander W. W. & Sarah A. M. Webster

James Tyler, adm. of Jesse Lankford

Levin Tyler, guardian to Sally N., Betsy, Henry & William T. White

Mary Williams, guardian to Adaline, Mary Anne & Priscilla Williams

James Stewart & John King to divide negroes between heirs of Hamilton Bell

Isaac Gibbons, exe. of John Gibbons

F. 200   Thomas Robertson & Daniel Dakes to view estate of John & Abraham Cottingham, in care of Henry Broughton, temporary guardian

Tues., Jan. 9, 1827   All Justices present

David Lankford appointed crier, vice Samuel Heath, dec.

James Goslee, adm. of John Green

Samuel Brown, exe. of Stephen Disharoon

F. 201   William Stewart, adm. of Robert Hitch

Orphan; Thomas D. Evans
Appointed Guardian; Marcellus Jones
Sureties; Jesse Hughes, George Jones (of Robt.)

Estate of Thomas D. Evans to be delivered to Marcellus Jones, guardian

John Cottman, temporary guardian to Sarah A. & Margaret E. Chapman

William Miles, guardian to William Gunby & others

Orphan; William B., Eleanor H., Josiah S. Crockett (of William)
Appointed Guardian; Hetty Crockett
Sureties; Charles Robinson, John P. Marshall

Estate of William B., Eleanor H. & Josiah S. Crockett to be delivered to Hetty Crockett, guardian

Dr. James Wilson & John H. Anderson to adjust accounts between James Polk, one creditor of William Crockett, dec., & Benjamin Bailey, adm. of said dec.

F. 202   Henry Lankford, adm. of Pearce Riggin, to sell negroes Peter, Isaac, Nace(?) & Saul

Winder Cannon, adm. dbn of Sally Cannon

James Russell, guardian to Thomas Russell & others

Isaac Harris, guardian to William H. Acworth

Posthumous account of William Harris, guardian to Thomas D. Evans

Tues., Jan. 23, 1827   All Justices present

Caroline Tull, exe. of Samuel Tull

F. 203   Orphan; Edmond (?) C., William Curtis (of John)
         Appointed Guardian; Richard E. Waters
         Sureties; Thomas Robertson, John Waters

John Miles, guardian to George Johnson

On 1 Mar., 1825, adm. of Isaac Dashiell granted to George P. Jones; adm. null & void, as letter received from Isaac, from Savannah, GA., showing he is alive; estate to be delivered to Isaac Denson & wife, former guardians

Thomas Marshall, guardian to Josias Marshall

Rosanna A. W. Wainright, guardian to Edward J. C. Wainright & others

John Leatherbury, adm. of Robert Jones

F. 204   Samuel Polk, appointed to view estate of Joseph B. & John A.
         H. Cottman (of Joseph), died; John H. Bell & Benjamin Bailey
to view estate

Tues., 13 Feb., 1827   All Justices present

F. 205   Humphrey Humphreys, guardian to George W. & Mary A. Humphreys

John S. Crockett & Matthias [no surname given], adms. of Josiah Dashiell

Joseph Barkley, adm. of Samuel Heath

Daniel Maddux, exe. of Marcy Maddux

Ann S. Collins, adm. of William Collins

F. 206   Levin Wilson & William King, who intermarried with Lanta
         Dickerson (adm. of Isaac Dickerson)

Levin Tyler, guardian to Henry White, to sell negro woman Grace & her two children

Henry Crawford, guardian to Elizabeth E. Nelson

Edmond(?) R. Goslee, guardian to Elizabeth Goslee, to sell negro woman Leah

Francis Humphreys, guardian to Leah McB. & Elizabeth McB. Humphreys

Isaac Nicols, guardian to Robert & William Russum

Willing Wright, guardian to Henry Wright

John P. Langford, guardian to Benjamin Lankford

John Newman, guardian to Samuel T. Bounds

John S. Evans, guardian to John, Robert & James W. Dougherty

Stephen Ward & wife, guardian to Thomas M. Ward

Orphan; Elizabeth J. C., Mary A. Stewart (of John C.)
        Appointed Guardian; William Miles (of Saml.)
F. 207   Sureties; William Costen, Matthias Miles

Orphan; Robert Phillips
Appointed Guardian; James Phillips
Sureties; John S. Evans, Thomas Russell

Tues., Feb. 27, 1827   George Jones (of R.), Thomas K. Carroll present

William Whayland, guardian to Joseph Price & others

William W. Johnston, guardian to Ellen R. Johnston

Sally U. Adams, guardian to Edward H. & Louisa U. Adams

Gatty Kellum, adm. of John Kellum

William Wilson, guardian to James Rhodes & others

Levin Morris, guardian to Alexander & Wilhelmina Waller

F. 208   Division of negroes from estate of Charles Rhodes, May 9, 1815, null & void, as some were later sold to pay debt due Philip Graham, on account of suretyship for Thomas Bedsworth, & this left some heirs with no share; Peregrine Weatherly & Samuel Walter to divide remaining negroes

John H. Bell & Joseph L.(?) Colgan to adjust accounts between John Powell, & Benjamin Bailey, adm. of William Crockett

Samuel G. Holbrook, guardian to Sarah Jane Holbrook & others

Margaret R. Long, adm. cwa of William Long, to sell negro woman Milcah

Isaac Harris, guardian to William H. Acworth

Isaac Harris & Jane Harris, adms. of William Harris

F. 209   Tues., Mar. 6, 1827   All Justices present

Henry Moore, guardian to William H. Moore

William W. Moore, guardian to Thomas P. Adams

William S. Aikman, guardian to Elizabeth R. Moore

Joseph S. Cottman, guardian to John A. H. & Joseph B. Cottman

Margaret R. Long, exe. of William Long, to sell negro girl Milcah

F. 210   Tues., Mar. 20, 1827   All Justices present

Zadock Long, adm. of Levin R. King

Benjamin Bailey & John H. Bell to view estate of John A. H. & Joseph B. Cottman, in care of Joseph S. Cottman, guardian

William Done to adjust accounts between Peter Guillett, & George Jones & Robert Jones, exes. of Charles Jones, according to a contract between them

On motion of John H. Cohoon, adm. dbn of Isaac Connor, William H. Curtis & Henry Lankford to adjust accounts between Samuel A. Cohoon & Isaac Conner

Joseph S. Cottman, one adm. of Sally Cottman

F. 211   James Denson, adm. of Elizabeth D. Willing

Elizabeth Byrd, guardian to John Byrd

Orphan; Mary R. Wingate (of Peter)
Appointed Guardian; Nathan Bloodsworth
Sureties; Henry White, George Waller

Tues., 10 Apr., 1827   All Justices present

John Mason & wife, guardian to Hamilton, Benjamin, Eleanor & Henry Evans

George Walter, guardian to Thomas Willin

James Smith, exc. of William Tilghman, to sell negro boy Levin

Stephen Taylor, adm. of Aaron Foxwell

F. 212   Cathell(?) & Humphrey Humphreys, exes. of Thomas Humphreys

Thomas Walker, guardian to Asbury, Hetty, Elizabeth & William Ansley

Leah Walston & James F. Kelly, adms. cwa of Thomas Walston

John Hurley, guardian to Elizabeth Hurley

Apprentice; Jesse Beauchamp
Bound to; James Gibbons
Trade; boot & shoemaking

Estate of Mary R. Wingate to be delivered to Nathan Bloodsworth, guardian

Richard E. Waters, guardian to Edmond C. Curtis

Elizabeth McBryde, guardian to John B. Slemons & Mary E.(?) M. McBryde

John Harskins, guardian to William Leatherbury

Jonathan Huffington, guardian to George & Sally Williss

Orphan; George, William E., Benjamin S. Foxwell (of Aaron)
       Appointed Guardian; Elzey Foxwell
F. 213   Sureties; Jonathan Huffington, Stephen Taylor

John H. Anderson & Arnold E. Jones to divide negroes from estate of Levin Winder

Tues., Apr. 24, 1827   All Justices present

Henry Lankford, adm. of Pearce Riggin

Samuel K. Handy, adm. of Simon Horsey

Sarah Slocomb, exe. of Thomas Slocomb

Samuel Gordon, adm. of William Willing

Apprentice; Thomas Langsdale
Bound to; Samuel McBryde
Trade; tanner & currier

Aaron Driskell, guardian to Levin J. M. & Isaac H. W. Stanford

Jehu Parsons, guardian to Henry A. Smyth

Ann Beauchamp, guardian to Isaac Beauchamp

F. 214   Cyrus Nelson, exe. of Hetty Porter

Orphan; William Long (of David)
Appointed Guardian; Whitty Fontaine
Sureties; John T. Fontain, Planner H. King

Orphan; Sally Ann Elzey (of James)
Appointed Guardian; Whitty Fontaine
Sureties; John T. Fontaine, Planner H. King

Whitty Fontaine, guardian to William Long & Sally Ann Elzey

Thomas Robertson & Daniel Dakes to view estate of John & Abraham Cottingham, in care of Henry Broughton, guardian

James Powell, guardian to Nathaniel J. Smulling

Orphan; George H., Charles, Alfred Jones (of Charles)
Appointed Guardian; Elizabeth Jones
Sureties; Robert Jones (of Geo.), William T. Wood

Orphan; George P., Henrietta, Maria S. Jones (of Levin D.)
Appointed Guardian; Robert Jones
Sureties; George Jones (of R.), William T. Wood

William Boggs, guardian to Thomas E. Gibbons

Covington Cordray & George D. Walter to view estate of James, William, Thomas & Ware Willing, in care of Samuel Gordon, guardian

F. 215   Negro man Moses, in inventory of Delila Dashiell, adm. of Joseph Dashiell, not property of dec.

George Jones, adm. of Ezekiel Gilliss

Eleanor Phillips, adm. of Noah Phillips

Tues., May 8, 1827   All Justices present

Ephraim K. Wilson & James Polk to adjust accounts between Lucretia Handy, adm. of Richard H. Handy, & Jesse Walter

James Stewart, adm. of George Layfield

F. 216   Charles Davis, adm. of Samuel Davis

Elizabeth Acworth, guardian to John L. Moore

Tues., May 22, 1827   William Williams, Thomas K. Carroll present

Littleton Aires & Benjamin I. Jones, appointed on 16 May, 1826, in accordance with will of Thomas Robertson, report; Robert Stewart to pay $40.00 to Thomas Robertson (of Benjamin) for land left him by Thomas Robertson, dec.; 11 Nov., 1826

Lucretia Handy, adm. of Richard H. Handy

Elijah Dougherty, guardian to Henry Matthews

Willin Wright, guardian to Henry Wright

James Herron, guardian to Ann C. J. Dashiell

Richard E. Waters, guardian to William Curtis

William Costen, exe. of Isaac Harris

George Twilley & wife, adms. of William Twilley

George Twilley, guardian to Samuel J. & Ann M. Twilley

Mary Mills, guardian to Margaret Mills & others

Lovitha Milbourn, adm. of Lodowick Milbourn

F. 218   Wed., May 23, 1827   All Justices present

Orphan; Algernon Johnson
Appointed Guardian; Benjamin Gravner
Sureties; Isaac Kennerly, William Hosaima(?)

Elihu Jackson, guardian to Joseph Leonard

Orphan; Mary, Eliza James (of Jacob)
Appointed Guardian; John Austin
Sureties; Isaac Harris, Henry Crawford

F. 219   Elizabeth Collier, guardian to William Broughton

Amelia Bell, guardian to Nathaniel Bell

Gertrude Kellum, adm. of John Kellum, to sell negro Martha

Thomas Robertson, guardian to Jacob Marshall

Isaac Harris & Jane Harris, adms. of William Harris

Zipporah Croswell, guardian to John Croswell & others

Marcellus Jones, adm. of William U. Waters

F. 220   John Austin & Henry Dorman to view estate of Azariah W. & William D. Donoho (of Philip M.), in care of Priscilla Donoho, guardian

John Austin & Henry Dorman to divide negroes from estate of Philip M. Donoho

Thurs., May 24, 1827   All Justices present

Priscilla Dashiell, guardian to Robert N., Edward, Ann, John H., Isabella, Priscilla & Sarah Dashiell

John H. Bell, adm. of Littleton Pollitt

Charles Venables, adm. of Margaret W. Venables

Tues., May 29, 1827   All Justices present

F. 221   Orphan; James, Louisa Waters (of William U.)
Appointed Guardian; Marcellus Jones
Sureties; Jesse Hughes, John S. Crockett

Lucretia Harris, guardian to John Harris

William Hopkins, guardian to Charles E. M. Collier

James Goslee & Henry Gale to view estate of Charles E. M. Collier, in care of William Hopkins, guardian

James Wilson & John H. Bell to view estate of Levin D. & Hiram Jones, & also of George H., Alfred & Charles Jones, in care of Elizabeth Jones, guardian

Henry Gale, exe. of Stephen Taylor

F. 222 Case of will of Thomas Williams; Jurors in Worcester County Court find that Thomas Williams was insane at time of writing of will

                          William B. Martin
                          Asa Spence

F. 223 18 May, 1827

                        John C. Handy, Clk. Wor. Coy. Court

Tues., 12 June, 1827   All Justices present

Aaron Driskell, guardian to Henry, William S. H., Levin J. M. W.(?) & Isaac H. W. Stanford, refuses to give counter security to Thomas Morris & William Mezick, his securities; guardianship revoked; Elijah Christopher appointed guardian to Henry, aged 20, last April;
F. 224 William S. H., aged 16 last May; Levin J. M. W.(?), aged 10 on 4th of last May; & Isaac H. W. Stanford, aged 7 on 15th of last Jan.; sureties; John Bounds, Levin D. Collier

James Goslee, adm. of John Green

Henry Gale, adm. of Isaac Anderson, to sell negro woman Esther

Joshua & John U. Humphriss, exes. of Elijah Humphriss

John Miles, guardian to George Johnson (of Josiah), to sell negro Adam

F. 225 William Done, Littleton P. Dennis & James Polk to adjust accounts between William T. G. Polk, adm. of Samuel Polk, & Lee P. Harcum

Robert J. H. King, adm. of Robert J. King

Wm. T. G. Polk, adm. of Samuel Polk

Samuel Walter, adm. of John Robertson

Beauchamp Acworth & Shiles Crockett to view estate of Robert, Nancy, John, William, Eliza, Sarah Jane, George, Thomas, James & Samuel Robertson (of John). in care of Samuel Walter, temporary guardian

F. 226 Adm. of Peter Dashiell & exes. of James Ritchie to grant indulgence to Handy H. Irving, trustee for sale of real estate of Esme M. Waller

Tues., June 26, 1827   All Justices present

William King & wife, & Levin Wilson, adms. of Isaac Dickerson

James Goslee & Henry Gale to view estate of Maria, George P. & Henrietta Jones (of Levin D.), in care of Robert Jones, guardian

Elijah Lawson, guardian to Emeline Lawson

Tues., July 10, 1827   All Justices present

F. 227   Joseph B. Brinkley, adm. dbn of William H. Horsey

Mary Anderson, wife of Zebedee, & late widow of John Green, dec., admits keeping back money from estate from James Goslee, adm.

George L. Ayres, adm. cwa of William Ballard

Orphan; Susan, Mary Jane, Sarah Ann Green (of John)
Appointed Guardian; Zebedee Anderson
Sureties; Littleton Mezick, George Dashiell (of Wm.)

John Dryden, guardian to Littleton Dryden

F. 228   William Williams files writing purporting to be will of Thomas Williams;
    1) All of estate to brother William Williams

Tues., July 17, 1827   All Justices present

F. 229   George L. Ayres, adm. cwa of William Ballard, to sell negro Spencer

Henry Lankford, adm. of Pearce Riggin, to sell negroes; woman Esther & child, Bob, Lydia & Maria

William Coulbourn & Peggy, his wife, file caveat against will of Thomas Williams

Court rejects will, orders William Williams to pay all court costs

F. 230   Zadock Long, adm. of Levin R. King, to sell negro child, aged 7 months

Whitty Fontain, adm. of William Long

Tues., 14 Aug., 1827   All Justices present

Margaret R. Long, adm. cwa of William Long, claimant, & George Jones (of Robert), acting exe. of Charles Jones, ask court to appoint James Polk, Register of Wills, to settle dispute between them

F. 231   Clement Goslee, exe. of Lenday(?) Goslee

Robert J. H. King, adm. of Robert J. King, to sell stock in Chesapeak & Delaware Canal

Scott Brereton, adm. of Smith Brereton

Benjamin I. Jones, adm. of Robert Moreton(?)

Benjamin I. Jones, adm. of Robert Jones, to sell negro woman Henny

F. 232   Orphan; Charlotte(?) R. Heath (of Samuel)
Appointed Guardian; Joseph Barkley
Sureties; George A. Dashiell, John N. Bowland

James Stewart & Charles Simson to view estate of Charlotte R. Heath, in care of Joseph Barkley, guardian

George M. Willing, adm. of Obadiah Stanford

Joseph Barkley, adm. of Samuel Heath

Burton Cannon, adm. dbn of Burton Cannon

Burton Cannon, adm. of Caleb N. Cannon

F. 233   Robert Stewart, exe. of Thomas Robertson

George Jones (of Robert), acting exe. of Charles Jones

Tues., Aug. 28, 1827   All Justices present

James Wilson, guardian to Arnold E. Waters, to rent part of Pocomoke farm

Henry Gale, adm. of Isaac Anderson

Henry Gale & Francis D. Nelson to view estate of Susan, Mary Jane & Sarah Ann Green, in care of Zebedee Anderson, guardian

F. 234   John S. Crockett, one of adms. of Josiah Dashiell

Daniel Ballard, guardian to Elizabeth Collins, to repair farm where Noah & John Carsley live

John Cottman, exe. of John Chapman; William Boggs & Littleton Dennis, Sen., to give him negroes in amount of overpayment he made

Orphan; Margaret E., Sarah A. Chapman (of John)
Appointed Guardian; Margaret B. Chapman
Sureties; William L. McCormick, John Cottman

Littleton Dennis, Sen., & William Boggs to view estate of Margaret E. & Sarah A. Chapman, in care of Margaret B. Chapman, guardian

Littleton Dennis, Sen., & William Boggs to divide negroes from estate of John Chapman

F. 235   Priscilla Donoho, adm. of Philip M. Donoho

Tues., Sept. 11, 1827   All Justices present

Zadock Long, claimant, & Robert J. H. King, adm. of Robert J. King, ask court to appoint William Done & James Polk to arbitrate between them

James Goslee & Henry Gale to view estate of Charles E. M. Collier, in care of George Hopkins, guardian

Elijah Parsons & Elizabeth McBryde, exes. of James Ritchie

Henry Gale & Francis D. Nelson to view estate of Susan, Mary Jane & Sarah Ann Green, in care of Zebedee Anderson, guardian

F. 236   Henry Gale & Francis D. Nelson, who viewed estate of Susan, Mary Jane & Sarah Ann Green, & Zebedee Anderson, guardian, report that dwelling & corn house need repair; guardian to reroof both

John Austin, guardian to Eliza James, sold negro girl Sophia without court order; sale approved

Isaac Nicols, adm. dbn of William Russum

Orphan; Lee, William Weatherly (of William)
Appointed Guardian; William H. D. Collier
Sureties; Philip Graham, James W. Dashiell

Isaac Gibbons, exe. of John Gibbons

F. 237   Tues., Sept. 18, 1827   All Justices present

William S. Aikman, guardian to Elizabeth R. Moore

Orphan; Samuel C., Patty Ann, Rebecca M. Broughton (of Isaac M.)
Appointed Guardian; Levin Tyler
Sureties; John Tyler, Stephen Coulbourn

Robert J. Henry & Henry Lankford to view estate of Samuel C., Patty Ann & Rebecca M. Broughton, in care of Levin Tyler, guardian

William Coulbourn & Peggy, his wife, by E. K. Wilson, their attorney, filed petition concerning will of her brother, Thomas
F. 238   Williams; ask court to reject 2nd will, since not witnessed, & Thomas already found insane

[F. 239 - 260;repeat of previous testimony concerning will of Thomas Williams]

F. 261   Henry Lankford, adm. of William H. Adams

Tues., 9 Oct., 1827   All Justices present

F. 262   Zadock Long, adm. of Levin R. King, to sell negro man Ephraim (an idiot)

Caroline Tull, exe. of Samuel Tull

Ballard Read & Henry Newman to divide negroes from estate of Thomas Ballard

John N. Whittington, adm. of John Milbourn, to sell negroes Harry, Bob, Henry & Harriet

Tues., Oct. 23, 1827   All Justices present

F. 263   Littleton D. Maddux, guardian to Henry D. & Sarah S. Maddux

Daniel Ballard, guardian to Elizabeth Collins

Elijah Phillips, guardian to William R. Phillips

Robert J. Henry & Henry Lankford to view estate of William S. Broughton, in care of John Howard, guardian

Robert J. Henry & Daniel Dakes to view estate of heirs of Pearce Riggin

On 7 Mar., 1827, William Done was appointed to adjust accounts between Peter Guillett, & George Jones (of Robert) & Robert Jones, exes. of Charles Jones; Ephraim K. Wilson appointed to help

F. 264   Travers Daniel & George Rowe to view estate of Berry T. T., Henry A. P., Alexander W. W. & Sophia A. M. Webster (of Michael), in care of Elizabeth Webster, guardian

Sale of estate of Philip Nutter, exhibited by John Insley, on 22 Nov., 1825, annulled

Orphan; George L. R. (aged 8, last Jan.), Ann M. D. Walter (aged 13, last Mar.)
Appointed Guardian; Sarah Walter
Sureties; Levin Walter, John Waters

Covington Cordray & George Hopkins to view estate of George L. R. & Ann M. D. Walter (of James), in care of Sarah Walter, guardian

Sarah Walter, exe. of James Walter

Shiles Crockett & Isaac Atkinson to view estate of Esther A. & Charlotte J. Nelson (of James T.), in care of Caleb Hughes & wife, guardian

F. 265   Case of will of Thomas Williams; William Williams answers
F. 266   caveat to 2nd will; sworn before George M. Willing, J. P.
         files interrogations to be propounded to Henry Lankford,
George Riggin, Thomas Handy & John P. Gale

F. 267   Henry Lankford testifies; states 2nd will in handwriting of
         Dr. Thomas Williams

F. 268   George Riggin testifies; knew William & Peggy Williams before
         they married, over 20 years; I am 62; went to school with
Thomas Williams

F. 269   Mon., Oct. 29, 1827   All Justices present

Levin Tyler, guardian to Thomas W. White, to sell negro girl Charity

John P. Gale testifies in care of will of Thomas Williams

F. 270   Tues., Oct. 30, 1827   All Justices present

William Coulbourn & Peggy, his wife, ask court to transfer case of
will of Thomas Williams to another court

F. 272 [no 271]   Justices transfer case to Somerset County Court

F. 273   William Williams, by Littleton P. Dennis & Thomas Bayly, his
         attorneys, objects

William Williams, Esq., presiding justice, & defendant in case,
withdrew from bench during case

Ann S. Collins, adm. of William Collins

Orphan; Kitty, Hambleton, Maria J., Marcella Moore (of Stephen)
Appointed Guardian; Job Moore
Sureties; William Roach, Joseph B. Brinkley

Jacob Byrd & Jacob Cullin to view estate of Kitty, Hambleton, Maria J.
& Marcella Moore, in care of Job Moore, guardian

F. 274   Job Moore, guardian to aforesaid orphans, to sell negro
         George

Samuel Brown, exe. of Stephen Disharoon, to sell unexpired time of
negro Marcus

Tues., Nov. 20, 1827   All Justices present

George D. Walter, adm. of Daniel Walter

Cathell(?) Humphreys, one of exes. of Thomas Humphreys

Robert J. H. King, adm. of Robert J. King

'58'

F. 275   Stephen Taylor, adm. of Aaron Foxwell, to sell negro girl
         Kizziah

David Lankford, adm. of Lova(?) Lankford

Benjamin Dashiell, adm. of Jonathan Moore

         Citation issued for William Wilson, guardian to James & Sarah
F. 276   Ann Rhodes, to shew cause why he cut wood on land of orphans

Edward Fowler, one of adms. of Orrell Kennerly

Samuel Gordon, guardian to Ware Willing

Wed., Nov. 21, 1827   All Justices present

Elizabeth McClester & Samuel Gordon, adms. cwa of John McClester

Orphan; William J., Mary E., Martha J., Sarah P., Isaac J. T., Alcy K.
Harris (of William)
Appointed Guardian; Jane Harris
Sureties; Marcellus Jones, John Hopkins

F. 277   Jesse Hughes & Henry Hyland to view estate William J., Mary
         E., Martha J., Sarah P., Isaac J. T. & Alcy K. Harris, in
care of Jane Harris, guardian

Samuel Gordon, guardian to William Willing

Tues., 11 Dec., 1827   George Jones (of R.), Thomas K. Carroll present

Gatty Kellum, adm. of John Kellum

Daniel Benson, adm. of Adrian Marshall

William Roach, Jun., guardian to Littleton Johnson

Levin Tyler, guardian to William T., Sally N. & Henry White

James Smith, exe. of William Tilghman

F. 278   Joseph Barkley, adm. dbn of Mary Milliway

Orphan; Samuel, Maria, George Taylor (of Isaac)
Appointed Guardian; William Costen, Jr.
Sureties; Burton Cannon, Winder Cannon

Mary Porter, exe. of Richard B. Porter

William Costen, adm. of Betsy Ann Taylor

Orphan; Thomas Robertson (of Thomas)
Appointed Guardian; George E. Robertson
Sureties; John S. Handy, John P. Langford

John Howard, guardian to William S. Broughton

Winder Cannon, adm. cwa of George B. R. Costen

F. 279   James Stewart & Benjamin Simson to view estate of Charlotte R. Heath (of Samuel), in care of Joseph Barkley, guardian

Tues., Jan. 28, 1828   All Justices present

John Austin & Henry Dorman to view estate of Azariah W. & William D. Donoho, in care of Priscilla Donoho, guardian

John T. Fontain, guardian to John E. & Eleanor A. E. Fontain

John Cottman, temporary guardian to Margaret E. & Sarah A. Chapman

Elizabeth Webster, guardian to Sophia A. M., Henry A. P., Alexander W. W. & Berry T. T. Webster

Daniel Ballard & John Waters to divide negroes from estate of William Turpin

Isaac Denson & wife, guardian to Henry J. W. Dashiell

Michael B. Carroll to shew cause why adm. of estate of Betsy Bayly shall not be granted to Thomas M. Hargis

F. 280   Winder Cannon, adm. cwa of George B. R. Costen

Tues., Jan. 15, 1828   William Williams, George Jones (of R.) present

Jonathan Huffington, exe. of Gabriel Banks

Henry Lankford, adm. of William H. Adams

Elisha E. Whitelock, claimant, & Esther Broughton, adm. of Josiah & John H. Broughton, ask court to appoint James Stewart & Isaac M. Adams to arbitrate between them

F. 281   Josiah Furniss, guardian to Henry J. C. Furniss

Levin Tyler, exe. of Samuel Milbourn

William Jones, guardian to William E. Waters

Isaac Harris, guardian to William H. Acworth

Robert J. Henry & Henry Lankford to view estate of Samuel C., Patty A. & Rebecca M. Broughton, in care of Levin Tyler, guardian

Nathaniel Dixon, adm. cwa of Thomas Jenkins

Orphan; Thomas G. R. Roberts
Appointed Guardian; Benjamin Roberts (father)
Sureties; Samuel Robertson, Solomon Harris

George H. Rencher, collector of Nelson Waller

F. 282   Covington Cordray & George Hopkins to view estate of Ann M.
         D. & George L. R. Walter, in care of Sarah Walter, guardian

Tues., Jan. 22, 1828   All Justices present

Citation issued for Winder Cannon, adm. dbn of Sally Cannon, at
instance of Littleton Long

Jesse Hughes & Henry Hyland to view estate of William J., Mary E.,
Martha J., Sarah P., Isaac J. T. & Alcy K. Harris (of William), in
care of Jane Harris, guardian

Clement Goslee, exe. of Landay(?) Goslee

F. 283   William Sudler, adm. of Emory S. Sudler

Tues., 12 Feb., 1828   All Justices present

George M. Willing, adm. of Obadiah Stanford

Isaac T. Marshall, adm. of Jacob Marshall

F. 284   George L. Ayres, adm. cwa of William Ballard

Josiah Johnson, adm. of Josiah Johnson

Orphan; George W., Mary A., Levin, Elizabeth Layfield (of George)
Appointed Guardian; John Layfield
Sureties; John J. Davis, James Layfield

George Hopkins, adm. of Henry Wilson (negro)

Thomas Morris, adm. of Josiah Morris

F. 285   [following two entries have 'exe. of Saml. Milbourn' squeezed
         in above them]

Levin Tyler, guardian to William S. Broughton

Levin Tyler, guardian to Patty Ann, Samuel C. & Rebecca M. Broughton

John Miles, guardian to George Johnson

Tues., Feb. 26, 1828   All Justices present

Sarah Tilghman, guardian to Esther E. W. Tilghman (of William)

Thomas Walker, guardian to Elizabeth, Thomas & Asbury Ansley

F. 286   Orphan; Edward Travers (of Matthew)
         Guardian; Priscilla Travers, revoked, due to insanity
         Appointed Guardian; John Travers

Jesse Hughes & George D. Walter to view estate of Edward Travers, in care of Matthew [see above] Travers, guardian

Orphan; Sarah Jane, Ann Rebecca Holbrook
Guardian; Samuel G. Holbrook, revoked
Appointed Guardian; William Jones (Monie)
Sureties; Joseph Cottman, John McKenzie

Tues., Mar. 11, 1828   All Justices present

F. 287   Jane W. Bell, adm. of William Bell

William Miles, guardian to John, Mary A. J. & James K. Gunby

James Herron, guardian to Ann C. J. Dashiell

At instance of John P. Giles, citation issued for Jesse Owens, adm. of John Phillips, to shew cause why he doesn't return an inventory

F. 288   Noah Holland, guardian to Smith & Samuel Holland

Thomas M. Hargis, collector of Betsy Bayly

Stephen Taylor, adm. of Aaron Foxwell

John Harskins, guardian to William Leatherbury

Robert J. Henry & Henry Lankford to view estate of William S. Broughton

Joshua Brattan & Charles Venables to view estate of William R. & Sophia R. Donoho, in care of Alexander Donoho, guardian

Travers Daniel & George Rowe to view estate of Berry T. T., Henry A. P., Alexander W. W. & Sophia A. M. Webster, in care of Elizabeth Webster, guardian

F. 289   Tues., Mar. 25, 1828   All Justices present

Michael B. Carroll, adm. cwa of Betsy Bayly

William Stewart, adm. of Robert Hitch

Sarah Walter, exe. of James Walter

Zipporah & John Bounds, exes. of William Bounds

F. 290   Account passed by John Laws, who intermarried with Mary Gunby, adm. of Kirk Gunby, is defective

Henry Moore, guardian to William Moore

Henry Crawford, guardian to Elizabeth Nelson

F. 291   Molly Cox, guardian to Sally Marshall

Tues., Apr. 1, 1828   William Williams, George Jones (of R.) present

Caleb Hughes & wife, guardian to Charlotte J. & Esther A. U. Nelson

Esther Ballard, adm. of William Ballard

Theodore G. Dashiell, adm. of John S. Ward; Stephen Ward & wife, late guardians of aforesaid dec. to pass final account

F. 292   Jesse Hughes & Henry Hyland to view estate of William J., Mary E., Martha J., Sarah P., Isaac J. T. & Alcy K. Harris (of William), in care of Jane Harris, guardian

Tues., Apr. 22, 1828   George Jones (of R.), Thomas K. Carroll present

Elizabeth Acworth, guardian to John L. Moore, to sell negroes Leah & Ara(?)

Tues., Apr. 29, 1828   George Jones (of R.), Thomas K. Carroll present

Marcellus Jones, adm. of William U. Waters

F. 293   May 13, 1828   All Justices present

Henry Lankford, crier pro tem

Theodore G. Dashiell, by William Done, his attorney, asked that adm. of John S. Ward, granted him on 1st of Apr., last, be revoked, as not according to law; new adm. granted to Theodore G. Dashiell & wife, Matilda T. Dashiell

F. 294   Elizabeth S. J. Evans, adm. of James Evans, to sell negroes Leah & John

Tues., May 20, 1828   All Justices present

David Lankford, crier

Humphrey Humphreys, guardian to George W. & Mary A. Humphreys

Orphan; Emeline Dickerson (of Isaac)
Appointed Guardian; Parker Dickerson
Sureties; George Miles, William Costen

William Costen, Sen., & Levin Wilson to view estate of Emeline Dickerson, in care of Parker Dickerson, guardian

Samuel Gordon, one of adms. of John McClester

F. 295   William Mezick, adm. of Covington Mezick

Orphan; Purnell, Ann Johnson (of William P.)
Appointed Guardian; Samuel Williams
Sureties; William Williams (of Saml.), Arthur Lankford

Elijah Christopher & Levin D. Collier to view estate of Purnell & Ann Johnson, in care of Samuel Williams, guardian

Elizabeth Mezick, adm. of Aaron Mezick, sold much of estate to Jacob
         Mezick, & took his bill obligatory, with Joshua B. Roberts,
F. 296   his surety; both principle & security unable to pay

Edward Fowler & Levisa(?) Kennerly, adms. of Orrell Kennerly

Ballard Reid & Henry Newman to divide negroes from estate of Thomas Ballard

Wed., Mary 21, 1828   All Justices present

Orphan; William Bell (of William)
Appointed Guardian; Levin D. Collier
Sureties; Peter Bell, Levin W. Ballard

Orphan; George, Elizabeth Bell (of William)
Appointed Guardian; Robert Hitch
Sureties; Peter Bell, Levin D. Collier

F. 297   James C. Coulbourn & wife, guardian to Emeline B. Parker

Elihu Jackson, guardian to Joseph Leonard

John Mason & wife, guardian to Benjamin & Hamilton Evans

Peregrine Weatherly & Samuel Robertson to divide negroes from estate of Charles Rhodes

Stephen Ward & wife, guardian to John S. Ward

Thurs., May 22, 1828   All Justices present

William Hopkins, guardian to Charles E. M. Collier

James Phillips, guardian to James R. H. Phillips

F. 298   Tues., May 27, 1828   All Justices present

Jacob W. Bayly, adm. of David Vance

Lucretia Handy, adm. of Richard H. Handy

Orphan; Mary A. Giles
Appointed Guardian; John P. Giles (father)
Sureties; James Rider, Perry T. Phillips

Wed., May 28, 1828   All Justices present

Levin Walter, adm. dbn of William Walter

F. 299   Levin Morris, guardian to Alexander & Wilhelmina Waller

William Whayland, guardian to Robert, John & Joseph Price

James Powell, guardian of Nathaniel H. Smulling

Thomas Marshall, guardian to Josias Marshall

Tues., 10 June, 1828   All Justices present

Handy H. Irving, William W. Handy & John Rider appointed to adjust accounts between the guardian of Purnell & Ann Johnson, & Hannah Hearn, exe. of William Hearn

Orphan; John, Charles Milbourn (of John)
Appointed Guardian; Lodowick Milbourn
Sureties; Daniel Boston, Isaac T. Marshall

Robert J. Henry & Levin Tyler to view estate of John & Charles Milbourn, in care of Lodowick Milbourn, guardian

F. 300   Isaac T. Marshall, adm. of Jacob Marshall

Henry Gale, exe. of Stephen Taylor

Theodore G. Dashiell, adm. of John S. Ward

Orphan; George P. Jones (of Levin D.)
Appointed Guardian; Robert Jones
Sureties; George Jones (of Robert), John Leatherbury

Orphan; Henrietta Jones (of Levin D.)
Appointed Guardian; John Leatherbury
Sureties; Robert Jones (of Geo.), George Jones (of Robt.)

James Goslee & Henry Gale to view estate of George P. & Henrietta Jones, in care of John Leatherbury & Robert Jones (of George), guardians

F. 301   Lucretia Harris, guardian to John Harris

Stephen Ward & wife, guardian to Thomas M. Ward

Jesse Hughes & George D. Walter to view estate of Edward Travers, in care of John Travers, guardian

Elizabeth McBryde, guardian to Mary E. McBryde

Tues., June 24, 1828   William Williams, Thomas K. Carroll

David Lankford, exe. of Lova(?) Lankford

Matthias Dashiell & John S. Crockett, adms. of Josiah Dashiell

Elizabeth McBryde, guardian to John B. Slemons

William Howarth & wife, guardian to John, Mary & Severn Croswell

Frances Humphriss, guardian to Elizabeth McB. & Leah M. McB. Humphreys

F. 302   Tues., July 8, 1828   George Jones (of R.), Thomas K. Carroll

Sarah Dashiell, adm. of John Dashiell

Orphan; John W. S., Ann Maria Hughes (of James)
Appointed Guardian; Henrietta Maria Hughes
Sureties; John Insley, Samuel Dickerson

Jonathan Huffington, guardian to George & Sally Williss

Tues., July 22, 1828   All Justices present

William Done, John H. Bell & Robert Stewart appointed to adjust claim of George Jones (of Robt.), exe. of Charles Jones, against William King (of Jesse), according to judgement of County Court

F. 303   Robert J. Henry, Daniel Dakes & Henry Lankford to value interests of Samuel C., Rebecca & Patty A. Broughton, infant children & divisees of Ann Broughton, in lands divised to them by Ann

Severn Mister, exe. of Richard Evans

Samuel Brown, exe. of Stephen Disharoon, to take action to secure debt due from real estate of Esme M. Waller, by taking obligation of Edward Fowler

Beauchamp Acworth & Shiles Crockett to view estate of Robert, Nancy, John, William, Eliza, Sarah Jane, George, Thomas, James & Samuel Robertson

F. 304   Tues., 12 Aug., 1828   All Justices present

Marcellus Jones, exe. of Keziah Jones

Henrietta B. Robinson, adm. of Charles Robinson

Hiram Lankford, adm. of James R. Hayman

F. 305   Ephraim K. Wilson, Henry K. Long & James Polk appointed to
         determine amount due in judgement of Count Court, rendered
May 28, 1828, in favor of George & Robert Jones,, exes. of Charles
Jones, vs. Esther Broughton, adm. of John H. Broughton

Henry K. Long & James Polk to award in case of Mary Broughton vs.
Esther Broughton, adm. of John H. Broughton

Jane Miles, guardian to Isaac T., Washington & Catherine Miles

Joseph S. Cottman, guardian to John A. H. & Joseph B. Cottman

Tues., Aug. 26, 1828   William Williams, George Jones (of R.) present

Severn Mister, exe. of Richard Evans

F. 306   Benjamin I. Jones, adm. of Robert Moreton(?), to sell horse

Tues., Sept. 9, 1828   All Justices present

Peregrine Weatherly & Philip Graham to divide negroes from estate of
John Kellum

George Maddux & Elizabeth Byrd, exes. of Thomas Byrd, ordered to
secure debt due from real estate of Esme M. Waller, by taking the note
of Edward Fowler

Adm. of Charles Robinson sold estate too cheaply

James Goslee & Henry Gale to view estate of George P. & Henrietta
Jones (of Levin D.), in care of Robert Jones & John Leatherbury,
guardians

F. 307   Tues., Sept. 23, 1828   William Williams, George Jones (of
                                  R.) present

George Todd, adm. of Spencer Todd

William Sudler, adm. of Emory S. Sudler

William T. Wood, adm. of Robert Jones (of Robert)

Edward Fowler & Alcy White, adms. cwa of Henry White

Theodore G. Dashiell, adm. of John S. Ward, claimant, & Stephen Ward,
ask court to appoint Thomas K. Carroll, Littleton Dennis, Sen., &
Daniel Ballard to settle dispute between them

[no F. 308]

F. 309   Orphan; Elisha B. Harcum
         Appointed Guardian; Henry L. Harcum
         Sureties; Lee P. Harcum, Thomas Goslee

Edward Fowler & Alcy White, adms. cwa of Henry White

Joseph S. Cottman, adm. of Daniel Whitney

F. 310   Tues., 14 Oct., 1828   George Jones (of R.), Thomas K. Carroll present

Orphan; John Josephus, William Charles Bell (of William)
Appointed Guardian; Jane W. Bell
Sureties; Elisha Gunby, John P. Langford

Stephen Horsey & David Lankford to view estate of John J. & William C. Bell (of William), in care of Jane W. Bell, guardian

William Miles & George Blake to view estate of Henry, Hamilton & Eleanor Evans (of Benjamin), in care of John Mason & wife, guardian

John Mason, adm. of Benjamin Evans

Orphan; James Morris (of Robert)
Appointed Guardian; Thomas Morris
Sureties; William Gunby, Lemuel Collins

Orphan; Ann William Bell [no comma] (of William)
Appointed Guardian; Harriet Bell
Sureties; Matthias Miles, Ware C. Pollitt

Orphan; Mary Anne Riggin (of Pearce)
Appointed Guardian; Henry Lankford
Sureties; Thomas Robertson, Isaac Beauchamp

Robert J. Henry & Daniel Dakes to view estate of Mary Ann Riggin (of Pearce), in care of Henry Lankford, guardian

John Miles, guardian to George Johnson, to rent farm

F. 311   George Hopkins, guardian to Leah, Jane & Margaret E. Dashiell

William Hopkins, guardian to John F. Collier

Tues., Oct. 28, 1828   All Justices present

Peregrine Phillips, exe. of William Phillips

Elijah Parsons, adm. of Peter Dashiell, to secure debt due from real estate of Esme M. Waller, by taking bond of Edward Fowler

F. 312   Tues., Nov. 18, 1828   William Williams, George Jones (of R.)

James Herron, agent for West & Sperry, claimant, & Benjamin Bailey, adm. of William Crockett, ask court to appoint William Done & Ephraim K. Wilson to settle dispute between them

Stephen Horsey & David Lankford to view estate of John J. & William C. Bell, in care of Jane W. Bell, guardian

Littleton D. Maddux, guardian to Henry D. & Sarah S. Maddux

Robert J. Henry & Levin Tyler to view estate of John & Charles Milbourn, in care of Lodowick Milbourn, guardian

Wed., Nov. 19, 1828   All Justices present

Joseph S. Cottman, adm. of Daniel Whitney

F. 313   Orphan; Matthias E. Willing (of Evans)
          Appointed Guardian; Robert J. H. King
          Sureties; Josiah Warwick, John Miles

Wed., Nov. 20, 1828   All Justices present

William Miles & George Blake to view estate of Henry, Hamilton & Eleanor Evans (of Benjamin), in care of John Mason & wife, guardian

Tues., Dec. 2, 1828   All Justices present

James Stewart, adm. of John C. Stewart; ordered that John H. Bell & Matthias Miles divide negroes from estate

Edward Coulbourn & Henry Lankford to divide negroes from estate of Isaac W. Connor

George Twilley, guardian to Samuel J. & Ann M. Twilley

James Russell, guardian to Levin Russell

F. 314   James Stewart, temporary guardian to Mary & Elizabeth Stewart

Jan. 6, 1829   George Jones (of R.), Thomas K. Carroll present

John Mason, adm. of Benjamin Evans

Orphan; Ann M. Morris
Appointed Guardian; Levin Morris
Sureties; William Whayland, Joshua Brattan

John Waters, adm. of William Boggs

Joseph Handy & John Curtis to divide negroes from estate of Emory S. Sudler

John Howard, guardian to William S. Broughton

Elizabeth Webster, guardian to Henry A. P., Berry T. T. & Sophia A. M. Webster

Daniel Ballard, guardian to Elizabeth Collins

Isaac Denson & wife, guardian to Henry J. Dashiell

F. 315 Peggy King, guardian to John U. & Henrietta King

John H. Bell & Matthias Miles to divide negroes from estate of John C. Stewart

Tues., Jan. 13, 1829   George Jones (of R.), Thomas K. Carroll present

Jonathan Huffington, guardian to George & Sally Williss, to have lands surveyed

Orphan; Eliza Ann, Alexander H., Robert Spencer Todd (of Spencer) Appointed Guardian; George Todd
Sureties; Jonathan Huffington, Cis Todd

Jehu Parsons & Thomas Hooper to view estate of Eliza Ann, Alexander H. & Robert S. Todd (of Spencer), in care of George Todd, guardian

John Beauchamp, guardian to Matthias C. T. Beauchamp

F. 316 Margaret B. Chapman, guardian to Sarah A. & Margaret E. Chapman

William Costen & Levin Wilson to view estate of Emeline Dickerson, in care of Parker Dickerson, guardian

Tues., Feb. 3, 1829   William Williams, George Jones (of R.) present

Henry Hyland, adm. of Abraham Barkley

Tues., 10 Feb., 1829   All Justices present

F. 317 Caroline Tull, exe. of Samuel Tull

Samuel Cooper & Priscilla Badley, adms cwa of Severn Badley

Apprentice; Matthias E. Willing
Bound to; John S. Zieber
Trade; printing

Benjamin Dashiell, adm. of Jonathan Moore

Samuel Cooper, exe. of Eleanor Cooper

Tues., Feb. 17, 1829   William Williams, George Jones (of R.) present

Stephen Riggin, adm. of William Cox

F. 318 Elijah Lawson, guardian to Emeline Lawson

Sarah U. Adams, guardian to Edward H. & Louisa U. Adams

John T. Fontaine, guardian to John E. & Eleanor A. E. Fontaine

George Hopkins, guardian to Margaret E., Leah & Jane Dashiell

Tues., Feb. 24, 1829   All Justices present

Edward Fowler, one adm. of Orrell Kennerly

James R. Hayman, adm. of James R. Hayman

Elijah Parsons & Elizabeth McBryde, exes. of James Ritchie, by William W. Handy, their attorney, state that they have a judgement to a considerable amount against Samuel McBryde, in Somerset County Court

F. 319   William Jones, guardian to Sarah J. & Ann R. Holbrook

Sally U. Adams, guardian to Edward H. & Louisa U. Adams

Levin Tyler, guardian to Samuel C., Patty A. & Rebecca M. Broughton

Peggy King, guardian to John U. King

Samuel Walter, temporary guardian to William Thomas, John, Eliza, James, George, Samuel, Nancy, Sarah J. & Robert Robertson

Tues., Mar. 10, 1829   All Justices present

Dispute between William Mezick, exe. of Covington Mezick, & James D. Adams, who intermarried with Leah W. Mezick, a claimant against estate of Covington Mezick

F. 320   Peter Collins, adm. cwa of Joseph Brewington

Cathell & Humphrey Humphreys, exes. of Thomas Humphreys

Marcellus Jones, exe. of Charles Palmer

Jesse Hughes & Littleton Aires to view estate of heirs of Charles Palmer, in care of Marcellus Jones, temporary guardian

Henry Gale, exe. of Stephen Taylor

F. 321   Joseph Handy & John Curtis to divide negroes from estate of Emory S. Sudler

James Russell, guardian to Levin Russell

Tues., Mar. 24, 1829   George Jones (of R.), Thomas K. Carroll present

Daniel Ballard qualifies as Justice

F. 322   John Waters, adm. of William Boggs

Rachel Howard & Samuel Phillips, adms. cwa of Joseph Howard

Orphan; Lovitha A. Milbourn (of Samuel)
Appointed Guardian; James Handy
Sureties; William T. Wood, Tubman Cox

William T. Wood, adm. of Robert Jones

Scott Brereton, adm. of Smith Brereton; William Done & James Polk to adjust accounts between Scott Brereton, & estate of dec.

[page number appears, off by one]

F. 322b Robert J. Henry & Levin Tyler to view estate of Lovitha Ann Milbourn (of Samuel), in care of James Handy, guardian

Orphan; Elizabeth, Levin Goslee
Guardian; Edmond R. Goslee, revoked
Appointed Guardian; John U. Turpin
Sureties; William T. Wood, John Turpin

Charles Elzey, guardian to William Kellum

Levin Morris, guardian to Alexander & Wilhelmina Waller

Caleb Hughes & wife, guardian to Esther A. U. & Charlotte J. Nelson

Noah Holland, guardian to Samuel & Smith Holland

John Dryden, guardian to Littleton Dryden

Tues., 14 Apr., 1829 Daniel Ballard, George Jones (of R.) present

Orphan; William W., Edward M., George K. Wise (of William)
Appointed Guardian; William W. Johnston
Sureties; George Handy, Mary S. Wilson

F. 323 John Cullen, adm. of Benjamin Ward

William W. Handy & George Todd to divide negroes from estate of Richard H. Handy

Thomas Robertson, exe. of Robert Riggin

John Dryden, adm. of Stephen Adams

Nathan Gordy, adm. of Thomas Connelly

F. 324 Jesse Hughes & Littleton Aires to view estate of heirs of Charles Palmer

Marcellus Jones, exe. of Charles Palmer

Stephen Riggin, adm. of William Cox

'72'

William Done, adm. cwa of Sally Gale

Henry Crawford, guardian to Elizabeth E. Nelson

Isaac Harris, guardian to William Acworth

Joseph Barkley, guardian to Charlotte R. Heath

Frances Humphreys, guardian to Leah McB. & Elizabeth McB. Humphreys

F. 325   John Hopkins, guardian to Kitturah Acworth

Elizabeth Collins, guardian to William Broughton

Henry Maddux, guardian to John Turpin

Elizabeth McBryde, guardian to Mary E. McBryde

Robert J. Henry & Daniel Dakes to view estate of Mary A. Riggin (of Pearce), in care of Henry Lankford, guardian

Tues., Apr. 28, 1829   All Justices present

Robert Stewart, adm. of Francis Brady

Philip Adams, adm. of Lazarus Adams

F. 326   Morris H. Adams, adm. cwa of Ruth Adams, to sell term of years of negro Margaret

Joseph B. Brinkley, adm. dbn of William H. Horsey

Orphan; John, Isaac, Grace, Travers, William, Harriet Lawson (of Isaac)
Appointed Guardian; Littleton Tyler
Sureties; James Lawson, Horsey Somers

William Roach & Isaac Lawson to view estate of John, Isaac, Grace, Travers, William & Harriet Lawson, in care of Littleton Tyler, guardian

Orphan; William J. T. B. Willing (of Evans)
Appointed Guardian; George M. Willing
Sureties; Joseph B. Brinkley, William Quinn

Tues., May 19, 1829   All Justices present

F. 327   Job Moore, guardian to Marcella, Maria J., Hambleton & Kitty Moore

Lorenzo D. Parker & Robert M. Parker, adm. cwa of John Parker

Benjamin Bailey, adm. of William Crockett

Levin Tyler, guardian to Samuel C. Broughton

Levin Tyler, guardian to Rebecca M. & Patty Ann Broughton, to repair dwelling house

Robert J. Henry & Mary D. Henry, exes. of Harriet G. Stevenson

F. 328   Robert J. Henry & Mary D. Henry, exes. of Harriet G. Stevenson

Elizabeth Acworth, guardian to John L. Moore

Isaac Nicols, guardian to William P. & Robert Russum

Jehu Parsons & Thomas Hooper to view estate of Eliza A., Alexander H. & Robert S. Todd, in care of George Todd, guardian

Robert J. Henry & Levin Tyler to view estate of Lovitha A. Milbourne, in care of James Handy, guardian

John Hopkins, guardian to Kitturah Acworth

Wed., May 20, 1829   All Justices present

William Done, claimant, & Joseph Barkley, adm. of Samuel Heath, ask court to appoint William W. Handy & John H. [incomplete]

F. 329   James Stewart, claimant, & Joseph Barkley, adm. of Samuel Heath, ask court to appoint John H. Bell & Isaac M. Adams to settle dispute between them

Philip Adams, adm. of Lazarus Adams

Tues., May 26, 1829   All Justices present

Humphrey Humphreys, adm. dbn of Elizabeth Wilson

William Mezick, exe. of Covington Mezick

Sarah Walter, guardian to Ann M. D. Walter

Levin Walter, adm. dbn of William Walter

Isaac Aires, through his agent, claimant, & Robert Stewart, adm. of
     George D. Atkinson, ask court to appoint Jesse Hughes & Henry
F. 330   Hyland to settle dispute between them

Orphan; Alcy K., William J., Mary E., Martha J., Isaac J. T. & Sarah P. Harris (of William)
Appointed Guardian; Isaac Harris
Sureties; Marcellus Jones, John Hopkins

William Whayland, guardian to George, Joseph & Robert Price

'74'

William S. Dashiell, guardian to Algernon S. Dashiell

George Twilley, guardian to Ann M. & Samuel J. Twilley

Sarah Walter, guardian to George L. R. Walter

John Mason, guardian to Hamilton Evans

William Howarth & wife, guardian to John, Mary & Severn Croswell

George Walter, guardian to Thomas Willing

Elihu Jackson, guardian to Joseph Leonard

F. 331   Tues., 9 June, 1829   Daniel Ballard, George Jones (of R.)

Robert Patterson, exe. of Leolin Stayton

Orphan; Theodore T.(?) Gibbons (of Isaac)
Appointed Guardian; William Smith (of Saml.)
Sureties; William T. Wood, David Lankford

[writing changes at this point]

David Ballard & William Sudler to view estate of Theodore T. Gibbons, in care of William Smith (of Saml.)

Rosanna A. W. Wainright, guardian to Edward J. C., Nancy F. D. & Rosanna E. M. J. Wainright

Lucretia Harris, guardian to John Harris

John Miles, guardian to Geo. Johnson

Esther Broughton, adm. of John H. Broughton, being sued by Elisha A. Whitelock in County Court

INDEX TO BOOK 1, 1823 - 1829

ACWORTH:

Beauchamp................52,65
Betsy.......................22
Elizabeth.......10,34,50,62,73
Kitturah................23,72,73
Kitturah H..................9,34
Samuel......5,6,17,24,26,39,44
Train........................25
William......................72
William H.............45,47,59

ADAMS:

Amelia......................43
B.D..........................8
Beauchamp D..................8
Edward..................5,6,41
Edward H...........26,47,69,70
Elizabeth...................43
Hope........................18
Isaac M.............8,11,59,73
James D.....................70
Jesse.......................43
John.....................13,18
Lazarus................43,72,73
Louisa................5,6,26,41
Louisa U.............47,69,70
Morris H....................72
Philip...................72,73
Ruth........................72
Sally U........5,6,26,41,47,70
Samuel......................11
Sarah U.....................69
Stephen..................18,71
Thomas...................38,42
Thomas P.............12,24,47
William H...............55,59

AIKMAN:

William................8,18,32
Willaim S............18,47,55

AIRES: (Ayres)

Betsy J....................1,24
George...................1,2,25
George L.................53,60
Littleton..6,17,19,26,32,36,41,
                  50,70,71,73

ANDERSON:

Isaac...............27,32,52,54
James...........15,16,31,32,36
John H.15,17,19,29,30,40,43,45,
                               49
Mary........................53
Zebedee...............53,54,55

ANSLEY:

Asbury...........14,17,29,48,60
Elizabeth........14,17,29,48,60
George...................13,14
Hetty.............14,17,29,48
Thomas......................60
William............14,17,29,48

ATKINSON:

Eliza A.....................25
George D..5,6,7,15,16,19,21,24,
                  25,28,30,73
George S....................25
Isaac.........15,25,33,38,41,56
Mary E......................25
William.....................25

AUSTIN:

Ann M....................38,39
Billy.....................2,3,4
Edward...................38,39
Eleanor (Ellena, Ellender)..1,2
George......................2,4
Harriet.....................1,2
John....1,2,3,4,5,6,36,51,55,59
Purnell...................1,2,4
Susan.......................39

(cont.)

(Austin cont.)

Susan L....................27
William..............1,2,3,4

AYRES (See Aires)

BADLY: (Bradley?)

Gideon..............24,34,35
Priscilla.................69
Severn....................69

BAILEY: (Bayley, Bayly)

Benjamin.31,38,40,43,45,46,47,
                  48,67,72
Betsy..................59,61
Jacob W.............33,36,63
Josiah....................12
Thomas...........1,14,19.57
Thomas D..................33

BALLARD:

Arnold H............10,15,25
Daniel...11,37,40,42,54,56,59,
              66,68,70,71,74
David.....................74
Edward....................25
Edward J..................10
Esther.................36,62
Henry.....................33
James..................33,36
Jarvis.................20,30
John......................32
Levin.....................37
Levin W...................63
Sarah..............20,30,37
Thomas.................56,63
William..........36,53,60,62

BANKS:

Gabriel................37,59
Gamaliel..................20
Henry.............20,22,26

BARGLUND:

John......................32
Jonas.....................36

BARKLEY: (Barkly)

Abraham...................69
James.....................16
Joseph..16,22,46,54,58,59,72,73

BARKLY (See Barkley)

BARRETT:

Don Carlos................22

BAYLEY, BAYLY (See Bailey)

BEAUCHAMP:

Aliceana (Alissanna).......8,22
Ann..................8,22,49
Anna.......................8
Isaac..........7,8,22,49,67
Jesse.....................48
John............1,10,20,34,69
Matthias C................13
Matthias C.T.......1,10,34,69
Matthias T.C..............20

BEDSWORTH:

Amelia.................10,25
Thomas.................24,47
Tubman..........18,37,38,39,40

BELL:

Amelia............11,22,35,51
Ann W.....................67
Betsy..................22,35
Elizabeth..............44,63
George....................63
Hamilton...............44,45
Harriet...................67
Jane W.............61,67,68
John H..6,19,39,46,47,48,51,52,
              65,68,69,73
John J.................67,68
Mary E....................44
Nathaniel..........11,22,35,51
Peter.....................63
Robert..........10,23,27,32,35
Thomas....................44
Thomas H...............39,44
William.....7,14,25,30,61,63,67
William C..............67,68

BENSON:

Daniel............33,39,42,58
Susan......................24

BIRD (See Byrd)

BLAKE:

George..................67,68

BLAND:

Theodorick.................39

BLOODSWORTH:

Nathan.....................48

BOGGS:

William...9,10,11,20,23,28,50,
                54,55,68,70

BOSMAN (See Bozman)

BOSTON:

Daniel.....................64
Margaret T.................13

BOUNDS:

Doughty (Doubty).....5,6,24,26
Elizabeth..................25
James....................7,20
John..............10,41,52,61
Samuel T...8,11,19,20,26,29,47
Stephen....................19
Tubman.....................13
William..................7,61
Zipporah...................61

BOWLAND:

John N.....................54

BOZMAN: Bosman)

Jesse....................3,6

BRADLEY: (Badley?)

Gideon......................7

BRADY:

Francis....................72

BRATTAN:

Joshua.13,26,27,32,34,38,40,61,
                            68

BRERETON:

Scott...................54,71
Smith...................54,71

BREWINGTON:

Joseph.....................70

BRINKLEY:

Joseph B............53,57,72

BROUGHTON:

Ann...............20,30,33,65
Betsy..................9,14,22
Edward..................40,41
Elizabeth..................35
Esther..15,31,32,39,40,59,66,74
Henry...................45,49
Isaac M.........30,32,33,42,55
James......................14
John H..........39,59,66,74
Josiah..15,17,31,32,34,40,42,59
Mary.......................66
Patty A...14,28,33,55,59,60,65,
                        70,73
Rebecca....................65
Rebecca M.14,28,33,55,59,60,70,
                           73
Samuel C..14,28,33,55,59,60,65,
                        70,73
William..........9,22,35,51,72
William S..9,28,33,35,42,56,59,
                     60,61,68

BROWN:

Samuel............21,45,57,65

BURROUGHS:

Arthur......................3
Arthur W....................6

BYRD:

Benjamin H..............22,33
Elizabeth..........22,33,48,66
Jacob......................57
John................22,33,48
Thomas.....................66

CANNON:

Burton............16,17,54,58
Caleb N....................54
Sally............34,35,45,60
Winder.16,17,34,35,45,58,59,60

CARROLL:

Henry J....................20
Michael B...............59,61
Thomas K.11,39,41,44,47,50,58,
         62,65,66,67,68,69,70

CARSLEY:

John.......................54
Noah....................31,54

CHAPMAN:

John...........31,38,42,54,55
Margaret B..............54,69
Margaret E......38,45,54,59,69
Sarah A.........38,45,54,59,69

CHRISTOPHER:

Elijah..................52,63
Harriet...............1,2,3,4

COHOON:

John H............14,24,26,48
Samuel A...................48

COLGAN:

Joseph L...................47

COLLIER:

Charles E.M..13,14,23,30,37,51,
                      52,55,63
Eleanor...............5,12,30
Elizabeth..................51
Esme................5,6,12,24
Francis....................36
George E.R.J...............33
John F............33,36,37,39,67
Levin D................52,63
William H.D.....33,36,37,39,55

COLLINS:

Ann S...................46,57
Elizabeth.....40,42,54,56,68,72
Francis....................33
Lemuel.....................67
Peter......................70
Stephen.9,14,20,22,28,29,33,35,
                         38,40
William.......21,28,33,35,46,57

CONNELLY:

Thomas..................44,71

CONNOR:

Isaac......................48
Isaac W....................68

COOPER:

Eleanor....................69
Samuel.....................69

CORDRAY:

Covington..........43,50,56,60

COSTEN: (Costin)

George B.R..1,11,12,13,34,35,59
Isaac H....................13
Isaac T.................20,21
Samuel S............13,20,21
William...13,15,16,17,18,20,21,
       28,29,30,35,38,47,50,58,62,69

COSTIN (See Costen)

COTTINGHAM:

Abraham...................45,49
John......................45,49
Mary..........................7
Nancy.........................5
Sally........................16
Thomas.................5,28,39

COTTMAN:

Esther H..................10,11
John...23,30,31,38,42,45,54,59
John A.H..11,30,31,46,47,48,66
Joseph.6,10,11,22,23,25,30,31,
                           46,61
Joseph B........30,46,47,48,66
Joseph S..30,31,47,48,66,67,68
Sally..............11,23,31,48
Sarah........................10

COULBOURN: (Coulbourne)

Alexander.................33,39
Betsy......................9,11
Edward.......................68
James C............10,25,37,63
John.......................9,11
Peggy.........34,40,41,53,55,57
Stephen......................55
William..24,26,27,29,34,35,40,
                     41,53,55,57

COX:

Mary.........................29
Molly..............5,17,43,62
Tubman.......................71
William..................69,71

CRAWFORD:

Henry.10,12,13,14,26,29,46,51,
                           62,72
John.........................12

CROCKETT:

Eleanor H....................45
Hetty........................45
John S..........39,46,51,54,65
Josiah S.....................45
Levin................1,4,14,17

Shiles...........4,41,52,56,65
William...6,17,18,25,38,40,43,
                     45,47,67,72
William B....................45

CROSWELL:

John............14,35,51,65,74
Mary...............14,35,65,74
Severn...............35,65,74
Severn T.....................14
William....................7,36
Zipporah..............14,35,51

CULLEN (See Cullin)

CULLIN: (Cullen)

Jacob..................13,24,57
John.........................71
Walter.................13,24

CURTIS:

Edmond C.................46,48
Edward W......................9
Elizabeth....................44
Elizabeth W...................9
Henry.........................9
Henry J.......................9
John..............44,46,68,70
Mary.......................9,29
Sarah T.......................9
Susan A.......................9
Thomas.....................9,10
W.H..........................41
William.................46,50
William H............41,42,48

DAKES:

Daniel...16,29,32,42,45,49,56,
                        65,67,72
Stephen...........16,22,29,32

DANIEL:

Travers (Traverse).....8,56,61

DASHIELL:

Algernon S...........26,44,74
Ann C.J..........8,19,32,50,61
Anne..................9,21,51
              (cont.)

(Dashiell cont.)

Benjamin.................58,69
Chapman........5,7,13,17,35,37
Delila......................50
Edward.................9,21,51
Eliza A.C............5,7,13,17
Elizabeth R............5,13,17
George.....................1,53
George A...............1,39,54
Henry J.....................69
Henry J.W........7,18,31,44,59
Henry W............5,7,13,17,35
Isaac.......................46
Isabella...............9,21,51
James........................7
James W..............5,13,55
Jane............11,23,35,67,70
John..1,9,18,20,21,22,26,27,65
John H......................51
Joseph...................37,50
Josiah.............39,46,54,65
L.F..........................6
Leah............11,23,35,67,70
Margaret.................11,23
Margaret E............35,67,70
Mary.....................26,27
Matilda T...................62
Matthias.........6,26,39,44,65
Peter.................9,52,67
Priscilla...........9,21,35,51
Robert..............9,18,21,35
Robert N....................51
Sally........................2
Sarah................9,21,51,65
Theodore G............62,64,66
Thomas...................39,43
William.....................53
William S............26,44,74

DAVIS:

Alexgean....................16
Ann.........................36
Ann E.......................16
Charles.....................50
Henrietta................16,26
Henry....................16,26
Jane A......................16
Jane E......................26
John J...................32,60
Nancy.......................16
Patty.......................16

Patty A.....................26
Samson..........16,19,20,26,36
Samuel......................50
Sophia L.................24,28
Turner...............16,19,20

DEAN:

Mary.................7,24,34,35

DENNIS:

L.P.........................41
Littleton..22,29,38,42,54,55,66
Littleton P..............52,57

DENSON:

Isaac.......7,18,31,44,46,59,69
James....................43,48

DICKERSON:

Emeline..................62,69
Isaac...........27,28,46,53,62
Lanta....................27,46
Lucretia....................17
Parker...................62,69
Samuel......................65
William.....................17

DISHAROON:

Stephen............21,45,57,65

DIXON:

John.........................3
Nathaniel................38,59

DONE:

Mary A......................24
William..5,6,48,52,55,56,62,65,
                  67,71,72,73

DONOHO:

Alexander...........37,40,42,61
Azariah W................51,59
James..4,6,9,14,18,22,30,37,38,
                      40,41,42
John............4,6,9,18,30,38

(Donoho cont.)

Philip M.....12,21,35,36,51,55
Priscilla....35,36,42,51,55,59
Richardson....6,14,22,36,38,41
Sophia R..................40,61
William.......................40
William D..................51,59
William R..................40,61

DORMAN:

Henry......................51,59

DOUGHERTY:

Elijah.................11,23,50
James........................18
James W..................9,21,47
John.......................9,47
Peter........................30
Robert...........9,18,21,28,47

DRISKELL:

Aaron..................35,49,52

DRYDEN:

John.........12,15,25,39,53,71
Littleton....12,15,25,39,53,71
Peggy.......................4,5
Stephen.....4,5,11,19,32,38,41

DUNN:

John L......................12
John S....................11,12
Margaret....................12
Peggy.....................11,12
Priscilla..............7,21,40

DUTTON:

Mary A.......................24

ELLEGOOD:

Elizabeth....................44
John H.......................44

ELZEY:

Charles....................14,71
James.........................49
Sally A.......................49

ENNIS:

Elijah......................2,3

EVANS:

Alexander S....................1
Benjamin......12,22,48,63,67,68
Eleanor..........12,22,48,67,68
Elizabeth S.J.............26,62
Hamilton...12,22,48,63,67,68,74
Henry.........12,22,35,48,67,68
James..................21,26,62
John S.....1,6,9,18,21,38,39,47
Peter........................37
Richard...................65,66
Thomas D..............10,26,45
William.......................8

FACK:

Louisa.......................16

FITCHETT:

Margaret..................11,12

FLEMING:

John.........................43
William......................14

FONTAIN: (Fontaine)

Eleanor A.E............30,59,70
John.........................44
John E................30,59,70
John T.............30,49,59,70
Whitty....................49,53

FOOKS:

Benjamin......................4

FOWLER:

Edward....17,58,63,65,66,67,70

FOXWELL:

Aaron..............48,49,58,61
Benjamin S..................49
Elzey.......................49
George......................49
William E...................49

FURNACE (See Furniss)

FURNISS:

Henry H.....................30
Henry J.C.................7,59
Josiah.................7,30,59
William..................7,30

GALE:

George H.................15,19
Henry..7,13,26,27,32,52,53,54,
                  55,64,66,70
John P......................57
Sally.......................72

GIBBONS: (Gibons)

Edward......................37
Isaac...........9,32,45,55,74
James.......................48
John.....................45,55
Theodore T..................74
Thomas....................9,23
Thomas E....................50

GIBONS (See Gibbons)

GIBSON:

Bennett......................8

GILES:

John P...................61,64
Mary A......................64

GILLISS: (Gillis)

Ezekiel.....................50
George......................39

Levin.......................39
Thomas......................18

GODDARD:

Thomas......................31

GORDON:

Samuel..32,34,38,43,49,50,58,63

GORDY:

Nathan...................44,71

GOSLEE:

Clement..................53,60
Edmond R..........41,42,46,71
Elizabeth.........41,42,46,71
James.4,5,10,14,24,26,32,35,36,
    37,39,40,43,45,52,53,55,64,66
John......................8,19
Landay (Lenday)..........53,60
Levin................41,42,71
Thomas.................6,10,66

GRAHAM: (Greyham)

Amy.........................43
Peter.......................43
Philip.............24,47,55,66

GRAVNER:

Benjamin....................51

GREEN:

Isaac.......................29
John.................45,52,53
Mary........................53
Mary J...............53,54,55
Sarah A..............53,54,55
Susan................53,54,55

GREYHAM (See Graham)

GUILLETT:

Peter................22,48,56

GUNBY:

Amelia......................12
Elijah......................17
Elisha...................20,67
Esther...................17,20
James K.................12,26,61
John.....................12,61
Kirk....................2,26,61
Mary.......................61
Mary A.....................12
Mary A.J...................61
William................12,45,67
William J..................26

HALL:

Levin...................19,21

HAMMOND

Charles....................16

HANDY:

George....................6,71
James.......11,24,28,31,71,73
John.......................40
John C.....................52
John S..................41,58
Joseph...10,11,20,28,31,36,39,
                         68,70
Lucretia..............39,50,63
Noah..................11,28,31
Richard H.........39,50,63,71
Samuel......................8
Samuel K...................49
Thomas..................29,57
William W.......24,64,70,71,73

HARCUM:

Elisha B...................66
Henry L....................66
Lee P.............21,38,52,66

HARGIS:

Thomas M................59,61

HARPER:

Joseph......................2

HARRIS:

Alcy K.............58,60,62,73
Isaac..15,18,21,30,34,35,38,45,
             47,50,51,59,72,73
Isaac J.T..........58,60,62,73
Jane..........34,47,51,58,60,62
John..........12,14,23,51,64,74
John L.....................37
Lucretia...12,14,23,37,51,64,74
Martha J...........58,60,62,73
Mary E.............58,60,62,73
Sarah P............58,60,62,73
Solomon....................60
William.6,10,17,24,26,34,39,45,
             47,51,58,60,62,73
William J..........58,60,62,73

HARSKINS:

John............19,26,33,49,61

HAYMAN:

Isaiah................21,22,25
James R.................65,70
Randal..................21,25

HAYWARD:

Sarah..................18,20,34

HEARN:

Hannah.....................64
William....................64

HEATH:

Charlotte R............54,59,72
Jos.........................7
Josiah S.W...............14,21
Josiah W.................21,22
Matilda....................22
Parthena...................22
Rebecca....................22
Samuel...1,17,33,45,46,54,59,73

HENDERSON:

Jacob......................28

HENRY:

Mary D......................73
Robert J.22,29,40,42,55,56,59,
    61,64,65,67,68,71,72,73

HERRON:

James.........8,19,32,50,61,67

HICKMAN:

Jonathan....................22

HILLMAN: (Hilman)

William...............13,14,27

HILLY:

William......................4

HILMAN (See Hillman)

HITCH:

Adam........................21
Levin.....................3,19
Robert...............45,61,63

HOLBROOK:

Ann R...................61,70
Edward............23,30,31,39
Edward H...................10
Jane S.....................18
Matilda C..................19
Rebecca...............23,30,31
Rebecca A..................10
Samuel.................30,31
Samuel G..10,18,20,23,30,47,61
Sarah J...10,23,30,31,47,61,70
William T..................20
William T.W................19

HOLLAND:

Betsy......................32
James.......4,5,11,19,32,38,41
Noah.............8,21,33,61,71
Samuel..........8,21,33,61,71
Smith..............8,33,61,71
Smith H....................21
Thomas.....................32

HOOPER:

Capt........................3
Thomas............34,36,69,73

HOPKINS:

Elizabeth..................21
George..6,11,21,23,28,34,35,37,
              55,56,60,67,70
John..........9,23,34,58,72,73
Matthias D............28,32,34
Stephen.................21,23
William...14,23,30,33,36,37,39,
              51,52,63,67

HORSEY:

Polly......................41
Simon....................8,49
Stephen..................67,68
William H................53,72

HOSAIMA:

William....................51

HOWARD:

David...................16,26
John.............42,56,59,68
Joseph.....................70
Rachel.....................70

HOWARTH:

William.................65,74

HUFFINGTON:

Jonathan.1,4,13,19,20,32,37,49,
                 59,65,69

HUGHES:

Ann M......................65
Caleb.............41,56,62,71
Henrietta M................65
James..............6,9,18,65
Jesse.4,7,19,25,45,51,58,60,61,
              62,64,70,71,73
John W.S...................65

HULL:

Edward....................25,27

HUMPHREYS: (Humphriss)

Cathell...............48,57,70
Elijah....................42,52
Elizabeth M.....31,34,46,65,72
Francis........31,34,46,65,72
George W...........31,34,46,62
Humphrey..31,34,46,48,62,70,73
John U....................42,52
Joshua....................42,52
Leah M..........31,34,46,65,72
Mary A.............31,34,46,62
Thomas.3,11,12,25,26,31,36,43,
                        48,57,70
William......................13

HUMPHRISS (See Humphreys)

HURLEY:

Elizabeth....................48
Elizabeth W...................7
John.......................7,48

HYLAND:

Henry...2,10,37,58,60,62,69,73
James C......................37
James C.H....................10
Lambert......................10
Sarah........................10

INSLEY:

John.......7,12,13,21,40,56,65

IRVING:

Handy H...................52,64
Leah.......................7,21
Levin......................7,21
Nancy.........................6

JACKSON:

Elihu.......4,16,26,34,51,63,74
George W.....................20

JAMES:

Eliza........................55
Eliza J......................51
Francis U.................15,16
Jacob........................51
Louisa....................15,16
Mary.........................51

JENKINS:

Thomas....................38,59

JOHNSON: (Johnston?)

Algernon.....................51
Ann.......................63,64
George.....27,35,46,52,60,67,74
Josiah...............29,52,60
Littleton.................27,58
Purnell...................63,64
William P....................63

JOHNSTON: (Johnson?)

Bridget......................38
Ellen........................27
Ellen R......................47
Henrietta....................27
John.........................12
Josiah.......................17
Littleton....................44
William......................27
William W.................47,71

JONES:

Alexander..........30,36,37,39
Alfred....................49,52
Almira.......................34
Arnold E............9,10,14,49
Benjamin......................6
Benjamin I.5,17,33,36,44,50,54,
                              66
Charles..4,8,13,14,22,27,29,37,
    40,42,48,49,52,53,54,56,65,66
David......................8,43
Dr...........................41
Eleanor (Ellena, Ellender)..1,2
Elizabeth.................49,52

(Jones cont.)

George...1,2,4,5,8,9,11,12,13,
14,15,16,18,19,20,21,22,23,24,
25,26,27,28,29,30,31,32,33,34,
35,37,38,39,40,41,43,44,45,47,
48,49,50,53,54,56,58,59,62,64,
        65,66,67,68,69,70,71,74
George H.................49,52
George J.............11,27,29
George P.4,5,21,46,50,53,64,66
Gertrude....................34
Henrietta...4,5,38,50,53,64,66
Henrietta M.................21
Hiram.......................52
James..............9,34,36,37
John.................9,23,39
Joshua....................1,2,3
Keziah......................65
Leah........................37
Levin.....................4,27
Levin D.5,11,14,50,52,53,64,66
Marcellus...25,29,37,38,45,51,
           58,62,65,70,71,73
Maria...............4,5,38,53
Maria S.....................50
Mary.......................4,5
Mary A.......................6
Matthias....................38
Milcah G....................38
Perry.......................38
R..25,39,41,43,44,47,58,59,62,
        65,66,67,68,69,70,71,74
Robert...1,2,4,5,8,9,11,12,13,
14,15,16,18,19,21,22,23,24,26,
27,28,30,31,32,33,34,35,37,38,
40,43,44,45,46,48,49,50,53,54,
                56,64,65,66,71
Sarah A.....................34
Susan J.....................27
Teresa A....................11
Thomas M....................11
W...........................15
William............15,59,61,70
William M...................11

KELLUM

Gatty....................47,58
Gertrude....................51
John.............47,51,58,66
William.....................71

KELLY:

Elizabeth............9,12,13,25
James F..................40,48
William............8,9,12,13,25

KENNERLY:

Isaac.......................51
Levisa......................63
Orrell................58,63,70

KER:

Dr..........................41
Samuel...................22,43

KING:

Henrietta................19,69
Henrietta F.................10
Jesse.......................65
John........10,14,39,42,44,45
John U..................19,69,70
John W....................7,11
L.R.........................14
Lanta.......................46
Levin.....................8,10
Levin R............31,48,53,56
Margaret....................10
Peggy...................19,69,70
Planner H................10,49
Robert J...........52,54,55,57
Robert J.H....20,52,54,55,57,68
Whittington............7,10,11
William.................46,53,65
William F...................19

LANGFORD (See Lankford)

LANGSDALE:

Thomas......................49

LANKFORD:

Aaron C.....................10
Arthur......................63
Benjamin...........12,20,27,46
Betsy.......................32
David......45,58,62,65,67,68,74
Henry..20,29,32,42,44,45,48,49,
53,55,56,57,59,61,62,65,67,68,
              (cont.)   72

(Lankford cont.)

Hiram..........................65
Jesse..........................44
John A.........................28
John P.........10,12,27,46,58,67
Lova........................58,65
Nathan J....................12,27
Stephen A......................28
William........................32
William H.......................2

LAWES: (Laws)

John..................1,2,3,4,61
Mary......................2,61

LAWS (See Lawes)

LAWSON:

Elijah...............1,17,53,69
Elijah S.......................35
Emeline..........1,17,35,53,69
Grace..........................72
Harriet........................72
Isaac..........................72
James..........................72
John...........................72
Kesandy.........................1
Mary............................1
Travers........................72
William........................72

LAYFIELD:

Elizabeth......................60
George......................50,60
George W.......................60
James..........................60
John...........................60
Levin..........................60
Mary A.........................60

LEATHERBURY:

Asa..........................8,19
Elizabeth H.................25,26
John.................34,46,64,66
Peregrine......................26
Robert.8,11,14,18,19,30,31,35,
                            36,37
Sarah A.....................15,38
William.........19,26,33,49,61

LEONARD:

John............................4
Joseph...4,16,26,28,34,51,63,74

LEWIS:

James..........................37

LLOYD:

Maria..........................23
Thomas.........................23
Zacheus........................23

LOE (See Lowe)

LONG:

David..........................49
Henry K..................9,10,66
Jesse...........................9
Littleton...................35,60
Margaret...............27,28,29
Margaret R............47,48,53
William....27,28,29,47,48,49,53
Zadock...........31,48,53,55,56

LOWE: (Loe)

Ralph..........................27

LOWES:

Ann.............................5
Tubman..........................5

MADDUX:

Daniel......................11,46
George......................19,66
Henry...............7,25,36,72
Henry D..........15,27,41,56,68
Littleton D..15,27,35,36,41,56,
                               68
Marcy..........................46
Sarah..........................27
Sarah S............15,41,56,68

MARSHALL:

Adrian......................42,58
Isaac..........................20
            (cont.)

(Marshall cont.)

Isaac T................9,60,64
Jacob.........9,18,34,51,60,64
John P.....................45
Josias..........9,20,31,46,64
Robert N................19,21
Sally...........5,17,29,43,62
Thomas..........9,20,31,46,64

MARTIN:

Robert N....................1
William B..................52

MASON:

George.....................37
John..12,14,22,35,37,48,63,67,
                        68,74
Juliet.....................37

MATHEWS (See Matthews)

MATTHEWS: (Mathews)

Benjamin...................23
Benjamin H.................11
George.....................31
Henry................11,23,50
John.......................24
William.................8,24

MEZICK:

Aaron......................63
Covington...........63,70,73
Elizabeth..................63
Jacob......................63
Leah W.....................70
Littleton..................53
William........35,52,63,70,73

MILAWAY (See Millaway)

MILBOURN:

Charles.................64,68
John........38,42,44,56,64,68
Lodowick.............50,64,68
Lovitha....................50
Lovitha A...............71,73
Samuel....28,30,32,33,59,60,71

MILES:

Catherine..............29,31,66
George........................62
Henry W....................15,33
Isaac J.......................31
Isaac T.......................66
Jane.......................31,66
John....27,35,46,52,60,67,68,74
Levin..........................7
Matthias.........6,7,47,67,68,69
Samuel..............35,38,40,47
Washington.............29,31,66
William.1,12,16,17,26,35,38,45,
                    47,61,67,68

MILLAWAY: (Milaway)

Mary.......................33,58

MILLS:

Benjamin................16,17,23
Eleanor A...............16,17,23
George W................16,17,23
Isaac.........................16
Margaret......................50
Maria G.................16,17,23
Mary.................16,17,23,50
Stephen.................16,17,23
William W...............16,17,23

MISTER:

Severn....................65,66

MITCHELL:

Amelia........................12
Francis....................12,36
Hamilton......................12
Henry T....................41,42
John..........................41

MOORE:

Benjamin...................37,39
E.R............................8
Elizabeth.....................18
Elizabeth R......10,18,32,47,55
Hambleton..................57,72
Henry............9,21,32,47,62
            (cont.)

(Moore cont.)

Jemima....................32
Job...................14,57,72
John L.......10,22,34,50,62,73
Jonathan..............22,58,69
Julia........................8
Kitty....................57,72
Marcella.................57,72
Maria J..................57,72
Stephen...............14,32,57
William.....................62
William H..........9,21,32,47
William R...................10
William W........7,12,24,29,47

MORETON (See Morton)

MORRIS

Ann M.......................68
Isaac..................1,2,3,4
Jacob.......................28
James.......................67
Josiah......................60
Levin..7,20,21,26,33,47,64,68,
                             71
Polly........................3
Robert......................67
Thomas..........28,35,52,60,67

MORTON: (Moreton)

Robert...............36,54,66

MURRAY:

James....................22,25

McBRYDE:

Elizabeth.5,27,31,34,49,55,65,
                          70,72
Mary E...........5,27,34,65,72
Mary E.M....................49
Samuel..........5,21,22,49,70

McCLESTER:

Elizabeth...................58
John.....................58,63

McCORMICK:

William L...................54

McCREE;

Eleanor.....................12

McGEE:

James.......................12
Peter.......................20

McINTIRE:

Jesse.......................41

McKENZIE:

John........................61

NELSON:

Charlotte.................4,18
Charlotte E.................41
Charlotte J.......4,18,56,62,71
Cyrus.......................49
E.E.........................14
Elizabeth...................62
Elizabeth E......10,13,26,46,72
Esther.......................4
Esther A.................41,56
Esther A.C...................4
Esther A.U...........18,62,71
Francis D.....12,13,23,36,54,55
James T........4,19,30,38,41,56

NEWMAN:

Henry..............15,33,56,63
John................20,26,47

NEWTON:

Thomas H....................13

NICHOLS: (Nicols)

Isaac..13,16,25,26,39,43,46,55,
                             73

NICHOLSON:

Betty..................3,11,43
Theophilus............27,36,39

NICOLS (See Nichols)

NUTTER:

Philip......................56

OWENS:

Jesse.......................61

PALMER:

Charles..................70,71

PARKER:

Emeline B..........10,25,37,63
John........................72
Lorenzo D...................72
Robert M....................72

PARKS:

Charles.....................14

PARSONS:

Elijah..........16,26,55,67,70
Jehu...14,25,34,36,40,49,69,73
John W B.................16,25

PATTERSON:

Robert......................74

PHILLIPS:

Asa......................13,40
Day G.......................35
Eleanor..............13,33,50
Elijah...................13,56
Francis.....................35
James....................47,63
James R.H...................63
John........................61
Margaret....................13
Noah.....................33,50
Peregrine...................67

Perry T.....................64
Robert......................47
Samuel......................70
Theodore....................13
William.....................67
William D...................13
William R...................56

POLK:

James...1,15,20,21,33,45,50,52,
                53,55,66,71
Samuel........11,31,33,46,52
Whittington..................8
William T................15,16
William T.G.................52

POLLITT:

Levin....................15,35
Littleton..........10,38,39,51
Ware C......................67
William..................3,7,25

PORTER:

Hetty.......................49
Mary........................58
Richard B...................58

POWELL:

James.........12,24,29,35,49,64
John.....................23,47
Sally.....................5,17

PRICE:

Eleanor...................8,23
George.................8,23,73
Isaac........................8
James.......................23
John.................8,17,64
Joseph........8,23,35,47,64,73
Robert............8,23,64,73

PRIOR:

Miss.........................2

PUZEY:

Benjamin....................21

QUINN:

William.....................72

RACKLIFFE:

John H......................25

RADISH (See Reddish)

READ: (Reid)

Ballard..................56,63

REDDISH: (Radish)

William..............11,28,31

REID (See Read)

RENCHER:

George H....................60

RHODES:

Beauchamp.......10.11,17,23,36
Charles...........17,24,47,63
James........10.11,17,29,47,58
Rachael...........10,11,17,29
Sarah A........10,11,17,29,58

RICHARDS:

Joseph...................14,16

RICHARDSON:

John.......................2,3

RIDER:

James................23,26,64
John.............6,13,44,64

RIGGIN:

George......................57
Henry........................6
Henry J.................29,44
John........................42
John T..............18,19,35
Louther.................19,25

Mary A..................67,72
Pearce.29,32,42,44,45,49,53,56,
                         67,72
Robert......................71
Stephen..................69,71

RITCHIE:

James........22,23,26,52,55,70

ROACH:

William....11,27,28,44,57,58,72

ROBERTS:

Benjamin....................60
Joshua B....................63
Mary........................22
Rencher.....................21
Thomas......................24
Thomas G.R..................60
Underwood...................21

ROBERTSON:

Benjamin.................36,50
Eliza................52,65,70
George............39,52,65,70
George E....................58
James................52,65,70
John.................52,65,70
Nancy................52,65,70
Robert...............52,65,70
Samuel.......2,52,60,63,65,70
Sarah E.....................32
Sarah J..............52,65,70
Thomas.18,32,33,34,36,37,39,44,
  45,46,49,50,51,52,54,58,65,67,
                            71
William..................52,65
William T...................70

ROBINSON:

Charles..............45,65,66
Henrietta B.................65
Thomas.......................9

ROSS:

Asa A.......................33

ROWAN:

James J..................25,26

RUCKLE:

Leah......................37

RUMBOLD (See Rumbolt)

RUMBOLT: (Rumbold)

John....................24,25

RUSSEL:

Eleanor....................30
Elizabeth..................30
James..........12,30,45,68,70
Levin.............12,30,68,70
Nelly......................12
Robert..................12,30
Susan......................30
Thomas...............30,45,47

RUSSOM (See Russum)

RUSSUM: (Russom)

Joseph B...................13
Robert...........13,26,46,73
William......13,16,25,26,46,55
William P..................73

SAMPSON: (Samson)

R..........................7
Richard...................22

SAMSON (See Sampson)

SCOFIELD: (Schoolfield)

Elizabeth..................43
Polly W.................40,41
William....................6
William A.................29

SCHOOLFIELD (See Scofield)

SHREVES: (Shrieves)

Handcock (Hancock).....8,16,24
Samuel....................38

SHRIEVES (See Shreves)

SIMPSON:

Benjamin.................6,59
Charles...................54

SIMSON (See Simpson)

SLEMONS:

John B...........5,27,34,49,65

SLOCOMB:

Sarah...................41,49
Thomas............15,18,41,49

SMITH: (Smyth)

Henry A..............14,40,49
James...................48,58
Mary.......................4
Moses C.................13,27
Samuel....................74
William...................74

SMULLING:

Henry.....................12
Henry J...................35
Mary A....................17
Mary A.P...................5
Nathaniel H...............64
Nathaniel H.J..........24,29
Nathaniel J...............49

SMYTH (See Smith)

SOMERS: (Summers)

Horsey............15,27,28,72
Isaac................15,27,28

SPENCE:

Asa.......................52

STANFORD:

Henry..................35,52
Isaac.....................23
Isaac H.W...........35,49,52
         (cont.)

(Stanford cont.)

John L.W..............12,21,42
Leah H...................12,23
Levin.......................23
Levin J.M...................49
Levin J.M.W..............35,52
Obadiah (Obediah)......6,54,60
William..................12,35
William S.H..............35,52

STAYTON:

Leolin......................74

STEPHENS (See Stevens)

STEVENS: (Stephens)

John.....................24,25
Levi.........................3

STEVENSON:

Harriet G...................73
Joseph.................8,16,24

STEWART:

Elizabeth...................68
Elizabeth J.C...............47
James..7,15,18,39,44,45,50,54,
                      59,68,73
John........................22
John C............6,7,47,68,69
Mary........................68
Mary A......................47
Nancy.......................42
Robert..5,7,16,19,21,24,25,28,
     30,33,36,37,39,40,50,54,65,72,
                            73
William..................45,61

STURGIS:

Littleton...................22
Sally........................2

SUDLER:

Emory S...........60,66,68,70
William............7,60,66,74

SUMMERS (See Somers)

SWIFT:

John........................44

TAYLOR:

Betsy A.............28,30,38,58
Elizabeth................14,20
George......................58
Isaac.......................58
Maria.......................58
Matthias C...........11,13,21
Samuel......................58
Stephen....48,49,52,58,61,64,70
William......................3

TEACKLE:

Littleton D.................14

TILGHMAN:

Esther E.W.....4,15,18,20,34,60
Noah........................19
Sarah.................4,15,60
William............15,48,58,60

TOADVINE:

Isaac........................3
Isaiah.......................3
James........................2
Priscilla....................2

TODD:

Alexander H..............69,73
Cis.........................69
Eliza A..................69,73
George..........30,66,69,71,73
Robert S.................69,73
Spencer.............30,66,69

TOWNSEND:

Cutter......................44
Mary..................6,13,19

TRAVERS: (Traverse)

Alce........................7
Edward................7,61,64
John....................61,64
Matthew.............7,17,61
Priscilla...........7,17,61

TULL:

Caroline............45,56,69
Levin......................10
Samuel.........27,28,45,56,69
Thomas.....................28
William................36,39

TURPIN:

E.L........................7
Elizabeth L...............25
John..........7,25,36,71,72
John U....................71
William.................7,59

TWILLEY:

Ann M........29,32,50,68,74
George...26,29,30,32,34,37,50,
                         68,74
Hester A..................27
Maria.....................14
Robert....................29
Samuel J......29,32,50,68,74
Thomas....................27
William.5,14,26,30,32,34,37,50

TYLER:

Ann...................12,28
James............7,28,30,44
John.....................55
Levin..6,17,28,29,33,40,42,44,
46,55,57,58,59,60,64,68,70,71,
                            73
Littleton...........12,28,72

VANCE:

David................33,36,63

VENABLES:

Charles...4,13,14,17,19,26,30,
           34,38,40,51,61

Margaret W................51
Robert.................32,36

VINCENT:

Benjamin................1,2,3
Eli.......................18
James.....................18
Patty A..............27,36,39
Samuel.....................3
Solomon...................27
Solomon F.............27,39

WAILES:

Eleanor.................6,23
Margaret................6,23
William...................23

WAINRIGHT:

Ann F.D....................7
E.J.C......................7
Edward J.C.........19,30,46,74
Elizabeth.................22
Jesse.....................15
Jesse H.................6,18
Matilda...................22
Nancy F.D..............19,74
Nancy T.D.................30
R.E.M.J....................7
Rosanna A..................7
Rosanna A.W........19,30,46,74
Rosanna E.M.J.........19,30,74

WALKER:

Thomas........13,14,17,29,48,60

WALLACE (See Wallis)

WALLER:

Alexander....1,7,21,33,47,64,71
Esme M.............52,65,66,67
George....................48
Jonathan..........16,17,23,27
Nelson....................60
Richard................22,27
Wilhelmina (Williamina)...1,21,
                     33,47,64,71
William....................7
William L..................1

WALLIS: (Willis,Wallace)

Betsy........................37
Elizabeth....................33
George.......13,15,32,49,65,69
Milcah A.....................37
Sally..........13,32,49,65,69

WALSTON:

Leah.........................48
Thomas.............15,18,40,48
Tubman.......................33

WALTER:

Ann M.D...............56,60,73
Asa..........................38
Benjamin.....................34
Daniel.......................57
George................34,48,74
George D.....32,43,50,57,61,64
George L.R............56,60,74
James...............19,42,56,61
Jesse.....................4,50
John..................9,23,38,39
Levin.................56,64,73
Samuel..........10,17,47,52,70
Sarah...........56,60,61,73,74
William............42,43,64,73

WARD:

Benjamin.....................71
Eleanor...............17,19,25
George F............9,10,20,32
James.................17,19,25
John H.......................10
John S............62,63,64,66
Stephen...9,10,20,32,47,62,63,
                          64,66
Thomas M......9,10,20,32,47,64

WARWICK:

Josiah.......................68
William R....................44

WATERS:

Arnold..................4,5,15
Arnold E..........18,26,29,54

Elizabeth...................4,6
Elizabeth A.W.......15,18,36,41
Elizabeth E..................16
Francis.................4,42,43
Francis H...1,4,6,7,8,13,14,16,
           17,19,22,25,29,32,42,43
James........................51
John.......35,36,46,56,59,68,70
Levin......................4,15
Levin L.............18,26,29
Louisa.......................51
Richard E..........29,46,48,50
Sarah D......................33
William E...........15,18,41,59
William G............5,15,20,36
William U...........29,37,51,62

WEATHERLY:

James......................7,13
John.........................12
John L....................37,40
Lee..........................55
Peregrine.10,17,18,27,33,36,38,
                    39,47,63,66
Polly............23,24,25,37,40
Royston (Roiston)...12,23,24,25
Royston C....................37
Susan........................39
William......................55

WEBSTER:

Alexander....................18
Alexander W.W..8,30,44,56,59,61
Benjamin T.T.................18
Berry T.T...8,30,44,56,59,61,68
Elizabeth..8,18,30,44,56,59,61,
                              68
Henry A.P..8,18,30,44,56,59,61,
                              68
John..........................8
Michael....................8,56
Sophia A.M.8,18,30,44,56,59,61,
                              68

WHAYLAND:

William.1,6,8,9,18,20,23,35,47,
                       64,68,73

WHITE:

Alcy....................66,67
Betsy......................44
Elizabeth............6,17,29
Henry..6,17,29,44,46,48,58,66,
                              67
Sally N..........6,17,29,44,58
Thomas W...................57
William T........6,17,29,44,58

WHITELOCK:

Elisha A...................74
Elisha E...................59

WHITNEY:

Daniel................6,67,68
Joseph...............31,34,39

WHITTINGTON:

John N.............38,42,44,56

WILKINS:

John.......................13
Seth.......................13

WILLIAMS:

Adaline....................44
Elijah.....................21
Mary.......................44
Mary A.....................44
Peggy...............41,55,57
Priscilla..................44
Samuel..................33,63
Thomas.34,40,41,43,52,53,55,57
William.1,2,4,5,6,7,8,9,12,16,
17,18,21,22,23,24,25,26,27,28,
29,31,33,34,35,37,38,40,41,43,
44,50,53,57,59,62,63,65,66,67,
                              69

WILLIN (See Willing)

WILLING:

Elizabeth D................48
Evans...................68,72
George M.....18,42,54,57,60,72
James......................50

Mary.......................38
Matthias E..............68,69
Thomas.............34,48,50,74
Ware.................38,50,58
William....32,34,38,43,49,50,58
William J.T.B..............72

WILLIS (See Wallis)

WILSON:

Abraham....................16
E.K........................55
Elizabeth..................73
Ephraim K..22,34,40,50,56,66,67
George S................ 9,14
Henry......................24
James...4,5,6,9,15,16,18,22,26,
                     29,45,52,54
Jesse................23,24,26
John C...................9.10
Levin...........27,46,53,62,69
Mary S.....................71
Nancy...................28,39
William...10,11,17,23,24,26,29,
                        36,47,58

WINDER:

Levin......................49

WINGATE:

Mary R.....................48
Peter......................48

WINSOR:

Isaac......................19

WISE:

Edward M...................71
George K...................71
William....................71
William W..................71

WOOD:

William T........49,50,66,71,74

WOOLFORD:

John........................17

WRIGHT:

Henry............8,19,32,46,50
Willing (Willin).8,19,32,46,50

ZIEBER:

John S......................69

LISTINGS LEFT OUT OF INDEX

BENNETT:

Edmond........................4
James T.......................8
Jane..................1,4,5,24
Joshua........................8
Martha J......................5
Samuel G.W....................5

ROWE:

George...................56,61

FREE NEGROES WITHOUT SURNAMES

John........................6

FREE NEGROES WITH SURNAMES

ALLAN:

Freeborn....................24

DONE:

John........................24

DUTTON:

Adam........................23

NUTTER:

Philiss.....................13

WILLIAMS:

William......................3

WILSON:

Henry.......................60

INDEX TO SLAVES

Adam....................52	Kizziah..................58
Alfred..................42	Leah............1,19,44,46,62
Ann...................8,28	Levin.........3,16,31,34,44,48
Ara.....................62	Littleton................37
Araminta................30	Lydia....................53
Arthur................34,44	Marcus...................57
Belinda.................37	Margaret.................72
Benjamin.................1	Maria..................5,53
Bob................19,53,56	Martha...................51
Charity.................57	Mary..................19,44
Charlotte.............5,42	Matilda...................9
Durham..................20	Matthias.................42
Ebben...................15	Mida.....................42
Ephraim.................56	Milcah.................47,48
Esther................52,53	Moses....................50
Flora...................15	Nace.....................45
Frank...................14	Ned...................15,19
George................44,57	Nelson...................42
Ginny...................24	Peter....................45
Grace...............1,20,46	Rachael..................42
Hamilton................15	Rhoda....................40
Hannah..................30	Robert...................15
Harriet.................56	Rose.....................30
Harry...................56	Sally....................40
Henny...................54	Sam....................5,11
Henry.................28,56	Sarah....................44
Ibby....................34	Saul...................1,45
Isaac..............15,28,45	Sophia...................55
Jacob.................6,9,44	Spencer..................53
James.................9,42	Tom......................5
Jenny...................34	Vilet.....................2
Jesse....................9	William...............19,25
Joe.....................28	York.....................1
John.................28,62	Zadock....................9

SOMERSET COUNTY, MARYLAND

ORPHANS COURT PROCEEDINGS

BOOK 4

June 23, 1829 - June 26, 1838

SOMERSET COUNTY REGISTER OF WILLS

(Orphans Court Proceedings)   MSA C 1794

'101'

SOMERSET COUNTY ORPHANS COURT PROCEEDINGS, 1829-38

F. 1   Tues., June 23, 1829

Justices; Daniel Ballard, George Jones (of Robt.), Thomas K. Carroll
Crier; David Lankford
Register; James Polk

Thomas Robertson, exe. of Robert Riggin

Littleton Long & Burton Cannon, adms. of Winder Cannon

18 Sept., 1827, caveat against admission to probate of paper purporting to be will of Thomas Williams filed originally by William Williams. Ephraim K. Wilson, solicitor, withdraws caveat

F. 2   Stephen Ward & wife, guardian to George F. Ward

James Powell, guardian to Nathaniel H. J. Smulling

William Hopkins, guardian to Charles E. M. Collier

Tues., July 14, 1829   All Justices present

Will of Thomas Williams admitted to probate. Letters of adm. with copy of will annexed granted to William Williams

John Cullen(?), adm. of Benjamin Ward

F. 3   James Handy, next friend of William S. Broughton, orphan. John Howard, guardian, to answer charges of improper conduct toward said orphan

John Dryden, adm. of Stephen Adams

Harriet Bell, guardian to Leah A. W. Bell

James C. Coulbourn & wife, guardian to Emeline Coulbourn

Joseph S. Cottman, guardian to John A. H. & Joseph B. Cottman

William Miles, guardian to Mary A. & Elizabeth J. Stewart

William Roach & Isaac Lawson to view estate of John, Isaac, Grace, Travers, William & Harriet Lawson, in hands of Littleton Tyler guardian

F. 4   Tues., 11 Aug., 1829   Daniel Ballard, George Jones (of Robt.)

Robert Stewart, adm. of Francis Brady

William F. Dashiell, adm. cwa of Amelia W. Nicholson

F. 5   Orphan; Asbury, Hetty, William, Elizabeth Ansley
       Appointed Guardian; Priscilla Walker
       Surety; William Huffington, James W. Badley

Shiles Crockett & Charles Venables to view estate of Asbury, Hetty, William & Elizabeth Ansley (of George), in hands of Priscilla Walker

Orphan; William S. Broughton (of Isaac M.)
Appointed Guardian; James Handy
Sureties; Joshua R. Handy, Lodowick J. Milbourn

Tues., Aug. 18, 1829   All Justices present

Henry Lankford Crier pro tem

Henry Lankford, exe. of John Howard

F. 6   William Done, adm. cwa of Sarah H. Gale, to sell negro Sandy

Tues., Sept. 8, 1829   Daniel Ballard, Thomas K. Carroll present

James Polk to settle dispute between Joseph S. Cottman (adm. of Daniel Whitney) & John King, Sr.

Orphan; Susan Jones Disharoon, minor
Appointed Guardian; William S. Disharoon
Sureties; Levin Dorman, Jr., Richard Waller

Sarah Hayward, guardian to Elizabeth E. W. Tilghman

John Mason, guardian to Hamilton Evans & others

Marcellus Jones, guardian to Thomas D. Evans

F. 7   George Waller & Samuel McBryde to divide negroes from estate of
       Samuel Heath

Tues., Sept. 22, 1829   Daniel Ballard, Thomas K. Carroll present

Littleton Long & Burton Cannon, adms. of Winder Cannon

William Done to settle dispute between Zadock Long & Josiah Bayly (adm. of Thomas Bayly)

Henry Crawford & Thomas Jones to view estate of heirs of Francis Brady, in care of Robert Stewart, temporary guardian

Daniel Ballard, exe. of William Miles

Sarah Handy, exe. of Thomas Handy

F. 8   George H. Rencher, adm. de bonis non of William L. Waller, to
       sell negro boy James(?)

Orphan; William S. Broughton (of Isaac M.)
Guardian; James Handy, revoked
Appointed Guardian; Sally Howard
Sureties; Henry Lankford, Daniel Benson

Henry Lankford, exe. of John Howard, to sell negro Sam

Isaac Nicols, guardian to William P. & Robert C. Russum

Tues., 13 Oct., 1829   All Justices present

Josiah Bayly, adm. of Thomas Bayly

F. 9   Joshua Humphriss & John U. Humphriss, exes. of Elijah Humphriss

James Polk to settle dispute between Esther Broughton & William Done (adm. cwa of Sarah H. Gale)

Rachel Howard & Samuel Phillips, adms. cwa of Joseph Howard

Littleton Long & Burton Cannon, adms. dbn of Sally Cannon

Littleton Long & Burton Cannon, adms. dbn of George B. R. Costen

F. 10   Mason Abbott appointed crier; David Lankford resigned

Tues., Oct. 27, 1829   All Justices present

Ann Holland, exe. of James Holland

James F. Kelly, adm. of Ebenezer D. Howard

Orphan; John S., Ann M. Hughes (of James)
Appointed Guardian; Thomas Bell
Sureties; George Hopkins, Levin Jones (of Levin)

F. 11   William Costen, exe. of Isaac Harris

William Williams, by Ephraim K. Wilson, his attorney, files petition concerning partnership between himself & Alexander Coulbourn, deceased. Adm., Daniel Benson; various documents given

F. 12   George H. Rencher, adm. dbn of William L. Waller to sell negro James

Henry L. Harcum, adm. cwa of Lee P. Harcum

F. 13   Tues., Nov. 3, 1829   All Justices present

James Tilghman, adm. of James Blaine

Thomas Bradley, adm. of Wilson Bradley

Isaac H. Johnson, adm. of Jesse Johnson

Daniel Benson (adm. of Alexander Coulbourn), by Littleton P. Dennis,
his attorney, files answer to petition of William Williams,
F. 14   in which said Williams claims property of said Coulbourn as
surviving partner in firm of Coulbourn & Williams. Benson
F. 15   claims all property solely owned by Coulbourn. 3 Nov., 1829,
Daniel Benson appears before Theodore G. Dashiell, Justice of
the Peace

Arnold E. Jones, exe. of William Jones

F. 16   Samuel G. Holbrook, guardian to Edward H. Holbrook

Littleton D. Maddux, guardian to Sarah S. & Henry D. Maddux

Elizabeth Byrd, guardian to John Byrd

John Layfield, guardian to Levin, George, Mary & Elizabeth Layfield

Elijah Phillips, guardian to William A. R. Phillips

William Wilson, guardian to James, Beauchamp & Sarah A. Rhodes

Zebedee Anderson, guardian to Mary J. & Susan E. Green

Chapman Dashiell, guardian to Elizabeth R., Henry W. & Eliza A. C.
Dashiell

Elizabeth Jones, guardian to George H., Alfred & Charles Jones

Tues., Nov. 24, 1829   All Justices present

George M. Willing, adm. of George Brown

F. 17   Josiah Bayly, adm. of Thomas Bayly

Levi Dougherty, exe. of John Dougherty

John Langsdale & wife, admx. of George Hopkins, to sell negro Jim

Peregrine Phillips, adm. of William Phillips

Stephen Mills to distribute apparel of George Waller

F. 18   John U. Dennis & Littleton U. Dennis, exes. of George
Robertson

Orphan; Henry C. Connor (of Isaac W.)
Appointed Guardian; Mary Connor
Sureties; Henry Lankford, Edward Coulbourn

Wed., Nov. 25, 1829   All Justices present

Isaac Giles & Elizabeth Waller, adms. of George Waller

Peter Collins, adm. cwa of Joseph Bruington

F. 19   Jesse Hughes & Levin Jones to view estate of Peter J. Palmer, in care of Marcellus Jones, temporary guardian

Robert J. Henry & Levin Tyler to view estate of Elizabeth Collins (of Stephen), in care of Daniel Ballard, guardian

James G.(?) Waller & Elijah C. Johnson to divide negroes from estate of Richard H. Handy

Orphan; James, William Collins (of William)
Appointed Guardian; Robert Morris
Sureties; Robert Mallone, Thomas Morris

George Jones & Isaac Denson to view estate of James & William Collins, in care of Robert Morris, guardian

Thurs., Nov. 26, 1829   All Justices present

Robert Stewart & John Austin to settle dispute between Henry Ballard & William Done (attorney for representatives of Thomas Bayly)

F. 20   William Done to settle dispute between George Jones (of Robt.), surviving exe. of Charles Jones, & William T. G. Polk, adm. of Samuel Polk

Orphan; George, Joseph, Robert Price (of George)
Guardian; William Whayland, revoked
Appointed Guardian; Benjamin Davis
Sureties; Thomas & Robert Morris

Chapman Dashiell, guardian to his children

Shiles Crockett & Charles Venables to view estate of Asberry, Hetty, William & Elizabeth Ansley, in care of Priscilla Walker, guardian

Daniel Ballard & William Sudler to view estate of Theodore T. Gibbons, in care of William Smith, guardian

F. 21   Tues., 8 Dec., 1829   George Jones (of Robt.), Thomas K. Carroll present

James Wilson, exe. of George Wilson

Nathan Gordy, adm. of Thomas Connelly

Charles Simpkins, adm. of Major Simpkins

Littleton Dennis, Sr., & Robert J. Henry to settle dispute between Levin Pollitt & Michael B. Carroll (adm. cwa of Betsy Bayly)

F. 22   James L. Waller & Elijah C. Johnson to divide negroes from
         estate of Richard H. Handy; cannot divide. Matthias O.
Toadvine & wife, adm. of Richard H. Handy, to sell negroes

Josiah Furniss, guardian to Henry J. C. Furniss

Samuel Williams, guardian to Ann & Purnell Johnson

John Austin, guardian to Mary & Eliza James

Whitty Fontaine, guardian to Sally A. Elzey & William Long

Elijah Christopher & Levin D. Collier to view estate of Ann & Purnell
Johnson, in care of Samuel Williams, guardian

Tues., Dec. 22, 1829   All Justices present

F. 23   Henry Hyland, adm. cwa of John Walter

Robert Stewart, adm. of George D. Atkinson

Levi Dougherty, exe. of John Dougherty

Ann Holland, exe. of James Holland

Adm. cwa of [Samuel crossed out] John McClester

Samuel Gordon, surviving adm. cwa of John McClester

F. 24   John Hopkins, adm. cwa of Samuel Acworth, to sell negro Levin

Henry L. Harcum, adm. cwa of Lee P. Harcum

Elijah Parsons, adm. of Peter Dashiell. Peter Guillett bought
property from estate. Sureties; Gideon Pearce, John Jones

Isaac Denson & wife, guardian to Henry J. Dashiell

[original minutes start at this point]

Tues., Jan. 12, 1830   Daniel Ballard, George Jones (of Robt.) present

Charles Simpkins, adm. of Major Simpkins

F. 25   Charles Leary(?) & Samuel Gordon to divide negroes from estate
         of Joseph Howard

James Wilson, exe. of Samuel Brown

Henry Lankford, exe. of John Howard

Mon., Feb. 8, 1830   Robert J. Henry, Arnold E. Jones present

F. 26   William Williams, Sr., Robert J. Henry & Arnold E. Jones
        commissioned Justices. Witness; Theodorick Bland, Chancellor

Benjamin Bailey, one of the exes. of James Anderson

F. 27   Tues., 9 Feb., 1830   Robert J. Henry, Arnold E. Jones present

Littleton Dennis & Levin Tyler to divide negroes from estate of James
Anderson

John D. Anderson & Benjamin Bailey, exes. of James Anderson

Isaac H. Johnson, adm. of Jesse Johnson

Joseph B. Brinkley & John P. Lankford to view estate of Isaac T. W. &
Catherine Miles (of Isaac), in care of Jane Miles, guardian

Tues., Feb. 16, 1830   Robert J. Henry, Arnold E. Jones present

William Williams qualifies as Justice

F. 28   Marcellus Jones, adm. cwa of Cheney Collier

Orphan; James K. Gunby (of Kirk)
Guardian; William Miles, revoked
Appointed Guardian; John Noble
Sureties; William Whayland, Jonathan Huffington

Isaac Denson & Jonathan Huffington to view estate of William Collins
(of William), in care of Robert Morris, guardian

Orphan; Lucinda Anderson (of James)
Appointed Guardian; Henry Adams
Sureties; John P. Langford, Seth Wilkins

Orphan; Stephen G. Anderson (of James)
Appointed Guardian; Isaac Covington
Sureties; William Anderson, George M. Willing

Orphan; James Anderson (of James)
Appointed Guardian; Benjamin Bailey
Sureties; Isaac Covington, Levin K. Leatherbury

Orphan; Gillis Anderson (of James)
Appointed Guardian; John D. Anderson
Sureties; John N. Bowland, Henry Adams

F. 29   Elzey Foxwell, guardian to William E. Foxwell

James Tilghman, adm. of James Blain

Tues., Feb. 23, 1830   All Justices present

Polly Cooper, adm. of Samuel Cooper

Betsy Bennett, adm. of James T. Bennett

F. 30   Henry Maddux, guardian to Elizabeth Turpin

Daniel Ballard, guardian to Elizabeth Collins

Isaac Harris, guardian to William H. Acworth

Noah Holland, guardian to Samuel & Smith Holland

Levin Morris, guardian to Alexander & Wilhelmina Waller

Elizabeth Webster, guardian to Berry T. T., Henry A. P. & Sophia A. M. Webster

Peregrine Weatherly & wife, guardian to Ann M. Austin

William Whayland, guardian to George, Joseph & Robert Price

Jane Miles, guardian to Catherine & Washington Miles

Samuel Gordon, guardian to Ware Willing

Jesse Hughes & Levin Jones to view estate of Peter J. Palmer, in care of Marcellus Jones

F. 31   Tues., Mar. 9, 1830   All Justices present

William W. Handy, adm. of Priscilla Dashiell

Covington Cordray & John Hopkins to divide negroes from estate of James Walter

Isaac Denson & Jonathan Huffington to view estate of William Collins (of William), in care of Robert Morris

Daniel Ballard & John Curtis [Carter?] to divide negroes from estate of William Tull

Marcellus Jones, adm. cwa of Cheney Collier

F. 32   Elizabeth R. Pollitt, exe. of William K. Pollitt

Arnold E. Jones, exe. of William Jones

Samuel G. Holbrook, adm. cwa of Elizabeth McClester

Margaret T. W. Barkley, adm. of David Barkley

Sarah Walter, guardian to George L. R. & Ann M. D. Walter

Robert J. Henry & Daniel Dakes to view estate of William S. Broughton, in care of Sally Howard, guardian

F. 33   Tues., Mar. 16, 1830   All Justices present

Jehu Parsons & William Williams to view estate of heirs of Richard H. Handy, in care of Matthias O. Toadvine & wife

Peter B.(?) Davis & wife, guardian to Martha J., Sarah P., Isaac J. T., William J., Alce K. & Mary E. Harris

Harriet Bell, guardian to Leah A. W. Bell

Tues., Mar. 30, 1830   All Justices present

Henry Lankford & Joseph B. Brinkley to settle dispute between James Johnson & Isaac H. Johnson (adm. of Jesse Johnson)

Morris H. Adams, adm. of Ruth Adams

F. 34   Tues., 13 Apr., 1830   All Justices present

Orphan; Mary Jane Green (of John)
Guardian; Zebedee Anderson, revoked, would not give counter security to Littleton Mezick
Appointed Guardian; Elisha Taylor
Sureties; Marcellus & Thomas Jones

John Leatherbury, adm. of George Jones (of Robt.)

Elizabeth R. Pollitt, exe. of William K. Pollitt

F. 35   Marcellus Jones, adm. of William M. Waters, to sell negro boy John

John Austin & James Goslee(?) to view estate of Mary Jane Green (of John), in care of Elisha Taylor

Tues., Apr. 20, 1830   All Justices present

Samuel McBryde & George M. Willing [Walton?] to divide negroes from estate of Samuel Heath

Levin Tyler, guardian to Sally N., William T. & Henry White

Jane W. Bell, guardian to John J. & William C. Bell

George Hargis & wife, guardian to William Broughton

Levin Tyler, guardian to Patty A., Samuel C. & Rebecca M. Broughton

Henry Crawford, guardian to Elizabeth E. Nelson

F. 36   Caleb Hughes, guardian to Charlotte J. & Esther A. U.(?) Nelson

Lodowick Milbourn, guardian to John W. & Charles Milbourn

James Handy, guardian to Luvitha Milbourn

Elijah Lawson, guardian to Emeline Lawson

John Miles, guardian to George Johnson

Tues., May 4, 1830   All Justices present

Negro woman Candis, and her child, to be sold by Elizabeth Alce Waters, guardian to William E. Waters

Apprentice; George Jenkins
Bound to; William Quinn
Trade; Coach Making, in harness making & trimming department

John Dryden, adm. of Stephen Adams, to sell negroes Elijah, John & Leah

F. 37   George M. Willing, adm. of George Brown

Tues., May 18, 1830   William Williams, Arnold E. Jones present

George Todd, guardian to Robert S., Alexander H. & Eliza A. Todd

Robert Leatherbury & Alexander Jones to divide negroes from estate of James Jones

John Travers, guardian to Edward Travers

George Walter, guardian to Ware Willing

Marcellus Jones, guardian to James & Louisa Waters

William Howarth & wife, guardian to Mary, Severn & John Croswell

Elizabeth Acworth, guardian to John L. Moore

Humphrey Humphreys, guardian to Mary A. & George W. Humphreys

F. 38   Wed., May 19, 1830   William Williams, Arnold E. Jones

James Wilson & James Polk to settle dispute between Edward Broughton & Esther Broughton (admx. of John H. Broughton)

James Wilson & James Polk to settle dispute between Edward Broughton & Esther Broughton (admx. of Josiah Broughton)

Apprentice; Louisa Summers
Bound to; George Drura
Trade; Female Waiter

John Austin, guardian to Mary & Elisa James

Littleton Tyler, guardian to John, Isaac, William & Harriet Lawson

Rosanna A. W. Wainright, guardian to Rosanna E. M. J., Ann F. D. & Edward J. C. Wainright, gives counter security to Levin Wainright. Sureties; James Stewart, Beauchamp D. Adams

F. 39   Thurs., May 20, 1830   William Williams, Arnold E. Jones

Orphan; George, Thomas, James, Sarah J., Samuel Robertson (of John) Appointed Guardian; Robert D. Robertson
Sureties; Train Acworth, Robert Venables

Shiles Crockett & Samuel Walter to view estate of George, Thomas, James, Sarah J. & Samuel Robertson, in care of Robert D. Robertson

Train Acworth & Robert Venables to divide negroes from estate of John Robertson

Robert D. Robertson, guardian to children of John Robertson, to sell property paid over to him by Samuel Walter, adm. of John

Tues., May 25, 1830   William Williams, Arnold E. Jones present

F. 40   Henry Hyland, adm. cwa of Abraham Barkly

Joseph Barkley, appointed trustee to sell house & lot in Princess Anne, left by Mary Milaway, in her will, to her brother Samuel Heath, & her brother Josiah W. Heath's three youngest children, viz.- Sarah Matilda A., Rebecca & Parthenia Mitchell Heath. Surety for Joseph Barkley; James Wilson

William Jones, guardian to Sarah J. & Anne R. Holbrook

F. 41   Tues., 8 June, 1830   All Justices present

Benjamin Gravner, adm. of James Graham

Rachel Howard & Samuel Phillips, adms. of Joseph Howard

Orphan; John Francis Collier (of Francis)
Appointed Guardian; Betsy Hopkins
Sureties; Philip Graham, William H. D. Collier

Tues., June 22, 1830   William Williams, Arnold E. Jones present

Lucretia Harris, guardian to John Harris

William Hopkins, guardian to Charles E. M. Collier

Stephen Ward & wife, guardian to George F. Ward

F. 42   Tues., July 6, 1830   All Justices present

'112'

Betsy Hopkins, adm. of William Hopkins

John Kirwan, adm. of Jacob Kirwan

Orphan; Abraham Wilson, John Thomas Cottingham
Appointed Guardian; Thomas P. Adams
Sureties; John M. Hall, Isaac H. Johnson

Thomas P. Adams, guardian to Abraham Wilson & John Thomas Cottingham

F. 43   Benjamin Lankford appointed crier in place of Mason Abbott (resigned)

Littleton P. Dennis & Ephraim K. Wilson appointed to settle dispute between Mrs. Elizabeth Jones (widow of Charles) & Levin Walter. Arnold E. Jones, adm. dbn. Charles sold parts of tracts of land to Levin Walter, viz.; 'Moorefield', 'Conclusion', 'Prickle Cox Hott', land not fully paid for, so Elizabeth to receive payment by right of dower

Tues., July 20, 1830   William Williams, Arnold E. Jones present

Sarah Landreth, adm. of John Landreth

F. 44   James Wilson, exe. of Samuel Brown

James Handy, guardian to Lovitha A. Milbourn, to sell negro man George

Job Moore, adm. of Aaron Moore

Job Moore, guardian to Marcella, Hambleton, Maria J. & Kitty Moore

F. 45   Tues., Aug. 3, 1830   All Justices present

Henry Gale, temporary guardian to Thomas, Hester Ann, Mary A., Zipporah, Sarah R. & John W. Fletcher

Littleton P. Dennis & Ephraim K. Wilson file award in case of Mrs. Elizabeth Jones (widow of Charles) & lands sold by Charles to Levin Walter

Jane Miles, adm. of Isaac Miles, to sell negro Sarah & her two children

Joseph B. Brinkley & John P. Langford to view estate of Washington, Isaac J. T. & Catherine Miles, in care of Jane Miles, guardian

Margaret B. Chapman, guardian to Sarah A. Chapman

F. 46   Tues., Aug. 10   All Justices present

Benjamin Gravner, adm. of James Graham

Orphan; Catherine T., John P., Juliet S, Emily H., William H. Jones
Appointed Guardian; Joshua Jones
Sureties; John Noble, Jonathan Huffington

William W. Handy, adm. of Priscilla Dashiell

Sarah Landreth, adm. of John Landreth

Tues., Aug. 24, 1830   All Justices present

F. 47   John Kirwan, adm. of Jacob Kirwan

Robert Stewart, adm. of Francis Brady, & temporary guardian to his children

James Wilson, guardian to Levin L. & Arnold E. Waters

Jane Miles, guardian to Washington & Catherine Miles

Frances Humphreys, guardian to Elizabeth Mc. B. & Leah Mc. B. Humphreys

John Insley, guardian to Priscilla Dunn

John Austin, guardian to Mary & Eliza James

James Powell, guardian to Nathaniel H. J. Smulling

James C. Coulbourn, guardian to Emeline B. Parker

Thomas Bell, guardian to Ann M. & John W. S. Hughes

Zebedee Anderson, guardian to Susan E., Mary J. & Sally A. Green

F. 48   Jacob Bird & Jacob Cullen to view estate of Kitty, Hambleton, Maria J. & Marcella Moore, in care of Job Moore

Daniel Ballard & John Curtis to divide negroes from estate of William Tull

Tues., Sept. 7, 1830   All Justices present

Job Moore, adm. of Aaron Moore

Levin Crockett, adm. dbn of Eleanor Cooper, to sell negro Daniel

Henry P. C. Wilson, exe. of John C. Wilson, Sen.

F. 49   Thomas K. Carroll to settle dispute between Sally Wilson (claimant of a certain negro called Parmen(?)), & Henry P. C. Wilson, exe. of John C. Wilson

Apprentice; George A. Noble
Bound to; George B. Waller
Trade; House Carpenter

Tues., Sept. 21, 1830   Robert J. Henry, Arnold E. Jones present

Sale of negro Daniel, property of Eleanor Cooper, deceased, by Levin
    Crockett, adm. dbn revoked, as Daniel is sick & infirm;
F. 50   negro Amelia to be sold instead

William H. Collier, guardian to Lee P. & William Weatherly

Sally Howard, guardian to William S. Broughton

Tues., 12 Oct., 1830   All Justices present

Henry P. C. Wilson, exe. of John C. Wilson

Orphan; Samuel, Francis Gibbons (of Isaac)
Appointed Guardian; William Smith (of Saml.)
Sureties; John Water, William T. Wood

Thomas Robertson & William Roads to divide negroes from estate of
Samuel Tull

William W. Handy, adm. of Priscilla Dashiell

F. 51   William W. Handy & Betsy K. Handy, exes. of William Handy,
        Sen.

19 Oct., 1830   All Justices present

Daniel Ballard, guardian to Elizabeth Collins, to repair dwelling
house on farm of orphan

John Leatherbury, adm. of George Jones (of Robert)

F. 52   Tues., Oct. 26, 1830   All Justices present

Belitha Christopher, exe. of Elijah Christopher

Orphan: Elizabeth McClester Fontain (of Henry)
Appointed Guardian; Whitty Fontain
Sureties; John P. Langford, Henry Fontain

Tues., Nov. 2, 1830   All Justices present

Thomas K. Carroll & Robert Stewart to settle dispute between William
Jones, Sen., deceased adm. of Thomas Jones, & Arnold E. Jones, son of
Thomas

F. 53   Tues., Nov. 16, 1830   All Justices present

David & Thomas [not in original minutes] White, exes. of William White

Joseph S. Cottman, guardian to Joseph B. & John A. H. Cottman

Elizabeth Jones, guardian to George H., Alfred & Charles Jones

John U. Turpin, guardian to Elizabeth & Levin Goslee

F. 54   Wed., Nov. 17, 1830   All Justices present

John Dryden, guardian to Littleton Dryden

Parker Dickerson, guardian to Emeline Dickerson

Orphan; Francis M. Johnson, legatee of Amelia W. Nicholson
Appointed Guardian; Elijah C. Johnson
Sureties; Jesse Walter, John W. B. Parsons

Samuel Williams, guardian to Purnell & Ann Johnson

Elijah Lawson, guardian to Emeline [Grace in original minutes] Lawson

Peregrine Weatherly & Philip Graham to divide negroes from estate of John Kellum

Thurs., Nov. 18, 1830   All Justices present

George Handy, adm. of Hope Handy

F. 55   Orphan; Amelia L. Disharoon
        Appointed Guardian; Thomas L. Disharoon
        Sureties; Levin W. Disharoon, Robert M. Smith

Tues., Nov. 30, 1830   All Justices present

Philip Covington, adm. of Thomas Jones, to sell estate (a schooner excepted). Also, to sell half of schooner, 'Swan'

William Costen, guardian to George W., Samuel & Maria Taylor

        Orphan; Gordon M. C., Alexander H., Elizabeth R., Esther G.
        Handy (of Richard H.)
        Appointed Guardian; Matthias O. Toadvine
F. 56   Sureties; Samuel Gordon, Purnell Toadvine

Alcy White & Edward Fowler, adms. cwa of Henry White

Mon., 20 Dec. [1830]   All Justices present

James F. Kelly, adm. of Ebenezer D. Howard

Henrietta B. Haynie, adm. of William Done

F. 57   Tues., Dec. 21, 1830   All Justices present

Elisha E. Whitelock & John Sanders, adms. dbn cwa of John H. Adams

Levin Ballard & James F. Kelly to view estate of orphan children of Henry White, in care of Alce White, temporary guardian

Tues., Dec. 28, 1830   William Williams, Arnold E. Jones present

Lee P. Harcum & wife, guardian to Maria, Henrietta & George P. Jones

William Smith, guardian to Theodore T. Gibbons

F. 58   Tues, Jan. 4, 1831   William Williams, Arnold E. Jones present

Jane W. Bell, adm. of William Bell, to sell negro boy Denwood

Tues., Jan. 11, 1831   All Justices present

William Porter, adm. of Parker Barnes

William W. Handy & James Polk to settle dispute between Arnold E. Jones (adm. dbn cwa of Charles Jones) & John Leatherbury (adm. of George Jones, of Robert)

F. 59   Joseph Barkley, adm. dbn of Jonathan Barkley [Hickman in original minutes]

Robert Hitch, guardian to George & Elizabeth Bell

Littleton D. Maddux, guardian to Henry D. & Sarah S. Maddux

John Layfield, guardian to Mary, George, Elizabeth & Levin Layfield

Robert Morris, guardian to William Collins

Thomas Robertson & William Roach to divide negroes from estate of Samuel Tull

Charles Leary & Samuel Gordon to divide negroes from estate of Joseph Howard

Tues., Jan. 25, 1831   Robert J. Henry, Arnold E. Jones present

John T. Fontaine, guardian to John E. & Eleanor A. E. Fontaine

F. 60   William Sudler & Daniel Benson to view estate of Samuel & Francis Gibbons, in care of William Smith, guardian

Tues., 8 Feb., 1831   Robert J. Henry, Arnold E. Jones present

Benjamin Davis, guardian to George Price

F. 61   Tues, Mar. 1, 1831   Daniel Ballard, Henry Hyland present

Daniel Ballard, Samuel Wilson Jones & Henry Hyland, M.D., commissioned Justices. Witnesses; Danl. Martin, Theodoricke Bland, Chancellor

Paper purporting to be will of Betty Dixon exhibited by Joseph B. Brinkley;

F. 62   Leaves whole of estate left her by her deceased husband to Elizabeth Dixon, wife of Joseph B. Brinkley

Witnesses;   17 Feb., 1831
    Jesse Benson
    Sarah White   Signed; Betty Dixon

Summons issued for near relations to appear; William Williams, Polly Horsey, Peggy Coulbourn

F. 63   Joshua Dougherty, adm. of John Lord

Belitha Christopher, exe. of Elijah Christopher

William W. Johnston, guardian to William W., Edward M. & George K. Wise

Rosanna A. W. Wainright, guardian to Nancy F. D., Rosanna E. M. J. & Edward J. C. Wainright

Tues., Mar. 8, 1831   Daniel Ballard, Samuel W. Jones present

Samuel W. Jones seated as Justice

F. 64   Levin Badley, adm. of William S. Robertson

Robert Patterson, exe. of Leolin Stayton

William Williams, by Littleton P. Dennis, attorney, & Ephraim K. Wilson, files caveat against will exhibited by Joseph B. Brinkley & Elizabeth, his wife, claiming to be will of Elizabeth Dixon

F. 65   Evidence produced to prove that Covington, Thomas J. W. & Levin J. M. P. Broadwater, are heirs of full age of James Broadwater, dec. (Quarter Master in the navy of Virginia in the Revolutionary War)

Orphan; Henry T., Julia Ann, Mary F., Samuel L. Tull (of Samuel)
Appointed Guardian; Caroline Tull
Sureties; William Roach, John P. Langford

Zipporah & John Bounds, exes. of William Bounds

Orphan; Henrietta Jones (of Levin D.)
Guardian; John Leatherbury (revoked)
Appointed Guardian; Thomas Jones
Sureties; Joshua Brattan, Robert Stewart

F. 66   Orphan; Thomas G. R. Roberts (of Benjamin)
         Appointed Guardian; Elizabeth Roberts
Sureties; John Leatherbury, Alexander Jones, Samuel G. Holbrook

Posthumous account of Elijah Christopher, guardian to William S.(?) H., Isaac H. W. & Levin J. M. W. Stanford

Noah Holland, guardian to Smith Holland

Tues., Mar. 15, 1831   Daniel Ballard, Samuel W. Jones present

Levin J. Irving, adm. of Leah Irving

Henrietta B. Haynie, adm. of William Done

Mary Langsdale, adm. of Huet Langsdale

F. 67   John Hopkins, adm. of George Dashiell (of Wm.)

William H. Waters, adm. dbn cwa of Sarah H. [not in orig.] Gale

Henry K. Long & Samuel McBryde to settle dispute between Joseph Barkley & Margaret T. W. Barkley (adm. of David Barkley)

F. 68   Robert J. Henry & Levin Tyler to view estate of Elizabeth
         Collins, in care of Daniel Ballard, guardian

Wed., Apr. 6, 1831   Daniel Ballard, Samuel W. Jones present

Joseph B. Brinkley, by William W. Handy, answers caveat of William Williams & Henry W. Coulbourn (for Peggy Coulbourn), against will of Betty Dixon

F. 69   Jesse Benson, witness to will of Betty Dixon, appears
         [long list of questions & answers follows thru F. 70]
He state that Capt. Joseph B. Brinkley steadied her hand while she signed will

F. 71   Sarah White, witness to will of Betty Dixon, examined by court
         [questions & answers follow] She states that she is now 60 years old, and Betty Dixon at death was 75 or 76; she did sign as witness; neither Joseph Brinkley, nor Elizabeth, his wife, were related to Betty Dixon by blood or marriage; Betty Dixon was aunt to William Williams & Mrs. Peggy Coulbourn (they being children of her half brother); she had great nephews & nieces (the grandchildren of John Turpin)

F. 72   Sarah White spoke to a Mrs. Philips after death of Betty Dixon

F. 73   Joseph B. Brinkley exhibits two other papers purporting to be
         the last will of Elizabeth Dixon; exhibit 'H';

Gives whole estate to Elizabeth Brinkley, wife of Joseph, including negroes; Sophia (6 years old), Nelly (4), Whitty (6), James (4), Sam (1), Henny (1 month)   19 Feb., 1824

Witnesses;   Exe.; Joseph B. Brinkley
Edward Howard
Thomas Philips   Signed; Bettey Dixon (widow of Wm.)

F. 74   Exhibit 'J';
Whole estate to Elizabeth, wife of Joseph B. Brinkley (exe.)

Witnesses;   14 Aug., 1819
Charles Hall
Thomas Holland   Signed; Betty Dixon

Thomas Goslee, adm. of Thomas Pollitt

John Dougherty, adm. of Robert Walter

F. 76   Tues., Apr. 12, 1831   Daniel Ballard, Samuel W. Jones
                                 A. H. Ballard, Deputy

Thomas Bradly, adm. of Wilson Bradly

Citation for Susan Rider & Messen(?) Dashiell to testify in behalf of M. S. Hall(?)

Samuel G. Holbrook, adm. cwa of Elizabeth McClester, to sell negro child Major

Wed., Apr. 13, 1831   Daniel Ballard, Samuel W. Jones present

Joseph B. Brinkley, by W. W. Handy, his attorney, vs William Williams, by E. K. Wilson & L. P. Dennis, his attorneys, in matter of will of Betty Dixon. Matter transferred to Somerset County Court

F. 78   Tues., Apt. 19, 1831   Daniel Ballard, Samuel W. Jones

John Mitchell, adm. of Ebenezer Mitchell

William T. Wood, adm. of Robert Jones

Betsy Hopkins, adm. of William Hopkins

William Porter, adm. of Parker Barnes

F. 79   William Freeney, adm. of William A. Hitch

Jane W. Bell, guardian to John J. & William C. Bell

Benjamin Lankford & Stephen Horsey to divide negroes from estate of William Bell

Summons issued for Robert Hitch & Isaac Vinson, witnesses to will of William A. Hitch

Tues., Apr. 26, 1831   Daniel Ballard, Samuel W. Jones present

James Polk & William W. Handy to settle dispute between Levin D. Jones & John Leatherbury (adm. of George Jones, of Robert)

Levin Crockett & Stephen Miles to view estate of William R. & Sophia R. Donoho (of James), in care of Alexander Donoho, guardian

F. 80   Tues., May 17, 1831   Daniel Ballard, Samuel W. Jones, Shiles Crockett present

Shiles Crockett seated as Justice

John Dennis, adm. of Littleton J. Dennis

F. 81   Arietta Williams, adm. of Levin Williams

Daniel Ballard, adm. of Sarah Garrettson

Peter Collins, adm. cwa of Joseph Brewington

Orphan; John W. McIntire (of Jesse)
Appointed Guardian; John Kirwin
Sureties; Elliott Kirwin, Risdon Bloodsworth

Orphan; Edward Pollitt (of James)
Appointed Guardian; Samuel Silverthorn
Sureties; Asbury C. Howard, Levin W. Disharoon

John Dougherty, adm. of John Lord

F. 82   Sarah Walter, guardian to George L. R. & Ann M. D. Walter

Isaac Denson & wife, guardian to Henry J. Dashiell

George Hargis, guardian to William Broughton

Elijah Lawson, guardian to Emeline Lawson

Wed., May 18, 1831   All Justices present

Henry L. Harcum, adm. cwa of Lee P. Harcum

Orphan; John W., Sarah R. & Hester Ann Fletcher (of Samuel)
Appointed Guardian; Noah Rider
Sureties; Charles Rider, Robert Dashiell

John Cullen, adm. of Benjamin Ward

John Dougherty, adm of Robert Walter

F. 83   John P. Giles, guardian to Mary A. Giles

Isaac Covington, guardian to Stephen G. Anderson

Levin Morris, guardian to Alexander & Wilhelmina Waller

Caleb Hughes, guardian to Esther A. U. & Charlotte J. Nelson

William Miles, guardian to James K. & Mary A. Gunby

William Miles, guardian to Mary A. & Elizabeth J. C. Stewart

John Miles, guardian to George Johnson

Daniel Ballard, guardian to Elizabeth Collins

Elijah Lawson, guardian to Grace Lawson

Priscilla Walker, guardian to Asbury, Hetty, William & Elizabeth Ansley

Frances Humphreys, guardian to Elizabeth M. B. & Leah M. B. Humphreys

Littleton Tyler, guardian to Travers, Harriet, Isaac, Grace, John & William Lawson

Matthias O. Toadvine, guardian to Esther G., Elizabeth R., Gordon McC. & Alexander H. Handy

George Todd, guardian to Robert J. Todd

F. 84   Mary Connor, guardian to Henry C. Connor

James Handy, guardian to Levitha Milbourn, enters into bond with John S. Handy & William H. Whittington, to indemnify William T. Wood & Tubman Cox

Thurs., May 19, 1831   Daniel Ballard, Samuel W. Jones present

Isaac M. Adams & Thomas M. Hargis to settle dispute between David Long & John A. Lankford (adm. of Thomas D. Atkinson)

Peregrine Weatherly & wife, guardian to Susan J. Jones

John D. Anderson, guardian to Gilliss Anderson

George Todd, guardian to Alexander H. & Eliza A. Todd

Wed., May 24, 1831   All Justices present

F. 85   Daniel Ballard, adm. cwa of Sarah Ballard, to sell negro girl Sally

Tues., May 31, 1831   All Justices present

Peggy [Elizabeth crossed out] K. Irving, exe. of Handy H. Irving

John A. Lankford, adm. of Thomas D. Atkinson

Mary Gunby, adm. of David Gunby

F. 86   Citation issued to Martha D. Adams & Rosanna A. W. Wainright to answer oath respecting property supposed by the adm. of Hope Adams, dec., to be held back

James Handy, guardian to Lovitha Milbourn

Samuel G. Holbrook, guardian to Edward H. Holbrook

Elisha Taylor, guardian to Mary J. Green

Margaret B. Chapman, guardian to Sarah A. Chapman

William Howarth, guardian to Severn, Mary & John Croswell

Tues., 14 June, 1831   All Justices present

James Brittingham, adm. of Hope Adams

Alexander Donoho, adm. of James Donoho

F. 87   Hetty Crockett, guardian to William B., Eleanor H. & Josiah Crockett

Benjamin Bailey, guardian to James Anderson

Peter Evans, guardian to Milcah A. & Betsy Wallace

George Twilley, guardian to Ann M. & Samuel J. Twilley

Tues., June 21, 1831   All Justices present

Mary Langsdale, adm. of Huet Langsdale

Henry Hyland, adm. cwa of John Walter

Tues., July 5, 1831   All Justices present

F. 88   Henrietta M. W. Sudler, exe. of Joseph Sudler

Tues., July 12, 1831   All Justices present

Arietta Williams, adm. of Levin Williams

Littleton Dennis, Sr., & Levin Tyler to settle dispute between Levin Pollitt & Michael B. Carroll (adm. cwa of Betsy Bayly)

James C. Coulbourn, guardian to Emeline B. Parker

Harriet Bell, guardian to Leah A. W. Bell

F. 89   Tues., July 26, 1831   All Justices present

Isaac H. Coulbourn, adm. of Thomas W. Coulbourn

Elizabeth Acworth, guardian to John L. Moore

Stephen Ward & wife, guardian to George F. Ward

Levin Tyler, guardian to Samuel C., Rebecca M. & Patty A. Broughton

Levin Tyler, guardian to William T., Sally N. & Henry White

Henry Crawford, guardian to Elizabeth E. Nelson

F. 90   Levin Crockett & Stephen Miles to view estate of William R. & Sophia R. Donoho, in care of Alexander Donoho, guardian

Tues., 9 Aug., 1831   All Justices present

Philip Covington, adm. of Thomas Jones (of Jas.)

James R. W. Conway, adm. of William Conway

Tues., Aug. 16, 1831   All Justices present

F. 91   Mary Gunby, adm. of David Gunby, to sell negro man Shadrach

Alexander Donoho, guardian to William R. & Sophia R. Donoho, to lease real estate of orphans for three years

Mary Gunby, adm. of David Gunby

Tues., Sept. 6, 1831   Samuel W. Jones, Shiles Crockett present

William H. Acworth, adm. of Isaac Harris

John U Humphriss, adm. of Sarah Humphriss, to sell negro woman Biddy

F. 92   Isaac H. Coulbourn, adm. of Thomas W. Coulbourn

James Brittingham, adm. of Hope Adams

James Wilson, exe. of George Wilson, Sr.

John A. Lankford, adm. of Thomas D. Atkinson

Tues., Sept. 20, 1831   Shiles Crockett, Samuel W. Jones present

F. 93   Joseph M. Puzey, adm. of John Puzey

Levin Ballard & James F. Kelly to view estate of orphan children of Henry White, in care of Alcy White, temporary guardian

William Jones, guardian to Ann R. Holbrook

John Dryden, guardian to Littleton Dryden

Tues., Oct. 18, 1831   Daniel Ballard, Shiles Crockett present

F. 94   Henrietta M. W. Sudler, exe. of Joseph Sudler

James Polk to settle dispute between Sarah M. Done & Henrietta B. Haynie (adm. of William Done)

Elizabeth Robertson, adm. of Eli Robertson

Thomas Johnson, adm. of Benjamin D. Johnson

F. 95   Peregrine Weatherly, adm. cwa of Mary James

Henry & Benjamin Lankford to divide negroes from estate of David Gunby

William W. Johnston, guardian to William W. Wise

Matthias O. Toadvine, guardian to Gordon M. C. Handy

Tues., Nov. 1, 1831   Daniel Ballard, Samuel W. Jones present

Robert D. Robertson & Bridget Venables, adms. of Robert Venables

Joseph B. Brinkley, exe. of Betty Dixon

F. 96   Eli Millican, adm. cwa of Isaac Millican

William M. Stone, exe. of Susanna Waters

Train Acworth & John S. Crockett to divide negroes from estate of John Robertson

F. 97   Evidence given that Mary Broadwater (widow), Covington, Thomas J. W., Levin J. M. P & Sally Broadwater (who intermarried with William Dryden & is since dec., leaving three children, to wit; James, Mary W. & John Dryden) are the only heirs & at full age of James Broadwater, Quarter Master in the navy of Virginia in the Revolutionary War

John Dennis, adm. of Littleton J. Dennis

Orphan; William, Ebenezer M., Mary E. Waller (of George)
Appointed Guardian; Elizabeth Waller
Sureties; Edward Fowler, Stephen Mills

John T. Adams, adm. of Jesse Adams, to sell negroes Nathan & Milly

'125'

Henry P. C. Wilson, exe. of John C. Wilson

Tues., Nov. 15, 1831   Daniel Ballard, Samuel W. Jones present

F. 98   Arnold E. Jones, exe. of William Jones, to sell negroes
Banda(?), Adam & Stephen

Thomas Jones, guardian to Henrietta Jones, to sell negro woman Harriet

Joseph Walker, adm. cwa of John Walker

John U. Humphriss, adm. of Sarah Humphriss

John Hopkins, adm. of George Dashiell (of Wm.)

F. 99   Thomas Goslee, adm. of Thomas Pollitt

Tues., Nov. 22, 1831   Daniel Ballard, Samuel W. Jones present

Levin Tyler, guardian to Patty A. & Rebecca M. Broughton

Wed., Nov. 23, 1831   Daniel Ballard, Samuel W. Jones present

Samuel Williams, guardian to Ann & Purnell Johnson

Littleton D. Maddux, guardian to Sarah S. & Henry D. Maddux

Sally Howard, guardian to William S. Broughton

Henry Adams, guardian to Lucinda Anderson

F. 100   Thurs., Nov. 24, 1831   Daniel Ballard, Samuel W. Jones

Orphan; Amelia P. Dashiell
Appointed Guardian; William F. Dashiell (father)
Sureties; John Morris, Levin J. E. Dashiell

William H. Acworth, adm. of Isaac Harris

Levin Crockett, adm. of Eleanor Cooper

John Hopkins, adm. dbn of Samuel Acworth, to retain in hand $300.00, the amount of claim against said deceased, in favor of Ebenezer Leatherbury, alleged to be absent from state

Letters of adm. dbn granted to Robert Jones (of George), on estate of Levin D. Jones, revoked. Thomas Jones appointed 2nd adm. dbn

Job Moore, guardian to Maria J., Kitty, Hamilton & Marcella Moore

Alexander Donoho, guardian to William R. & Sophia R. Donoho

F. 102   Tues., Jan. 17, 1832   Samuel W. Jones, Shiles Crockett

Samuel Williams, adm. of Cotter(?) Jones

F. 103   Mary S. Gunby, adm. of David Gunby

Samuel Williams, adm. of Cotter Jones

James Goslee, adm. of John W. Leatherbury

John H. Bell & William Miles (of Samuel) to divide negroes from estate of David Barkley

Nancy McDorman, adm. of Lewis McDorman, to sell schooner 'Exchange'

F. 104   Henry Riggin, adm. of Thomas Davis

Orphan; Alcy K., Mary E., Isaac J. T., Sarah P., Martha J. Harris (of William)
Appointed Guardian; John Hopkins
Sureties; Matthias Dashiell, George L. H. Woolford

Matthias Dashiell & Jesse Hughes to view estate of Alcy K., Mary E., Isaac J. T., Sarah P. & Martha J. Harris (of William), in care of John Hopkins, guardian

Henry White, adm. of William Hilman

F. 105   Isaac Denson & wife, guardian to Henry J. Dashiell

Tues., Jan. 24, 1832   All Justices present

Betsy Brinkley, adm. of Joseph B. Brinkley

Thomas Robertson & Robert Stewart to divide negroes from estate of Charles Palmer

James R. W. Conway, adm. of William Conway

F. 106   William H. Acworth, adm. of Isaac Harris

William H. Acworth, adm. of Alcy Harris

William H. Acworth, adm. of Isaac Harris, to sell 40 shares of stock in Bank of Salisbury

Orphan: Peter J., Brannas(?) N. Palmer (of Charles)
Appointed Guardian; James Adams
Sureties; John D. Anderson, James Tilghman

Thomas B. Robertson & Robert Stewart to view estate of Peter J. Palmer, in care of James Adams, guardian

F. 107   Tues., Jan. 31, 1832   Daniel Ballard, Samuel W. Jones

Thomas Dorsey, adm. of William Walston

James Russell, adm. of Abram Lankford

John W. King, adm. cwa of John King

F. 108   Tues., 14 Feb., 1832   Daniel Ballard, Henry Hyland present

Henry Hyland seated as Justice

John B. Slemons, adm. of Handy Phillips

F. 109   Thomas Brown, exe. of David Brown

Robert Morris, adm. of Ann S. Collins

John W. King, adm. cwa of John King

Henrietta B. Haynie, adm. of William Done

F. 110   Tues., Feb. 21, 1832   Daniel Ballard, Henry Hyland present

George M. Willing & Arnold H. Ballard to divide negroes which fell to Sarah S. & Henry D. Maddux from grandfather Daniel Maddux

William K. Coulbourn & William H. Curtis, adms. of Edward Coulbourn

Thomas Dorsey, adm. of William Walston

John Austin, adm. of Samuel Green

John Austin, adm. of John Wilson

F. 111   John W. Nelson & Levin Jones, exes. of Francis D. Nelson

Jabuz Travers & John Austin to view estate of Horatio, Eleanor & Almira Nelson (of Francis D.), in care of John W. Nelson & Levin Jones, temporary guardians

William Smith, guardian to Isaac F. & Samuel S. Gibbons

Tues., Mar. 6, 1832   Daniel Ballard, Henry Hyland present

Thomas H. Dougherty, adm. of Stephen Dougherty

James K. Bradley, adm. of Jesse Owens

F. 112   Margaret Hayman, exe. of Isaiah Hayman

Samuel Gilliss, adm. of Thomas Gilliss, to give additional security to Jesse Walter

John Austin, adm. of John Wilson

John W. Nelson & Levin Jones, exes. of Francis D. Nelson

James Goslee, adm. of John W. Leatherbury

F. 113   John E. Harris, by William W. Handy, attorney, petitions to admit to probate instrument of writing purporting to be will of William Hopkins; accepted

John Dougherty, adm. of Robert Walter

Esther Dougherty, adm. of Joshua Dougherty

F. 114   James K. Badley, adm. of Jesse Owens

John W. Nelson & Levin Jones, exes. of Francis D. Nelson

Henry Gale & Thomas Jones to view estate of Miranda & Eleanor Leatherbury (heirs of John M. Leatherbury), in care of James Goslee, temporary guardian

Benjamin Davis, adm. of Isaac Harris

John B. Slemons, Jr., adm. of Handy Phillips

F. 115   William Whayland & Thomas Goslee to view estate of Isaac Harris (of Isaac), in care of Benjamin Davis, temporary guardian

Tues., Mar. 20, 1832   Daniel Ballard, Henry Hyland present

James Goslee, adm. of John W. Leatherbury

Covington Cordray & John Hopkins to divide negroes from estate of James Walter

Nancy McDorman, adm. of Lewis McDorman

William Handy, adm. of Levi Moore

F. 116   John T.(?) Darby, adm. of Thomas Darby

John S. Crockett, adm. of Shiles Crockett, to sell estate to pay note due Bank of Salisbury

Eli Milligan, adm. cwa of Isaac Millican

Caleb Kennerly, adm. of William King (of Jesse)

F. 117   Thomas Walker & Willing Wright to view estate of Richard B. & Benjamin T. Darby (of Thomas), in care of John T. Darby, temporary guardian

Samuel Gillis, adm. of Hiram Gillis

Samuel Gillis, adm. of Thomas Gillis, adm. revoked; granted to Thomas Langsdale

Citation at instance of Obed Riggin, for John N. Whittington (adm. of John Milbourn), to pass final account

Joshua Dougherty, late adm. of John Lord

Orphan: Caroline J., Martha J. Holland (of James)
Appointed Guardian; Ann Holland
Sureties; John & James Dryden

Thomas Johnson, adm. of Benjamin D. Johnson

F. 118   William H. Acworth, adm. of Alcy Harris

Isaac Gibbons, adm. of John Gibbons

Orphan; Maria C., Sarah E., Elizabeth Ann Adams (of Stephen)
Appointed Guardian; Eleanor N. Adams
Sureties; John & James Dryden

Littleton U. Dennis & John A. Lankford to view estate of Maria C., Sarah E. & Elizabeth Adams, in care of Eleanor N. Adams, guardian

Tues., Mar. 27, 1832   Daniel Ballard, Henry Hyland present

William K. Coulbourn & William H. Curtis, adms. of Edward Coulbourn

F. 119   Isaac Coulbourn, exe. of Nancy Coulbourn

Benjamin Davis, adm. of Isaac Harris

Thomas Langsdale, adm. of Thomas Gilliss

John T. Adams, adm. of Jesse Adams

Lodowick Milbourn, guardian to Charles & John W. Milbourn

Sarah Walter, guardian to George L. R. & Ann M. D. Walter

F. 120   Noah Holland, guardian to Smith Holland

Elijah Lawson, guardian to Emeline & Grace Lawson

Margaret B. Chapman, guardian to Sarah A. Chapman

Matthias O. Toadvine, guardian to Gordon M. C. Handy

Matthias O. Toadvine, guardian to Alexander H., Elizabeth R. & Esther G. Handy

George M. Willing & Arnold H. Ballard to divide negroes from estate of Daniel Maddux, grandfather to Sarah S. & Henry D. Maddux

Tues., 10 Apr., 1832   All Justices present

F. 121   Peter Bell seated as Justice

Joshua Brattan & Willing Wright to view estate of Richard B. & Benjamin T. Darby, in care of John T. Darby, guardian, since Thomas Walker refuses to serve

Josiah Chittam, exe. of John Chittam

William Phillips, adm. of James Hurst

F. 122   Edward Fowler, exe. of Underwood Roberts

John H. Bell & Samuel W. Jones to settle dispute between Zadock Long & John Dennis (adm. of Littleton P.(?) Dennis)

Ann Handy, adm. of Joseph Handy

John Kirwan, adm. of Jacob Kirwan, to sell negro boy Isaac

F. 123   William Miles (of Samuel) & John N. Bowland to settle dispute between Margaret W. Polk & William T.(?) G. Polk (adm. of Samuel Polk)

Tues., Apr. 24, 1832   Daniel Ballard, Henry Hyland present

Court called by Wm. J. Dashiell
A. H. Ballard for James Polk, Reg.

Alexander Kibble, adm. of Mary Dorman

Levin Tyler, adm. of Peter Carsley

F. 124   John T.(?) Darby, adm. of Thomas Darby

Commission to Matthias Dashiell & Jesse Hughes to view estate of Alcy K., Mary E., Isaac J. T., Sarah P. & Martha J. Harris, in care of John Hopkins, renewed

Apprentice; Zorobabel Smulling
Bound to; Townsend & Hale [company?]
Trade; Coach Gig & Harness Making

Tues., May 8, 1832   All Justices present

Henry Riggin, adm. of Thomas Davis

F. 125   Joseph B. Brinkley, adm. dbn cwa of Betty Dixon

Isaac Coulbourn, exe. of Nancy Coulbourn, to sell unexpired time of negro Titus

John Dougherty, adm. of Robert Walter

Thomas Langsdale, adm. of Thomas Gilliss

William Phillips, adm. of James Hurst

F. 126   Margaret T. Barkly, adm. of David Barkly

John S. Evans, guardian to Robert Dougherty & others

Isaac Covington, guardian to Stephen G. Anderson

Elisha Taylor, guardian to Mary J. Green

Henry Adams, guardian to Lucinda Anderson

John H. Bell & William Miles (of Samuel) to divide negroes from estate of David Barkley

Tues., May 15, 1832   Daniel Ballard, Henry Hyland present

Josiah Chittam, exe. of John Chittam, to sell negro Sarah

F. 127   Tues., May 22, 1832   All Justices present

William Handy, adm. of Levi Moore

Thomas H. Dougherty, adm. of Stephen Dougherty

Eli Millican, adm. cwa of Isaac Millican

Ralph Lowe & Tubman Bedsworth to divide negroes from estate of Ebenezer Mitchell

George A. Dashiell, guardian to Levin & George Gilliss

Thomas Jones & Henry Gale to view estate of Miranda & Eleanor Leatherbury

F. 128   Thomas B. Robertson & Robert Stewart to view estate of Peter J. Palmer

Thomas B. Robertson & Robert Stewart to divide negroes from estate of Charles Palmer

Wed., May 23, 1832   All Justices present

William T. Wood, adm. of Robert Jones

Orphan; William J. Harris (of William)
Appointed Guardian; Levin Jones
Sureties; Marcellus Jones, Robert Stewart

James Russell, adm. of Abram Lankford

Levin [William in orig.] Morris, guardian to Alexander & Willhelmina Waller

John Hopkins, guardian to Kitturah H. Acworth

George Hargis & wife, guardian to William Broughton

Parker Dickerson, guardian to Emeline Dickerson

William Howarth & wife, guardian to Severn (Levin?), John & Mary Croswell

F. 129   Friday, May 25, 1832   All Justices present

Apprentice; Edward M. Wise
Bound to; William W. Johnston, Merchant
Trade; Merchant

James Wilson, exe. of George Wilson

George Twilley, guardian to Samuel J. & Maria A. [Ann M. in orig.] Twilley

George Todd, guardian to Robert S.(?), Alexander H. & Eliza A. Todd

John U. Turpin, guardian to Levin & Elizabeth Goslee

Jabez Travers & John Austin to view estate of Horatio, Almira & Eleanor Nelson (of Francis D.), in care of John W. Nelson & Levin Jones, temporary guardians

Tues., 12 June [1832]   All Justices present

Morris H. Adams, exe. of Thomas Adams

F. 130   John Waters & William Sudler to divide negroes from estate of Thomas Adams

Caleb Kennerly, adm. of William King

Hezekiah Hayman, adm. of Benjamin Milbourn

Hambleton B. Bennett, exe. of George Bennett

F. 131   Tues., June 19, 1832   All Justices present

Court called by Wm. J. Dashiell

John S. Crockett, adm. of Shiles Crockett

Bridget Venables & Robert D. Robertson, adms. of Robert Venables

Frances Robertson, adm. cwa of Elias Robertson

'133'

Biddy White, widow of Gowan White, files petition against Marcellus Jones, adm., to have adm. granted to Isaac S. Hopkins. Test.; Ann Morton(?)

F. 132   Evidence given that Elijah & Beauchamp White, of full age, are sons & only heirs of John White, gunner in the Revolutionary War, aboard galley fitted out by state of Virginia

Evidence given that Bruff Brattan & Margaret Kelly, of full age, are only heirs of Obadiah Kelly, who served in Revolutionary War from state of Virginia

Evidence given that James Cannon, of full age, is grandson & only heir of William Powell, who served in Revolutionary War from state of Virginia

Evidence given that Henry, John & Priscilla Cottman are grandchildren & only heirs of Elijah McCallahan, who served in Revolutionary War from state of Virginia

F. 133   July 10, 1832   All Justices present

William H. Collier, adm. of George M. Hopkins

Marcellus Jones, adm. of Gowan White, by Littleton T. Dennis & William W. Handy, his attorneys, files answer to petition of Biddy White; states Gowan White died more than eighteen months ago, & Biddy, being out of state, did not apply for letters of adm. for herself, or any other, within six months; states Isaac Hopkins has no right
F. 134   to adm., as he is neither creditor, nor heir. He had estate appraised by George D. Walter & Philip Covington; had property (negroes exclusively) deposited in county jail for safe keeping, which were later sold [testimony continues through F. 135]

F. 136   Tues., July 24, 1832   All Justices present

Orphan; Emily S., Thomas J., John E., Wesley S. Tull (of William) Appointed Guardian; Hester Tull
Sureties; William H. Tull, Eliza A. Tull

Alexander Kibble, adm. of Mary Dorman

Isaac Gibbons, adm. of John Gibbons

Citation at instance of William W. Maddux, for George Hopkins, guardian to Leah & Margaret Dashiell

Frances Humphreys, guardian to Elizabeth McB. & Leah M. McB. Humphreys

Rosanna A. W. Wainright, guardian to Nancy F. D., Rosanna E. M. J. & Edward J. C. Wainright

Thomas Jones, guardian to Henrietta E. Jones

Ralph Lowe & Tubman Bedsworth to divide negroes from estate of Ebenezer Mitchell

F. 137   Covington Cordray & John Hopkins to divide negroes from estate of James Walter

Train Acworth & John S. Crockett to divide negroes from estate of John Robertson

William Whayland & Thomas Morris (Goslee in orig.) to view estate of Isaac Harris (of Isaac), in care of Benjamin Davis, temporary guardian

Mary Connor, guardian to Henry C. Connor

Daniel Ballard, guardian to Elizabeth Collins

Tues., 14 Aug., 1832   All Justices present

Hetty Disharoon, adm. cwa of James Disharoon

[No F. 138 or 139]

F. 140   George M. Willing & Teagle Townsend to view estate of Leah J. W. Walston (of William), in care of Thomas Dorsey, temporary guardian

Orphan; John W. (aged 2 years on 25th of June last), Sally Ann (aged 3 years on 26th of April last) & Mary E. Johnson (aged 1 year on 1st of Jan. next); children of Benjamin D. Johnson
Appointed Guardian; Julia Ann Johnson
Sureties; Robert Dashiell, Benjamin Parsons

James Stewart & Jehu Parsons to view estate of John W., Sally Ann & Mary E. Johnson, in care of Julia A. Johnson

John H. Bell & George A. Dashiell to view estate of Thomas W. Stone, a devisee of Susanna Waters, deceased, in care of Wm. M. Stone, temporary guardian

John H. Bell & George A. Dashiell to view estate of James M. Stone, a divisee of Susanna Waters, deceased, in care of William M. Stone, temporary guardian

Hetty Disharoon, adm. cwa of James Disharoon, by Edward Long, her attorney, files petition against John Disharoon (of James), stating that he is withholding part of estate; money, bonds & notes against Richard Jenkins, Ben Pasons (Taylor), Thomas Morris & Ebenezer Disharoon

F. 141   Hetty her * Disharoon
                                                 mark
Subpoena issued for John Disharoon

Hetty Disharoon, adm. cwa of James Disharoon, files similar petition against William Disharoon (of James)

Subpoena issued for William Disharoon

Orphan; Francis A., Mary J., Caroline L., John W., William H. S. & Stephen D. Gunby (of David)
Appointed Guardian; John S. Handy
Sureties; Theodore G. Dashiell, Thomas G. Beauchamp

Orphan; Isaac T., Francis Barnes (of Parker)
Appointed Guardian; Margaret Barnes
Sureties; James Polk, Robert J. H. King

F. 142   Tues., Aug. 28, 1832   All Justices present

Betsy Hopkins, adm. of William Hopkins. to sell negro man Joshua

Jehu Parsons & Anthony B. Bennett to view estate of Alexander H., Eliza A. & Robert S. Todd (of Spencer), in care of George Todd, guardian

Levin Jones, exe. of Helena Collier

Rachel Dougherty, adm. of John Dougherty

James Tilghman & Elizabeth Catlin, adms. of Nehemiah Catlin

F. 143   Tues., Sept. 18, 1832   Daniel Ballard, Peter Bell present

John S. Crockett & James Wilson to view estate of William, Ebenezer M. & Mary Eleanor Waller (of George), in care of Elizabeth Waller, guardian

Levin Tyler & Stephen Coulbourn to view estate of George A., Mary E., Joseph B. & William T. Cox (of Tubman), in care of Ann Cox, temporary guardian

F. 144   Case of Biddy White vs. Marcellus Jones (adm. of Gowan White) on motion of Thomas A. Spence, attorney, continued until 2nd Tues. in Oct.

Ann Cox, adm. of Tubman Cox

William H. Curtis & William K. Coulbourne, adms. of Edward Coulbourn

John Dryden, guardian to Littleton Dryden

F. 145   Tues., 9 Oct., 1832   Daniel Ballard, Henry Hyland present

John S. Crockett, adm. of Charles Venables

Levin Wilson, adm. of William Cluff

Leah Trehearn, adm. of Teagle Trehearn

Matthias Dashiell & Benjamin I. Jones to divide negroes from estate of Helena Collier

F. 146   Thomas Robertson & William Sudler to divide negroes from estate of Joseph Handy

John B. Slemons, exe. of Rev. John B. Slemons

John W. Jones & William Whayland to divide negroes from estate of Samuel Fletcher

William Sudler, adm. of Emory S. Sudler

Biddy White vs. Marcellus Jones (adm. of Gowan White); witnesses for Marcellus Jones; Levin Walter (mentions, but doesn't name, son of Biddy White); Thomas Walter; Elizabeth Dickerson (states
F. 148   Gowan White died in VA 2 years ago last fall; Biddy returned to MD shortly after & told her Capt. Marcellus Jones would adm. estate & that he would bring suit against James Donoho & Joseph Barkley); Thomas Bell (Gowan White resided in VA & died in the fall of 1829)

Tues., Oct. 23, 1832   Henry Hyland, Peter Bell present

Samuel Adams, adm. of Levin Williams

Arnold E. Jones & Levin Ballard (of Jarvis) to divide negroes from estate of Ann R. Holbrook

F. 149   William Jones, guardian to Ann R. Holbrook

Matthias Dashiell & Jesse Hughes to view estate of Alcy K., Mary E., Isaac J. T., Sarah P. & Martha J. Harris (of William), in care of John Hopkins

Littleton U. Dennis & John A. Lankford to view estate of Maria C., Sarah E. & Elizabeth Adams, in care of Eleanor N. Adams

Anthony B. Bennett & Jehu Parsons to view estate of Alexander H., Eliza A. & Robert S. Todd, in care of George Todd, guardian

George M. Willing & Teagle Townsend to view estate of Leah J. Walston (of William E.), in care of Thomas Dorsey, temporary guardian

Robert D. Robertson, guardian to Thomas, James & Samuel Robertson

Tues., Nov. 6, 1832   All Justices present

F, 150   Sally Broughton, adm. of Henry Broughton

Marcellus Jones, adm. of Gowan White

Wed., Nov. 7, 1832   All Justices present

Arnold E. Jones & Levin Ballard, Jr. (of Jarvis), to divide negroes from estate of Ann R. Holbrook; cannot divide, recommend sale of Eben, 32; James, 70; Sarah, 29, and her children; Stephen, 8; Tom(?), 7; Thos., 2, rickety; Edmund, 9 months. Money to be divided among heirs (one in Jamaica, one a minor). Samuel G. Holbrook, adm. to sell

F. 151   14 Aug., 1832, Hetty Disharoon, adm. of James Disharoon, by her attorney, Edward Long, filed petition or bill of complaint, marked exhibit 'A'; Petition of Hetty Disharoon, adm. cwa of James Disharoon, believes John Disharoon, son of James, has certain money she is entitled to, plus sundry bonds & notes against Richard Jenkins, Ben Parsons (tailor), Thomas Morris & Ebenezer Disharoon

Appeared on the 28th instant Hetty Disharoon, adm. cwa of James Disharoon, with Edward Long & Littleton Dennis, his (sic) attorneys, & John Disharoon, with William W. Handy, his attorney

F. 152   Proceedings continued to 6th Nov., next, at which time Register laid before Court answer of John Disharoon, exhibit 'B' (original filed 10 Sept., 1832); Denies having any money or notes belonging to his father's estate, except certain notes assigned to him by his father before his death

F. 153   Ebenezer Disharoon appears in behalf of petitioner, states that he was present when notes were assigned to John by his father, with exception of note against Benjamin Parsons, which couldn't be found. Assignment of notes on the Tuesday preceding the Thursday of the death of James, Sr. Further states that James was not capable of making a valid contract. Ebenezer Disharoon's wife is daughter of Hetty Disharoon

Sally Cullen appears, also states that James Disharoon not capable of knowing what he was doing. Under cross-examination she does admit that when visited by Dr. Lemmon, James was able to ask the amount of the doctor's bill, and to pay it himself

F. 154   Sally Cullen is a daughter of Hetty Disharoon

James Polk appears, says that John Disharoon came to his office with certain notes, which he said were not his, only assigned to him to collect. Recommended he turn them over to adm., which he seemed willing to do

F. 155   7 Nov., 1832   Caleb Disharoon appears, states that James Disharoon, Sr., was in his right mind, most of the time, and asked that notes be divided between John, Hetty and grandson, William

F. 156   Further stated that James could right some, but not at time of these events; could only make his mark with assistance

Thomas Disharoon appears, states that his father was in his right mind

William Disharoon appears, states that his grandfather was in his right mind

James Disharoon appears, states that his father was not in his right mind, when he came later in the afternoon

F. 157   Judges dismiss petition, Judge Hyland dissenting; appeal filed & granted

William Disharoon answers petition against him by Hetty Disharoon; has no money or notes belonging to his grandfather's estate, except $9.29, which he has with him to pay into estate, and $8.00, given him by James, and not part of estate. Statement made 8 Sept., 1832, before Elijah C., Johnson, Justice of the Peace

F. 158   13 Nov., 1832   Daniel Ballard, Henry Hyland present

Matthias Dashiell & Benjamin I. Jones to divide negroes from estate of Helena Collier; cannot divide. Levin Jones, exe., to sell negroes

John B. Slemons, exe. of Rev. John B. Slemons

Sarah Moore, adm. of James Moore

F. 159   Tues., Nov. 20, 1832   All Justices present

Margaret B. Chapman, guardian to Sarah A. Chapman

James Polk, adm. of John Done

Biddy Walter, adm. of George Walter

Elizabeth Robertson, adm. of Eli Robertson

Jesse Walter & George Bounds to view estate of John & James Robertson (of Eli), in care of Elizabeth Robertson, temporary guardian

F. 160   Hezekiah Hayman, adm. of Benjamin Milbourn

Edward Fowler, exe. of Underwood Roberts

David White, one of the exes. of William White

Wed., Nov. 21, 1832   All Justices present

Levin Tyler, adm. of Peter Carsley

Biddy Walter, adm. of George Walter, to sell vessel to pay debts due in Baltimore

F. 161   John W. King, adm. cwa of John King

Tues., 11 Dec., 1832   Daniel Ballard, Henry Hyland present

Joseph Cantwell, adm. of John Cantwell

Josephus Humphriss, adm. of Joshua Humphriss

Noah Rider & Anthony B. Bennett to divide negroes from estate of James Disharoon

F. 162   Daniel Boston, adm. of Daniel Boston

Margaret Hayman, adm. of John H. Hayman

William & Joseph Harris, adms. of Ephraim K. Harris

Josiah Chittam, exe. of John Chittam

Sally Broughton, adm. of Henry Broughton

F. 163   Henry P. C. Wilson, exe. of John C. Wilson, & John D.. Anderson and Benjamin Bailey, exes. of James Anderson, ask that George Handy & John H. Bell be appointed to settle dispute between them

William T. Wood, adm. dbn of John W. Leatherbury

William Miles, guardian to Mary A. & Elizabeth J. C. Stewart

John Leatherbury, guardian to Henrietta E. Jones

Tues., Dec. 18, 1832   Daniel Ballard, Henry Hyland present

John J. Dashiell, adm. of James W. Dashiell

F. 164   Thurs., Jan. 1, 1833   Daniel Ballard, Henry Hyland present

Joseph Cantwell, adm. of John Cantwell

Peter Puzey, surety of Joseph M. Puzey (adm. of John Puzey), asks for counter security

Citation against Nancy Wilson, adm. of Thomas Cottingham, to issue final account

F. 165   John S. Handy, guardian to Mary Jane & Caroline Gunby, asks that negro boy Henry, when apprehended, be sold

Robert Patterson, agent for Nancy McDorman (adm. of Lewis McDorman), to sell negro man Adam

Tues, Jan. 15, 1833   All Justices present

William M. Stone, exe. of Susanna Waters

Thomas Robertson & William Sudler to divide negroes from estate of William Tull

F. 166   Tues., Jan. 29, 1833   All Justices present

James B. Moore, adm. cwa of Benjamin Moore

Sarah L. Goslee, exe. of James Goslee

Henry Gale, adm. of Samuel Fletcher

Nancy Connor, exe. of Elijah Connor

James Tilghman, one of the adms. of Nehemiah Catlin

F. 167   Nancy Connor, exe. of Elijah Connor

Robert J. Henry & John A. Lankford to divide negroes from estate of Stephen Adams

Tues., 12 Feb., 1833   Daniel Ballard, Henry Hyland present

Orphan; Samuel, Thomas Cottingham
Appointed Guardian; David Cottingham
Sureties; William Wilson, James Johnson

John T. Darby, adm. of Thomas Darby, to sell negro woman Priscilla & child

Joseph Humphriss, exe. of Joshua Humphriss

F. 168   James B. Moore, adm. cwa of Benjamin Moore

Orphan; William H., Joseph Weatherly (of Peregrine)
Appointed Guardian; Edward Weatherly
Sureties; Ralph Lowe, Lee P. Weatherly

Thomas Robertson & Daniel Benson to view estate of Mary Ann T. Broughton (of Henry), in care of Sally Broughton, temporary guardian

Orphan; John W., Hester A., Sarah R. Fletcher (of Samuel)
Appointed Guardian; Thomas W. Fletcher
Sureties; Noah Rider, Charles Rider

Tues., Feb. 26, 1833   All Justices present

Daniel Boston, adm. of Daniel Boston

F. 169   William Whayland, exe. of William Bounds

Orphan; Isaac J. H. Bounds (of Douty, & one of the heirs of Isaac Harris)
Appointed Guardian; William A. D. Bounds
Sureties; John L. Moore, John Kirwan, Jr.

James Wilson, adm. of John C. Wilson

'141'

Marcellus Jones, temporary guardian to Peter J., Elizabeth, Mary & Brennas(?) Palmer

Robert Leatherbury, guardian to John T. Riggin

William W. Johnston, guardian to William W. Wise

Harriet Bell, guardian to Leah A. W. Bell

Littleton D. Maddux, guardian to Henry D. Maddux

John D. Anderson, guardian to Gilliss Anderson

F. 170   Isaac Denson & wife, guardian to Henry J. Dashiell

Thomas Robertson & William Sudler to divide negroes from estate of Joseph Handy

Tues., Mar. 12, 1833   Daniel Ballard, Henry Hyland present

Henry Gale, exe. of Stephen Taylor

F. 171   Robert Pollitt, adm. cwa of George Pollitt

John Dashiell, adm. of James W. Dashiell

James Goslee, late adm. of John W. Leatherbury

Tues., Mar. 26, 1833   Daniel Ballard, Henry Hyland Present

Joseph Leonard, William Gordy & Henry Bacon, exes. of George Parker

F. 172   George W. Robertson, exe. Samuel Robertson

Eliza R. W. Waters, adm. of Levin L. Waters

Orphan; Amelia A., John P. J. Morris
Appointed Guardian; John Morris (father)
Sureties; Martin Bowen, Zadock Powell

Sarah Moore, adm. of James Moore

George Waller & Andrew W. Anderson to view estate of heirs of Benjamin Moore, in care of James B. Moore, temporary guardian & adm. cwa

George Waller & Andrew W. Anderson to view estate of Elizabeth A. G. & Sarah E. Moore (of James), in care of Sarah Moore, temporary guardian

F. 172b   Tues., 9 Apr., 1833   All Justices present

William & Joseph C. Harris, adm. of Ephraim K. Harris

Samuel Adams, adm. of Levin Williams

Biddy Walter, adm. of George Walter

Jesse Walter & Joseph Windsor to view estate of heirs of George Walter, in care of Biddy Walter, temporary guardian

Thomas Robertson & Nathaniel Bell to view estate of Joseph B., Sarah A., Thomas, Francis L. & Henry F. Brinkley (of Joseph B.), in care of Betsy Brinkley, temporary guardian & adm.

Thomas Robertson & Nathaniel Bell to divide negroes from estate of Joseph B. Brinkley

F. 173   Tues., Apr. 23, 1833   Daniel Ballard, Henry Hyland present

John S. Handy, guardian to Francis A. Gunby, to sell negroes Polly & Sarah

Alexander S. D. Evans, adm. of Levin Evans

Joseph M. Puzey, adm. of John Puzey, revoked; adm. dbn granted to Peter Puzey

F. 174   Levin Tyler, guardian to Samuel C., Patty A. & Rebecca M. Broughton

Daniel Ballard, guardian to Elizabeth Collins

Levin Tyler, guardian to Henry, William T. & Sally N. White

Matthias O. Toadvine, guardian to Gordon Mc., Alexander H., Elizabeth R. & Esther G. Handy

Posthumous account of William Hopkins, guardian to Charles E. M. Collier

Tues., May 7, 1833   Daniel Ballard, Henry Hyland present

Levin Wilson, adm. of William Cluff

Eliza R. W. Waters, adm. of Levin L. Waters

F. 175   Tues., May 21, 1833   Daniel Ballard, Henry Hyland present

Alexander S. D. Evans, adm. of Levin Evans

Louisa Larmore, exe. of. James Larmore

Josiah Chittam, exe. of John Chittam, to sell negroes Peggy & Betsy

Matthias Dashiell & Robert Stewart to view estate of heirs of William Conway

F. 176   Wed., May 22, 1833   Daniel Ballard, Henry Hyland present

Orphan: William Q.(?), Albert N., John Q.(?), Maria Morris (of Joseph)
Appointed Guardian; Thomas Holbrook
Sureties; Samuel G. Holbrook, Severn Ballard

[This entry crossed out] John S. Evans, guardian to John Dougherty, to sell negro men, Isaac & Jack, late property of his brother Robert Dougherty

Thurs., May 23, 1833   Daniel Ballard, Henry Hyland present

Hamilton B. Bennett, exe. of George Bennett

Thomas Boothe, of Somerset Co., Md., is brother & only heir of William Boothe, formerly master in the state navy of Virginia, in the Revolutionary War

Henry & Elizabeth Marshall, of Somerset Co., Md., are nephew & niece, and only heirs, of John Marshall, formerly boatswain in the state navy of Virginia, in the Revolutionary War

Levin Jones, temporary guardian to Horatio Nelson

George Hargis & wife, guardian to William Broughton

Thomas Robertson & William Sudler to divide negroes from estate of William Tull

F. 177   Thomas Robertson & Nathaniel Bell to view estate of Joseph B., Sarah A., Thomas, Francis L. & Henry F. Brinkley

Levin Tyler & Stephen Coulbourn to view estate of George A., Mary E., Joseph B. & William T. Cox, in care of Ann Cox

Thomas Robertson & Daniel Boston to view estate of Mary A. T. Broughton, in care of Sally Broughton, temporary guardian

Thomas Robertson & Nathaniel Bell to divide negroes from estate of Joseph B. Brinkley

John S. Crockett & James Wilson to view estate of William, Ebenezer M. & Mary E. Waller, in care of Elizabeth Waller, guardian

Seth Wilkins, by Edward Long, his attorney, files petition: Seth Wilkins, & Martha, his wife, daughter of Thomas Beauchamp, deceased, was owed money from said Thomas, and adms., Isaac & Ann Beauchamp, did not list debt in inventory.

F. 178   Isaac & Ann Beauchamp summoned to answer charge

Tues., 11 June, 1833   All Justices present

Robert C. Pollitt, adm. cwa of George Pollitt

John U. Dennis, exe. of Littleton U. Dennis

F. 179   Isaac Beauchamp, by Isaac D. Jones, his attorney, files
         answer to petition of Seth Wilkins; states that notes in
question, against George Beauchamp, were settled before inventory

F. 180   Ann Beauchamp states same

F. 181   Seth Wilkins presses claim

Eliza R. W. Waters, temporary guardian to her children

F. 182   Orphan; Miranda, Eleanor Leatherbury (of John N.[?])
         Appointed Guardian; Lucretia Harris
         Sureties; John J. Davis, John E. Harris

Tubman Bedsworth & Caleb Kennerly to view estate of Miranda & Eleanor
Leatherbury, in care of Lucretia Harris, guardian

Tues., June 25, 1833   Daniel Ballard, Henry Hyland present

Joseph Leonard, William Gordy & Henry Bacon, exes. of George Parker

Levin H. Patrick & Robert Hitch to view estate of Edwin L. D., George
J. & Sarah Ann E. Parker (children of Daniel, & devisees of George,
dec.), in care of Joseph Leonard, William Gordy & Henry Bacon,
temporary guardians

Elizabeth Badley, adm. of Thomas Badley

F. 183   James Phoebus, adm. of Henrietta B. Robinson

Tues., July 9, 1833   All Justices present

Orphan; Washington, Mary, Sarah, Joseph Brewington (of Joseph)
Appointed Guardian; Josiah Ellingsworth
Sureties; John B. Slemons, William W. Stevens

Levin H. Patrick & Joshua Hitch to view estate of Washington, Mary,
Sarah & Joseph Brewington (of Joseph), in care of Josiah Ellingsworth,
guardian

Josiah Chittam, exe. of John Chittam

Henry Lankford & Robert Cluff to view estate of Elizabeth Collins, in
care of Daniel Ballard, guardian

F. 184   Tues., July 23, 1833   All Justices present

Ann Handy, adm. of Joseph Handy

Zipporah & John Bounds, exes. of William Bounds

Planner H. King, adm. of John W. King

Orphan; Mary Priscilla, Eliza Ann R., William R. Atkinson (of George D.)
Appointed Guardian; Henrietta Atkinson
Sureties; Robert Stewart, Joseph Nicols

Matthias Dashiell & Marcellus Jones to view estate of Mary Priscilla, Eliza Ann R. & William R. Atkinson, in care of Henrietta Atkinson, guardian

Orphan; George S., Isaac S. Atkinson (of George D.)
Appointed Guardian; Joseph Nicols
Sureties; Robert Stewart, Henrietta Atkinson

Matthias Dashiell & Marcellus Jones to view estate of George S. & Isaac S. Atkinson (of George D.), in care of Joseph Nicols, guardian

Peter Bell & Jehu Parsons to divide negroes from estate of Benjamin D. Johnson

F. 185   Thomas Robertson & William Sudler(?) to view estate of heirs of Joseph Handy, in care of Ann Handy, temporary guardian

George Parsons (of J.), exe. of Levin Dorman

Orphan; Bayard Kennerly (of Orrell)
Appointed Guardian; Henry Kennerly
Sureties; Matthias Dorman, Robert D. Robertson

Jesse Walter & James Wilson to divide negroes from estate of Orrell Kennerly

James Phoebus, adm. of Henrietta B. Robinson

Orphan; Caroline, Irving Kennerly (of Orrell)
Appointed Guardian; Edward Fowler
Sureties; Ralph Lowe, John Bounds

Thomas Holbrook, guardian to orphans of Joseph Morris, to sell downed timber to cover repairs of house & barn

F. 186   Louisa (?) Kennerly & Edward Fowler, temporary guardians to heirs of Orrell Kennerly

Peter Puzey, 2nd adm. of John Puzey, revoked; adm. granted to Thomas A. Spence

Tues., 13 Aug., 1833   Daniel Ballard, Henry Hyland present

Hamilton Bayly, adm. of James Bayly

F. 187   Mary Langsdale, adm. of Huet Langsdale

Orphan; Horatio Nelson (of Francis D.)
Appointed Guardian; Cyrus Nelson
Sureties; John Bounds, John McDaniel

Orphan; Almira Nelson (of Francis D.)
Appointed Guardian; John McDaniel
Sureties; Cyrus Nelson, James Bounds

Jabus Travers & George Twilly to view estate of Almira Nelson (of Francis D.), in care of John McDaniel, guardian

Joseph Nicols, guardian to Isaac S. & George S.(?) Atkinson, & Henrietta Atkinson, guardian to Mary Eliza Ann & William Atkinson, asks that property of said orphans, from estate of Isaac Atkinson, be sold

Joshua Brattan, claimant, and Robert Stewart, adm. of Thomas Jones (of Thos.), ask that Levin Jones be appointed to settle dispute between them

Jabus Travers & William H. Collins to view estate of Horatio Nelson (of Francis D.), in care of Cyrus Nelson, guardian

F. 188   Orphan; William H., John A. Brown (of Samuel)
         Appointed Guardian; Henrietta Brown
         Sureties; Leah Disharoon, John Sanders

William W. Maddux, adm. of Margaret E. Dashiell

Henry Hyland, adm. of Priscilla Atkinson

Tues., Aug. 27, 1837 [33]   Daniel Ballard, Henry Hyland present

Negro man Frank, late slave of Jacob Tyler, sold to James Lawson (on condition he could buy is freedom) before passage of Act of Assembly, passed 12 Mar., 1832, entitled 'Act relating to people of color', having paid for same, is granted permission to remain in state. Manumission date, 13 July, 1833

F. 189   Marcellus Jones, adm. of Gowan White

Henry Hyland, adm. of Priscilla Atkinson

Nancy Cullen, adm. of Jacob Cullen

William Roach & Job Moore to view estate of Isaac W. & Samuel S. Cullen (of Jacob), in care of Nancy Cullen, temporary guardian

Hetty Disharoon, adm. of James Disharoon

William Smith, guardian to Francis & Samuel Gibbons, to repair porch & cook house, and ditch property of said orphans

'147'

Levin Ballard & John Jones to view estate of Underwood Williams (of Elijah, & devisee of Underwood Roberts), in care of Edward Fowler, guardian

F. 190   George Todd, guardian to Alexander H., Robert S. & Eliza A. Todd

William Miles, guardian to Elizabeth J. H. & Mary A. Stewart

Parker Dickerson, guardian to Emeline Dickerson

John Austin, guardian to Mary & Eliza James

Margaret B. Chapman, guardian to Sarah A. Chapman

Elijah Lawson, guardian to Emeline Lawson

Elisha Taylor, guardian to Mary J. Green

George Twilly, guardian to Ann Maria & Samuel J. Twilly

Tues., Sept. 17, 1833   Daniel Ballard, Henry Hyland present

William H. Curtis & Henry Lankford to view estate of Mary A. T. Broughton (of Henry), in care of Elijah Broughton, temporary guardian

Mary F. Porter, adm. cwa of Mary Porter

F. 191   Robert Stewart, adm. of Thomas Jones

John U. Dennis, exe. of Littleton U. Dennis

Elizabeth A. W. Waters, guardian to William E. Waters, to sell negroes Nehemiah & Sally

Orphan; Juliana M. J. Jones (of William G. H.)
Appointed Guardian; William Jones
Sureties; Thomas D. Jones, George B. Waller

Orphan; Lucinda Anderson
Guardian; Henry Adams, revoked
Appointed Guardian; John D. Anderson

Tues., Oct. 1, 1833   Daniel Ballard, Henry Hyland present

F. 192   William Dix, adm. of Cassan(?) Ker

Nathaniel Bell, adm. of Sally Broughton

Sarah H. Nelson, exe. of John W. Nelson

Isaac Nicols & Joseph Weatherly to view estate of William, Elizabeth & Jane Evans (of Levin), in care of Alexander S. D. Evans, temporary guardian

Planner H. King, adm. of John U. King

F. 193   Tues., 8 Oct., 1833   Daniel Ballard, Henry Hyland present

Elijah Broughton, adm. dbn of Henry Broughton

Wed., Oct. 23, 1833   Daniel Ballard, Henry Hyland present

Court called by Henry A. White

James Burnett, exe. of Ann Holland

Louisa Larmore, adm. of James Larmore

F. 194   Nancy Cullen, adm. of Jacob Cullen

Tues., Nov. 5, 1833   Henry Hyland, Peter Bell present

Orphan; Henry C. Connor (of Isaac)
Appointed Guardian; Levin Connor
Sureties; James Burnett, Aaron C. Lankford

William T. G. Polk, adm. of Samuel Polk

Orphan; Francis, Isaac T. Barnes
Guardian; Margaret Barnes (mother), revoked
Appointed Guardian; Alice Broughton
Sureties; William Anderson, Margaret Barnes

Levin H. Patrick & Jehu Parsons to divide negroes from estate of Levin Dorman

George Parsons, exe. of Levin Dorman

E. K. Wilson, granted adm. of Robert T. Walker (of Georgia)

F. 195   Tues., Nov. 19, 1833   Daniel Ballard, Peter Bell present

Levin H. Woolford, adm. of Stephen Hopkins

Elijah Broughton, adm. of Henry Broughton

Elijah Robertson & William Bennett to view estate of heirs of Thomas Bradly, in care of Elizabeth Bradley, temporary guardian

Samuel T. Connor, adm. cwa of Mary Connor

George Waller & Andrew W. Anderson to divide negroes from estate of James Moore

F. 196   Levin Tyler & John Matthews to divide negroes from estate of Tubman Cox

Wed., Nov. 20, 1833   Daniel Ballard, Peter Bell present

William H. Curtis & Henry Lankford to view estate of Henry C. Connor, in care of Levin Connor, guardian

James Wilson, exe. of Samuel Brown

John N. Whittington, adm. of John Milbourn

James Handy, guardian to Lovitha A. Milbourn, to sell negro man Sam

Robert Stewart, adm. of Thomas Jones

Orphan; Henrietta Jones (of Levin D.)
Appointed Guardian; Marcellus Jones
Sureties; Robert Stewart, Caleb Hughes

Thurs., Nov. 21, 1833   All Justices present

F. 197   Frances Robertson, temporary guardian to children of Elias Robertson

Daniel Ballard, guardian to Elizabeth Collins, to repair farm Cluff now resides on

Littleton D. Maddux, guardian to Henry D. Maddux

John Hopkins, guardian to Kitturah H. Acworth

John S. Evans(?), guardian to James & Robert Dougherty, allowed account against John Dougherty

Isaac Covington, guardian to Stephen G. Anderson

Peregrine Weatherly & wife, temporary guardian to Ann M. Austin

Levin Morris, guardian to Alexander & Wilhelmina Waller

Henry Lankford & Robert Cluff to view estate of Elizabeth Collins, in care of Daniel Ballard, guardian

Levin H. Patrick & Robert Hitch to view estate of Edwin L. D., George J., Sarah A. E. & George Parker, in care of Joseph Leonard, William Gordy & Henry Bacon

William H. Curtis & Henry Lankford to view estate of Mary A. T. Broughton, in care of Elijah Broughton, temporary guardian

Levin H. Patrick & Joshua Hitch to view estate of Washington Brewington, in care of Josiah Ellingsworth, guardian

F. 198   Levin H. Patrick & Robert Hitch to view estate of Edwin L. D., George J. & Sarah Ann E. Parker, in care of Joseph Leonard, William Gordy & Henry Bacon, temporary guardians

'150'

Levin Ballard & John Jones to view estate of Underwood Williams, in care of Edward Fowler, temporary guardian

Jabez Travers & George Twilley to view estate of Almira Nelson, in care of John McDaniel, guardian

Thomas Robertson & William Sudler to view estate of heirs of Joseph Handy, in care of Ann Handy, temporary guardian

James Stewart & Jehu Parsons to view estate of John W., Sally A. & Mary E. Johnson, in care of Julia A. Johnson, guardian

Matthias Dashiell & Robert Stewart to view estate of heirs of William Conway, in care of James R. W. Conway, temporary guardian

Tues., 10 Dec., 1833   Daniel Ballard, Henry Hyland present

James Brittingham & wife, guardian to Rosanna E. M. J., Edward J. C. & Ann F. D. Wainright (of Jesse H.)

F. 199   Orphan; Sarah Graham (of James), 4 years old on 12 Dec., 1833
         Appointed Guardian; Benjamin Gravner
         Sureties; Thomas Graham, Levin Phillips

William H. Wailes & Elijah Badley to view estate of Sarah Graham (of James), in care of Benjamin Gravner, guardian

Orphan; Edward Pollitt (of James S.)
Guardian; Samuel S. Silverthorn, revoked
Appointed Guardian; Levin W. Disharoon
Sureties; John S. Crockett, Thomas Aires

Sarah L. Goslee, exe. of James Goslee

William Smith, guardian to Samuel S., Isaac F. & Theodore T. Gibbons

Joseph Barkley & Isaac Anderson to view estate of Edward Pollitt (of James), in care of Levin W. Disharoon, guardian

Jabez Travers & William H. Collins to view estate of Horatio Nelson, in care of Cyrus Nelson, guardian

William Roach & Job Moore to view estate of heirs of Jacob Cullen, in care of Nancy Cullen, temporary guardian

F. 200   Levin Tyler & John Matthews to divide negroes from estate of
         Tubman Cox

Robert J. Henry & John A. Lankford to divide negroes from estate of Stephen Adams

Matthias Dashiell & Marcellus Jones to view estate of George S. & Isaac S. Atkinson, in care of Isaac [Joseph in orig.] Nicols, guardian

Matthias Dashiell & Marcellus Jones to view estate of Mary P., Eliza A. R. & William R. Atkinson, in care of Henrietta Atkinson, guardian

Jesse Walter & James Wilson to divide negroes from estate of Orrell Kennerly

Stephen Horsey & Benjamin Lankford to divide negroes from estate of William Bell

Tues., Dec. 24, 1833   Daniel Ballard, Henry Hyland present

Orphan; William H., Zadock J. Long (of Zadock, dec.)
Appointed Guardian; Zadock Long
Sureties; John Miles, Henry K. Long

F. 201   Eliza R. W. Waters, adm. of Levin L. Waters

Samuel T. Connor, adm. cwa of Mary Connor

Southy Whittington, adm. of William C. Whittington

Tues., Jan. 14, 1834   Daniel Ballard, Henry Hyland present

James Wilson, adm. of John C. Wilson

F. 202   Amelia Perkins, adm. of William Perkins

John M. Heath, claimant, & Robert C. Pollitt, adm. cwa of George Pollitt, ask court to appoint John H. Bell, Benjamin Simpson & Benjamin Bailey to settle dispute between them

Henry S. Handy & wife, guardian to John J. & William C. Bell

Nathaniel Bell, adm. of Sally Broughton

Tues., Jan. 28, 1834   Daniel Ballard, Henry Hyland present

John Robertson, adm. of George W. Robertson

F. 203   Orphan; Levin, Leah R. Dorman (of Levin)
Appointed Guardian; Benjamin Gordy
Sureties; William W. Stevens, William Disharoon

Levin H. Patrick & Asbury C. Howard to view estate of Levin & Leah R. Dorman, in care of Benjamin Gordy, guardian

Covington Cordray & James Denson to view estate of Andrew & Washington Robertson (of Samuel), in care of John Robertson, temporary guardian

John Robertson, adm. of George W. Robertson

John Robertson, adm. dbn cwa of Samuel Robertson

John H. Bell & George A. Dashiell to divide negroes from estate of
Mary Dorman

William Costen(?), Jr., guardian to Samuel, Maria & George W. Taylor

John Dryden, guardian to Littleton Dryden

James Brittingham & wife, guardian to Rosanna E. M. J., Edward J. C. &
Ann [Nancy in orig.] F. D. Wainright

F. 204   Tues., 11 Feb., 1834   All Justices present

Southy Whittington, adm. of William C. Whittington

Samuel T. Connor, adm. cwa of Mary Connor, to sell negroes Meda(?),
William & Isaac

Edward Fowler, exe. of William Roberts

Orphan; James K. Gunby
Guardian; John Noble, revoked
Appointed Guardian; William Gunby
Sureties; William H. Lankford, Tubman Lankford

Henry Lankford, exe. of Daniel Dakes

F. 205   Fri., Feb. 25, 1834   All Justices present

Paper purporting to be will of John Jones (of Benj.) exhibited

Orphan; Matthias E. Willing
Guardian; Robert J. H. King, revoked
Appointed Guardian; George M. Willing
Sureties; James Phoebus, Samuel G. Holbrook

John D. Anderson & Benjamin Bailey, exes. of James Anderson

Sarah H. Nelson, exe. of John W. Nelson

Tues., Mar. 18, 1834   All Justices present

William Whayland & Joseph Barkley to view estate of Maria, Albert N.,
John Q. & William Q. Morris, in care of Henry [Thomas in orig.]
Holbrook, guardian

F. 206   Hamilton Bayly, adm. of James Bayly

William Roach, exe. of Patty Dix

Josiah Furniss & Jonas Hartman(?) to divide negroes from estate of
David Long

'153'

Arrangements between Robert Stewart, adm. of George D. Atkinson, & George Dashiell (of John), approved; George D. Atkinson was surety for George Dashiell

John S. Crockett & John S. Evans to view estate of William H. Weatherly, in care of Edmond Weatherly, guardian

John S. Crockett & John S. Evans to view estate of Joseph Weatherly, in care of Edmond Weatherly, guardian

Whitty Fontaine, guardian to Sally Ann Elzey & Elizabeth Fontaine

Whitty Fontaine, guardian to William Long

Noah Rider, late guardian to John W., Hester A. & Sarah R. Fletcher

F. 207   Tues., Mar. 25, 1834   Daniel Ballard, Henry Hyland present

Edward Fowler, exe. of William Roberts, to sell negroes David & William James(?)

John Cullen, one of the representatives of Jacob Cullen, files petition; asks that Nancy Cullen, adm. of Jacob, apply extra funds listed in final account to mortgage debt due James Lawson, now in equity court; by his attorney, J. D. Jones

F. 208   Tues., 8 Apr., 1834   Daniel Ballard, Henry Hyland present

Levin Tyler & Lodowick Milbourn to divide negroes from estate of Patty Dix

Tues., Apr. 22, 1834   All Justices present

F. 209   Mary F. Porter, adm. cwa of Mary Porter

Robert W. Swan, exe. of Harriet Dryden

Adm. of estate of Littleton P. Dennis granted to James Polk. Sureties; Robert J. H. King, John Dennis

William Miles, guardian to Elizabeth & Mary A. Stewart

George Hargis & wife, guardian to William Broughton

Tubman Bedsworth & Caleb Kennerly to view estate of Miranda & Eleanor Leatherbury, in care of Lucretia Harris, guardian

Noah Rider & Anthony B. Bennett to divide negroes from estate of James Disharoon

Tues., May 6, 1834   All Justice present

John S. Crockett & Ralph Lowe to divide negroes from estate of Jacob James Weatherly

'154'

F. 210   Orphan; Martin, Elizabeth E., Severn Cooper (of Samuel)
          Appointed Guardian; Levin Cooper
          Sureties; Polly Cooper, Levin English

Elizabeth Phillips & William H. Wailes, adms. of William Phillips

Wed., May 14, 1834   Daniel Ballard, Henry Hyland present

25 Feb., 1834, paper purporting to be will of John Jones (of Benj.)
          exhibited by Benjamin I. Jones, marked exhibit 'A';
F. 211   1) To wife Betty, all property during her lifetime; after
          death to son Benjamin Jones for support of my little
grandson, John Quincy Adams Jones (son of my son George Withear Jones,
dec.) [following line crossed out;] If he die before reaching 21,
property to be divided between my grandsons John Claggett Dashiell &
Samuel Dashiell Jones. [following line substituted;] ...to be the
right of my son Benjamin Jones
2) To my daughter Betsy Withear Disharoon, home & support, and slaves;
David, Littleton, Metilda & Priscilla; after her death, slaves to go
to her daughters, Susan Jones Disharoon & Betsy Eleanor Jones
Disharoon
3) To my granddaughter Betsy Eleanor Jones Disharoon, negro lad Sam
Chase
[following section crossed out through signature;] 4) To the children
of my daughter, Nelly Dashiell (dec.), wife of George Dashiell,
property; Gideon, Philip, Rachel & Sarah Ann
5) To my Grandson Isaac Dashiell Jones, desk
6) To my granddaughter Betsy Dashiell Jones, negro fellow Joe
7) To my grandson John Quincy Adams Jones, property; Messer,
Washington, Cloe, Ann, Lucretia, Rachel, Lydda, Sarah Ann
8) Remainder to my granddaughters Betsy Withear Disharoon, Amanda
Elenor Jones Dashiell & Susan Jones Dashiell
9) Exe., son Benjamin Jones

F. 212   1 Aug., 1832   John Jones (of Benj.)

[next part added after crossed out section;]
1) To my grandson John Quincy Adams Jones, negroes; Joe, Messen,
Philip, Washington, Ann, girl Sarah Ann
2) To my son Benjamin Jones, negro Gideon
3) To granddaughter Amanda Eleanor Jones Dashiell, negro girl Lydda
4) To granddaughter Betsy Dashiell Jones, $200 due me from George
Dashiell (of John)
5) To my grandson Benj. Jones Dashiell
6) To my grandson George Washington Dashiell
7) To my grandson Isaac Dashiell Jones, money due me from George
Dashiell (of John)
8) I appoint my son Benjamin Jones to be guardian to my grandson John
Quincy Adams Jones & exe. of my will

Court issues summons to widow & near relations

F. 213   Benjamin J. Dashiell, one of the nearest relations of John
          Jones (of Benj.), by his attorneys, William W. Handy &
Charles C. Carroll, files caveat against will, marked exhibit 'B';
objects to admission of will presented by Benjamin I. Jones (of John)
for the following reasons;

1) Contains evidences of frequent changes of intention by its erasures
& interlineating
2) Paper is unfinished & unexecuted
3) John Jones (of Benj.) was not prevented from finishing it, but
didn't; shows it was not meant as his last will
          4) Will revoked and annulled by erasures & cross-outs
F. 214   5) Last part of will doesn't contain his name, and isn't
          signed or dated

Benjamin I. Jones files answer to caveat, by his attorney Thomas A.
Spence, marked exhibit 'C';

F. 215   Denies reasons for invalidating will, stating that it
          contains no ambiguities, is clearly expressed, is in the
handwriting of John Jones (of Benj.), and it was kept by him & found
among his most private & valuable papers

Benjamin J. Dashiell files in caveat a replication, marked exhibit
'D', stating he can prove his allegations

Benjamin I. Jones files certain interrogations, marked exhibit 'E'

F. 216   George D. Walter summoned to answer interrogations; 1) Has
          seen John Jones (of Benj.) write; will & signature both his
writing. 2) Called by widow to witness Isaac D. Jones open desk where
will was found; will in same condition now, as when found

Covington Cordray summoned, answers same to question '1', knows
nothing of question '2'

F. 217   Isaac D. Jones summoned, answers same to question '1'; in
          answer to question '2', states, I was asked by widow to open
desk & look for will in presence of family, & George D. Walter, Thomas
Walter & Samuel B. D. Jones; found will in envelope marked 'The Last
Will & Testament of John Jones of Benjamin'

Court dismisses caveat of Benjamin J. Dashiell, admits will, grants
adm. to Benjamin I. Jones

F. 218   14 May, 1834   Daniel Ballard
                                              Henry Hyland

Benjamin I. Dashiell appeals, granted

F. 219   Tues., May 20, 1834   Daniel Ballard, Henry Hyland present

Elizabeth [always Betsy in orig.] Insley, adm. of John Insley

Elizabeth Bradley, adm. of Thomas Bradley

Orphan; Isaac W., Samuel S. Cullen (of Jacob); Isaac, 19 on 6 Oct., 1833; Samuel, 17 on 19 Sept., 1833
Appointed Guardian; James Lawson
Sureties; William Roach, Henry Ward

Noah Rider & Anthony B. Bennett to divide negroes from estate of James Disharoon

William H. Collier, acting adm. of Charles E. M. Collier

James Russel, adm. of Abraham Lankford

F. 220   Wed., May 21, 1834   Daniel Ballard, Henry Hyland present

John S. Crockett & Ralph Lowe to divide negroes from estate of Jacob J. Weatherly, cannot divide, recommend sale

James Polk, adm. of Littleton Purnell Dennis

Thurs., May 22, 1834   Daniel Ballard, Henry Hyland present

Theodore G. Dashiell, adm. of William H. Fountaine, revoked; Adm. granted to Sally Ann Fountaine, the widow. Sureties; Whitty Fountaine, Henry Fountaine

F. 221   Tues., June 10   All Justices present

Appeal of Benjamin J. Dashiell vs Benjamin I. Jones; Somerset County Court upholds decision of Orphans Court in favor of Benjamin I. Jones

27 May, 1834   Asa Spence
                                          Wm. Tingle

10 June, 1834   Geo. Handy, Clk. Coty. Court

Filed June 10, 1834   James Polk, Reg. Wills

Adm. granted to Benjamin I. Jones. Sureties; Isaac D. Jones, John D. Adams

Lodowick J. Milbourne, one of the persons appointed to divide the negroes from the estate of Patty Dix, is near relative of one of the legatees. As this is illegal, division made by he, & Levin Tyler, is null & void

F. 222   Levin Tyler & William H. Curtis to redivide negroes

Robert Pollitt, adm. cwa of George Pollitt

Tubman Bedsworth & Caleb Kennerly to view estate of Miranda & Eleanor Leatherbury, in care of Lucretia Harris, guardian

William Bennett & Elijah Robertson to view estate of heirs of Thomas Bradley

Levin Morris, guardian to Alexander & Wilhelmina Waller

George Twilley, guardian to Samuel J. & Ann M. Twilley

Henry Kennerly, guardian to Bayard Kennerly

Tues., June 24, 1834   Daniel Ballard, Henry Hyland present

Jesse Walter & Joseph Windsor to view estate of Olivia & George Walter (of George), in care of Biddy Walter, temporary guardian

William A. D. Bounds, guardian to Isaac J. H. Bounds

F. 223   John U. Turpin, guardian to Levin & Elizabeth Goslee

William T. Wood, temporary guardian to Eleanor & Miranda Leatherbury

Joseph Leonard, William Gordy & Henry Bacon, temporary guardians to Edwin L. D., George J. & Sarah A. Parker, & to George Parker (of George) [of E. in orig]

Tues., July 8, 1834   All Justices present

Benjamin I. Jones, exe. of John Jones (of Benj.)

Orphan; Levin L., Ann E. E. Waters (of Levin L.)
Appointed Guardian; Eliza R. W. Waters
Sureties; John Jones (of Thos.), Lambert W. Hyland

John H. Bell & George M. Willing to view estate of Levin L. & Ann E. E. Waters, in care of Eliza R. W. Waters, guardian

Citation against Thomas Bell, guardian to Ann M. & John S. Hughes, to give counter security to Levin Jones (of Levin), one of his sureties

William H. Collier, acting adm. of Charles E. M. Collier

F. 224   Orphan: James M. C. Fountaine (of James R. J. M. C.)
         Appointed Guardian; Charles Rider
         Sureties; John S. Crockett, Thomas W. Fletcher

Covington Cordray & Jesse Hughes to view estate of James M. C. Fountaine, in care of Charles Rider, guardian

Hannah Hearn, claimant, & Thomas Johnson, adm. of Benjamin D. Johnson, ask court to appoint Jehu & Benjamin Parsons to settle dispute between them

Orphan; Joseph, Matthias J. Sudler (of Joseph)
Appointed Guardian; Samuel W. Jones
Sureties; Henrietta M. W. Sudler, John N. Bowland

George M. Willing & Charles W. Harding to view estate of Joseph &
Matthias J. Sudler, in care of Samuel W. Jones, guardian

William H. Curtis & Henry Lankford to view estate of Henry C. Connor,
in care of Levin Connor, guardian

Tues., July 22, 1834   Daniel Ballard, Henry Hyland present

Apprentice; Samuel M. Hopkins
Bound to; Henry K. Long
Trade; Tavern clerk & steward, and barkeeper

Henry Lankford, exe. of Daniel Dakes

F. 225   Orphan; Betsy E. J. Disharoon
          Appointed Guardian; William S. Disharoon (father)
          Sureties; Levin W. Disharoon, John Sanders

Tues., Aug. 5, 1834   All Justices present

George W. Hitch, adm. of Robert Hitch

Orphan; Ann M., John S. Hughes (of James)
Guardian; Thomas Bell, revoked, for failing to give counter security
to Levin Jones, one of his sureties
Appointed Guardian; Robert Stewart
Sureties; Henry Hyland, James Stewart

Orphan; Theodore, Sarah Margaret Hayman (of Isaiah)
Appointed Guardian; Margaret Hayman
Sureties; Benjamin Simson, John Pollitt

F. 226   George L. H. Woolford, adm. of Stephen Hopkins

James Polk, adm. of Littleton P. Dennis

Tues., 12 Aug., 1834   Daniel Ballard, Henry Hyland present

William H. Wailes, acting adm. of William Phillips

Tues., Aug. 26, 1834   All Justice present

Nancy Cullen, adm. of Jacob Cullen, gives counter security to John
Cullen, one of her sureties. Sureties; James Lawson, William Roach

Mary A. Milbourn & Levin Connor, adms. of Josiah Cottingham

F. 227   Levin Wilson, acting adm. of John W. Long

Ralph Lowe, acting exe. of John Bounds

Tues., Sept. 9, 1834   Daniel Ballard, Henry Hyland present

Joseph Weatherly & Joseph Windsor to view estate of William, Elizabeth
& Jane Evans (of Levin), in care of Alexander S. D. Evans, temporary
guardian

F. 228   Joseph Weatherly & Joseph Windsor to divide negroes from
         estate of Levin Evans

Orphan; Ebenezer T., Mary D., Joshua James Bennett (of James)
Appointed Guardian; Elizabeth Bennett
Sureties; Isaac Taylor, John B. Taylor

Joshua Brattan & Samuel Gordon to view estate of Ebenezer T., Mary D.
& Joshua J. Bennett (of James), in care of Elizabeth Bennett, guardian

John Leatherbury, adm. of George Jones (of Robt.), & William T. Wood,
adm of Robert Jones (of Robert), ask court to appoint James Polk to
settle dispute between them

Samuel McBryde, adm. of Jesse H. Wainright

Thomas Mitchell & wife, adm. of James Moore

Alexander S. D. Evans, adm of Levin Evans

William H. Wailes & Elijah Badley to view estate of Sarah Graham, in
care of Benjamin Gravner, guardian

F. 229   Tues., Sept 23, 1834   Daniel Ballard, Henry Hyland present

James B. Moore, adm. dbn of James Bailey

James Polk, adm. of Littleton P. Dennis

James Stewart, exe. of Benjamin Simpson

Orphan; Samuel, George W., Francis, Mary J., John Quincy, Henry Clay
Robertson (of Elias)
Appointed Guardian; Frances Robertson
Sureties; John Robertson, Samuel White

Jesse Hughes & James Denson to view estate of Samuel, George W.,
Francis, Mary J., John Quincy & Henry Clay Robertson, in care of
Frances Robertson, guardian

Tues., Oct. 7, 1834   All Justices present

Ware C. Pollitt, acting exe. of William Pollitt

F. 230   Samuel McBryde & Samuel Pollitt [G. Holbrook in orig.] to
 divide negroes from estate of William Pollitt

William Sudler & John Waters to divide negroes from estate of
Henrietta Long

Tues., Oct. 14, 1834   All Justices present

William Sudler & John Waters to divide negroes from estate of Henrietta Long; recommend sale. Daniel Ballard, adm., to sell

Robert D. Robertson, adm. of John Robertson

F. 231   George Todd, guardian to Alexander H., Robert S. & Eliza A. Todd

Robert Morris, guardian to William Collins

Isaac Covington, guardian to Stephen G. Anderson

Daniel Ballard, guardian to Elizabeth Collins

Report of John Noble, late guardian to James K. Gunby, exhibited by William Gunby

Harriet Bell, guardian to Leah A. W. Bell

Parker Dickerson, guardian to Emeline Dickerson

Littleton Maddux, guardian to Henry D. Maddux

John Dryden, guardian to Littleton Dryden

Tues., Oct. 28, 1834   All Justices present

Matilda McDorman & John W. Carew, adms. of Tubman McDorman

F. 232   Priscilla Walker, adm. of William Huffington

Benjamin I. Jones, exe. of John Jones (of Benj.)

Samuel McBryde, adm. of Jesse H. Wainright, revoked, for refusal to give counter security to George M. Willing & Benjamin Bayly; adm. granted to George M. Willing. Sureties; Benjamin Bailey, John McKenzie

Tues., Nov 11, 1834   All Justices present

Elizabeth Insley, adm. of John Insley

F. 233   Elizabeth Insley, adm. of John Insley, gives counter security to James Stewart, exe. of Benjamin Simpson (who was one of her sureties). Surety; Charles Simpkins

Orphan: Sarah A. Williams (of Levin)
Appointed Guardian; John M. Hall
Sureties; Henry S. Handy, Henry Ward

Tues., Nov. 18, 1834   Daniel Ballard, Henry Hyland present

Henrietta B. Haynie, adm. of William Done, files petition;
I became adm. of estate of William Done on 18, Mar., 1830. Received
letter from Nathaniel Williams, Esq., of Baltimore, District Attorney
for the U.S., stating that the U.S. had a claim on the estate.

F. 234   She deposited moneys in Bank of Md., toward claim by U.S., which bank failed, and money cannot be recovered

F. 235   Asks that no blame be attached to her as she acted in good faith

                                          Henrietta B. Haynie
                                          30 Mar., 1831

Court finds in her favor

Cost of suits in cases of Hetty Disharoon, adm. of James Disharoon, vs. John & William Disharoon, to be defrayed by Hetty from estate

Robert Morris, guardian to William Collins

James Brittingham & wife, guardian to Rosanna E. M. J., Ann F. D. & Edward J. C. Wainright, revoked, for refusal to give counter security to Robert Stewart, adm. of George D. Atkinson (one of the sureties of Rosanna Wainright). James Brittingham appointed guardian.

F. 236   Sureties; John W. B. Parsons, Marshall McDaniel

Wed., Nov. 19, 1834   All Justices present

Orphan; Margaret C. Dashiell (of Ichabod)
Appointed Guardian; William F. Dashiell
Sureties; James Stewart, John B. Slemons

Orphan; George A. C. Walter
Appointed Guardian; George Walter (father)
Sureties; Alexander Donoho, Thomas Walter

Thurs., Nov. 20, 1834   Daniel Ballard, Peter Bell present

Elizabeth Insley, adm. of John Insley, ordered to give counter security to John Turner

Levin Tyler & William H. Curtis to divide negroes from estate of Patty Dix, list slaves; Sandy, Isaac, Cyrus, Lazarus, Tamar.

F. 237   Cannot be fairly divided among four heirs, to wit; Harvey(?), Patty & Isaac T. Marshall, & Sophia Milbourne. William Roach, exe., to sell negroes

John McDaniel, guardian to Almira Nelson

Henry Adams, guardian to Lucinda Anderson

Covington Cordray & James Denson to view estate of Andrew & Washington Robertson, in care of John Robertson, temporary guardian

Joshua Brattan & Willing Wright to view estate of Richard B. & Benjamin T. Darby, in care of John T. Darby, temporary guardian

George M. Willing & Charles W. Harding to view estate of Joseph & Matthias J. Sudler, in care of Samuel W. Jones, guardian

Josiah Furniss & Jonas Hartman to divide negroes from estate of David Long

Levin H. Patrick & Asbury C. Howard, to view estate of Levin & Leah M. Dorman, in care of Benjamin Gordy, guardian

Covington Cordray & Jesse Hughes to view estate of James M. C. Fountaine, in care of Charles Rider, guardian

F. 238   Tues., Nov. 24, 1834   All Justices present

John M. Carew, one of the adms. of Tubman McDorman

Henry P. C. Wilson & Benjamin Bayly, adms. of Col. John C. Wilson, & John D. Anderson, exe. of James Anderson, ask court to appoint James Stewart & Col. George Handy to settle dispute between them

William Sudler & Daniel Benson to view estate of Samuel & Isaac [Francis in orig.] F. Gibbons, in care of William Smith, guardian

Joshua P. Horsey, exe. of Anda Horsey

Levin Tyler, exe. of Samuel Milbourne, to sell negro boy Henry

F. 239   Tues., 9 Dec., 1834   Henry Hyland, Peter Bell present

Charles Parks, adm. of Charles Parks

Nathan Gordy, adm. of Hannah Hearn

James Stewart, exe. of John H. Bell

James H. Spicer & John Freeney to divide negroes from estate of Hannah Hearn

John S. Crockett & John S. Evans to divide negroes from estate of Charles E. M. Collier

F. 240   Tues., Dec. 23, 1834   Daniel Ballard, Henry Hyland present

William Roach, exe. of Patty Dix

Caleb Hughes, adm. dbn cwa of James T. Nelson

David & Thomas White, exes. of William White

William T. G. Polk & Thomas Morris to divide negroes from estate of Isaac Harris

F. 241   Negro Tom, freed by will of Phillis Robertson, given
         permission to remain in county for 12 months

Tues., Jan. 20, 1835   All Justices present

Tubman DeBonne, adm. of Leah Walston

Mary Anderson, adm. of Peter Anderson

F. 242   Isaac B. Jackson, exe. of Elihu Jackson

Henry Hyland, adm. of Priscilla Atkinson

Joshua P. Horsey, exe. of Anda Horsey

Tues., Feb. 3, 1835   Daniel Ballard, Henry Hyland present

Joseph Cantwell, adm. of Thomas Ritchie

F. 243   James Wilson, exe. of Josiah Warwick

Orphan; William, Elizabeth R. Bounds (of William)
Appointed Guardian; James H. Bounds
Sureties; Richard S. Bounds, Thomas Mallone

Tues., Feb. 17, 1835   Daniel Ballard, Henry Hyland present

Tubman DeBonne, adm. of Leah Walston

William S. Disharoon, by Edward Long, his attorney, files petition;
John Jones (of Benj.), in his will left negro, Littleton, to my wife;
He also left negro lad, Sam Chase, to his granddaughter, Betsy Eleanor
         Jones Disharoon, to whom I am father & guardian. Asks that
F. 244   Benjamin I. Jones, exe. of John Jones, deliver these
         legacies. Court so orders

William Roach, adm. of John J. Davis

William Whayland, exe. of William Bounds

Orphan; William Roberts
Appointed Guardian; Thomas Roberts (father)
Sureties; Charles Simpkins, Thomas Robertson

Benjamin Davis, adm. of Isaac Harris

Thomas A. Spence, adm. of John Puzey

F. 245   Charles Parks, adm. of John Hurst

Orphan; John T. Handy (of Joseph)
Appointed Guardian; James Burnett
Sureties; Levin Connor, Daniel Benson

Orphan; Leah J. Walston (of William)
Appointed Guardian; Tubman DeBonne
Sureties; John W. B. Parsons, John M. Heath

Tues., Mar. 3, 1835   Daniel Ballard, Henry Hyland present

John W. Crisfield, adm. of Littleton Redden

Peter D. Weatherly, adm. of James Weatherly

F. 246   George M. Willing & Marshall McDaniel to view estate of Leah J. Walston, in care of Tubman DeBonne, guardian

Joseph Cantwell, adm. of Thomas Ritchie

Rebecca Nelson, adm. of Tubman Nelson

John Leatherbury & William T. G. Polk to divide negroes from estate of Thomas Ritchie

John U. Turpin, guardian to Elizabeth Goslee

William T. G. Polk & Thomas Morris to divide negroes from estate of Isaac Harris

Benjamin Davis, guardian to Isaac Harris

Tues., Mar. 17, 1835   Daniel Ballard, Peter Bell present

F. 247   James Wilson, M.D., appointed Justice

Levin Wilson & Henry Long, adms. of John W. Long

William H. Curtis & John P. Langford to divide negroes from estate of James Blain

Robert J. Henry & Reubin Adams to view estate of Mary W., Littleton & Elizabeth H. S. Landen (of Samuel, & heirs of William Perkins, dec.), in care of Amelia Perkins, temporary guardian

Isaac B. Jackson, exe. of Elihu Jackson

Admx. of John Insley to give counter security to John Turner

F. 248   Sarah Graham & William H. Collier, adms. of Charles E. M. Collier

Henry Hyland, adm. of Priscilla Atkinson

Joseph Weatherly & Joseph Windsor(?) to divide negroes from estate of Levin Evans; cannot divide. Alexander S. D. Evans, adm., to sell

Charles Rider, adm. cwa of James R. J. McClester Fountaine

Tues., Mar. 31, 1835   All Justices present

William H. Curtis appointed Justice

F. 249   Isaac M. Adams & John A. Lankford to divide negroes from estate of William Cluff

Clement Goslee, adm. of Elias Taylor

William T. G. Polk & John Leatherbury to divide negroes from estate of Thomas Ritchie; cannot divide. Joseph Cantwell, adm., to sell

F. 250   Orphan; Susan U.(?) P. Dashiell (of Ichabod) Appointed Guardian; William F. Dashiell Sureties; James Stewart, John N. Bowland

Levin Wilson, temporary guardian to Mary E. & Sally A. Cluff

Tues., 14 Apr., 1835   Daniel Ballard, William H. Curtis present

Letitia Pollitt & Ware C. Pollitt, exes. of William Pollitt

William H. Collier & Noah Handy do divide negroes from estate of Benjamin Moore

20 Jan., 1835, William H. Tull, adm. of Ann Handy, by his attorney, Samuel J. K. Handy, files petition, marked exhibit 'A'; states that James Burnett is concealing notes & belongings of Ann Handy
F. 251   (died Dec., 1834)   James Burnett is of age

James Burnett summoned by court, Samuel G. Holbrook, sheriff

James Burnett, by his attorney, Charles C. Carroll, answers petition, marked exhibit 'B'; Since July, 1833, I have handled Mrs.
F. 252   Handy's business affairs. My wife was her first cousin.
Prior to her death, she suffered occasional mental derangement, which she ascribed to the unkind & undutiful behavior of Sarah Ann Tull, wife of William H. Tull. A bad feeling existed between Mrs. Handy & her daughter, and she stated often that she would leave no part of her estate to Mrs. Tull. Mrs. Handy came to live with me on 14 May, 1833. On 12 Sept., 1833, she sold her possessions. I acted as her agent. She asked me to retain notes received from the sale for her children, John & Thomas. She also gave property to her sons before her death, including negro girl Harriet, child of
F. 253   Sarah

Sworn 17 Feb., 1835, before Geo. M. Willing, J. P.

Thomas Robertson, George F. Ward, Susan Gladden & Mary Burnett summoned to testify in behalf of James Burnett

William H. Tull files amended petition asking for accounting of all notes in possession of James Burnett

F. 254   James Burnett gives inventory of notes, but denies intent to
          conceal them; notes of hand include; John S. Crisp, William
          H. Curtis, George F. Ward, Henry Lankford, Littleton Redden,
F. 255   Stephen Coulbourne, Daniel Benson, Littleton D. Maddux,
          Thomas Robertson, Thomas P. Adams, Wm. H. Beauchamp, John W.
Pool, Sally Adams. Also, judgement against George Dashiell, in hands
of Samuel G. Holbrook, sheriff, and execution, in favor of Mrs. Handy,
in hands of William H. Curtis & James Gibbons

F. 256   Further lists his accounts of Mrs. Handy's business dealings;
          mentions Levin Conner, Ephraim Outten, Josiah Horsey, George
          & Joe Maddux, Wm. Howard, negro Steve, Thomas Robertson,
F. 257   James Polk, Wm. H. Tull, Charles C. Carroll, Wm. Benson, Wm.
F. 258   H. Merrill, John Powell, Meriah Handy, Wm. German, Alexander
F. 259   Bird, Wm. Howard, Wm. Parker, Nathan Tull, Henry Lankford,
          Wm. Wilson, negro Durham, Daniel Benson, Wm. Roach, Sr. [The
above is a day by day list of every expense incurred from May, 1833 to
Oct., 1834]

F. 260   William H. Tull & James Burnett file interrogations

F. 261   Mary Burnett, wife of James, rejected as witness

Henry Lankford testifies; notes in hand, of James Burnett, were for
her sons, and she didn't want Wm. H. Tull to have a cent of her
property. Mr. Burnett & I were sureties for Mrs. Handy, as adm. of
her husbands estate

F. 262   Mary A. Milbourne & Levin Connor, adms. of Josiah Cottingham

James Stewart, exe. of John H. Bell

James Stewart, exe. of Benjamin Simpson

F. 263   Margaret B. Chapman, guardian to Sarah A. Chapman

Tues., Apr. 21, 1835   Daniel Ballard, William H. Curtis present

William H. Collier & Noah Handy to divide negroes from estate of
Benjamin Moore, state that there is only one negro, boy Tubman (9 to
10 years old), and four heirs; James B. Moore, adm. cwa, to sell

George M. Willing & John P. Langford to view estate of Jane,
Elizabeth, Thomas & Sarah Blain, in care of James Tilghman, guardian

Orphan; Jane, Elizabeth, Thomas, Sarah Blain (of James)
Appointed Guardian; James Tilghman
Sureties; John T. Adams, James Dryden

F. 264   George M. Willing & John P. Langford to view estate of Jane,
          Elizabeth, Thomas & Sarah Blain, in care of James Tilghman,
guardian

Elizabeth Insley, adm. of John Insley, gives counter security to John Turner. Sureties; John L. Moore, John Robertson, Thomas Robertson, Charles Simpkins

Mary Miles, exe. of George Miles

Tues., May 5, 1835   All Justices present

Mary Anderson, adm. of Peter Anderson, to sell negro John

Orphan; Samuel S., Isaac F. Gibbons (of Isaac)
Guardian; William Smith (of S.), revoked
Appointed Guardian; Theodore T. Gibbons
Sureties; William Smith (of Jno.), William Maddux

William H. Curtis & John P. Lankford to divide negroes from estate of James Blain; cannot divide. James Tilghman, adm., to sell

F. 265   Mary Anderson, adm. of Peter Anderson

George M. Willing & Marshall McDaniel to view estate of Leah J. Walston, in care of Tubman DeBonne, guardian

Joseph Weatherly & Joseph Windsor to view estate of William, Elizabeth & Jane Evans, in care of Alexander S. D. Evans, temporary guardian

William Sudler & Daniel Benson to view estate of Samuel S. & Isaac F. Gibbons, in care of William Smith, guardian

Joshua Brattan & Samuel Gordon to view estate of Ebenezer T., Mary D. & Joshua J. Bennett, in care of Betsy Bennett, guardian

Jesse Hughes & James Denson to view estate of Samuel, George W., Mary J., Francis, John Quincy & Henry Clay Robertson, in care of Francis Robertson, guardian

William Miles, guardian to Mary A. & Elizabeth Stewart

Margaret Hayman, guardian to Theodore & Sarah M. Hayman

William H. Wailes, guardian to Levin J. M. W. & Isaac H. W. Stanford

Benjamin Davis, temporary guardian to Isaac W. Harris

George Hargis & wife, guardian to William Broughton

Elisha T. Taylor, guardian to Mary J. Green

John Dryden, guardian to Littleton Dryden

F. 266   Sarah H. Nelson, exe. of John W. Nelson (late guardian to Eleanor Nelson)

Tues., May 19, 1835   Daniel Ballard, Peter Bell present

Thomas Walter, adm. of Peggy Porter

Zipporah Graham, exe. of Philip Graham

John A. Lankford, adm. of Thomas D. Atkinson, to sell negro Cipio

Wed., May 20, 1835   Daniel Ballard, Peter Bell present

F. 267   Orphan; Sarah Elizabeth Weatherly (of Peregrine)
          Appointed Guardian; Susan L. Weatherly
          Sureties; John Austin, Richard Lemmon

Apprentice; John Gunby (colored, age 15 on May 15, 1835)
Bound to; Henry T. Tull

Rebecca Nelson, adm. of Tubman Nelson

Henry Ward, adm. of Stephen D. Gunby & John W. Gunby, to sell negro Abraham

Whitty Fontaine, guardian to William Long, bought of Daniel Ballard, adm. of Henrietta Long, negroes for use of his ward, one of the heirs of Henrietta

Tues., May 26, 1835   Daniel Ballard, Peter Bell present

Mary F. Porter, adm. of Mary Porter, to sell negro woman Charlotte

F. 268   Isaac B. Jackson, exe. of Elihu Jackson

Rebecca S.(?) Hayman, exe. of Josiah Hayman

Mary Anderson, adm. of Peter Anderson, gives counter security to James Brittingham & George Drura. Sureties; Henry Ward, John Wilson

Orphan; Sally A., Mary E. Cluff (of William)
Appointed Guardian; Levin Wilson
Sureties; John A. Lankford, William Costen

F. 269   Tues., 9 June, 1835   Daniel Ballard, Peter Bell present

Frances Robertson, guardian to Samuel, George William, Francis, Mary Jane, John Q. & Henry C. Robertson (of Elias), to sell timber to cover cost of repairing dwelling house & out houses

William H. Hall, adm. of George Hall

Orphan; James Collins
Guardian; Robert Morris, revoked
Appointed Guardian; James Mallone
Sureties; Robert Mallone, William Collins

Henry T. Tull, adm. of Caroline Tull

F. 270   Tues., June 23, 1835   Daniel Ballard, Peter Bell present

William H. Tull, Adm. of Ann Handy

Elijah Williams, adm. of Eleanor Fowler, to sell a negro in child

Orphan; George, Thomas B., Perry W. Moore (of Benjamin)
Appointed Guardian; John Taylor
Sureties; John W. Taylor, James B. Moore

Orphan; Edwin L. D., George J., Sarah A. Parker (of Daniel, and divisees of George Parker)
Appointed Guardian; William Gordy
Sureties; William T. Wood, George Vincent

Jehu Parsons & Samuel Leonard to view estate of Edwin L. D., George J. & Sarah A. Parker, in care of William Gordy, guardian

George H. Rencher, adm. of Nelson Waller, to sell negro boy David

Sally Pollitt, exe. of Nehemiah Pollitt

F. 271   Matthias Dashiell & Benjamin I. Jones to divide negroes from estate of William Conway

William Whayland & Thomas Morris to divide negroes from estate of James Bayly

Tues., July 7, 1835   Daniel Ballard, Peter Bell present

Levin Connor, guardian to Henry Q.(?) Connor, to ditch property

Elizabeth Insley, adm. of John Insley

F. 272   Tues., July 28, 1835   Daniel Ballard, Peter Bell present

Nancy Wilson, adm. of Levin Wilson

Samuel G. Holbrook, adm. of Edward H. Holbrook

Citation, at instance of Purnell Toadvine, against Edmond & Joseph Weatherly, & Mary Ann Goslee, next of kin to William H. Weatherly, dec., to show cause why they do not administer estate

Nathan C. Connor granted adm. of estate of Samuel T. Connor.
Sureties; William Wilson, Levin Connor

Nathan C. Connor, adm. dbn cwa of Mary Connor, to sell negro George

F. 273   Levin Ballard & James Phoebus to divide negroes from estate of Edward H. Holbrook

Tues., Aug. 18, 1835   Daniel Ballard, Peter Bell present

'170'

Samuel S. Boggs, adm. of Elizabeth Boggs

Robert J. Henry & Henry Lankford to view estate of John T. Handy (of Joseph), in care of James Burnett, guardian

John A. Lankford, temporary guardian to Sally E. Atkinson

Orphan; Sally E. Atkinson (of Thomas D.)
Appointed Guardian; Levin Atkinson
Sureties; John N. Bowland, Levin Pollitt [Powell in orig.]

F. 274   William Miles & Joseph Richards to view estate of Sally E. Atkinson, in care of Levin Atkinson, guardian

Tues., Sept. 1, 1835   Daniel Ballard, Peter Bell present

Orphan; Elizabeth A. G., Sarah E. Moore (of James)
Appointed Guardian; Thomas Mitchell
Sureties; Levin W. Dashiell, Edwin Dashiell

George Twilley & George Waller to view estate of Elizabeth A. G. & Sarah E. Moore, in care of Thomas Mitchell, guardian

Henry T. Tull, temporary guardian to children of Caroline Tull, to build smoke house, and ditch farm

William C. Kellum, adm. of Henrietta Elzey

John Lowe & Robert Twilley to view estate of heirs of William Phillips, in care of Elizabeth Phillips & William H. Wailes, temporary guardians

Thomas Ward, exe. of John Ward

F. 275   Orphan; Margaret H., John T. Banks
          Appointed Guardian; Henry Banks (father)
          Sureties; George Price, Henry Banks., Jr.

Isaac Nicols & Samuel Gordon to divide negroes from estate of Mary Porter

Peter D. Weatherly, adm. of James Weatherly

Tues., Sept. 15, 1835   All Justices present

Matthias Dashiell appointed Justice

F. 276   Levin Ballard & James Phoebus to divide negroes from estate of Edward H. Holbrook; cannot divide. Samuel G. Holbrook, adm., to sell

Robert J. King & Benjamin Lankford to view estate of heirs of Caroline Tull, in care of Henry T. Tull, temporary guardian

Henry Thomas, adm. cwa of Aaron Sterling

William H. Curtis & George M. Willing to view estate of Levin L. & Ann E. E. Waters (of Levin L.), in care of Eliza R. W. Waters, guardian

Indenture dated 24 July, 1822, bound certain free negroes apprentices to Joseph B. Brinkley. Upon his death negroes were listed in inventory as slaves & included in division of estate by Thomas Robertson & Nathaniel Bell. Division is null & void. Adm., Elizabeth Brinkley

F. 277 Robert J. King & Daniel Benson to divide negroes from estate of Joseph B. Brinkley

Orphan; Sarah A., Thomas, Francis L., Henry F. Brinkley (of Joseph B.)
Appointed Guardian; Elizabeth Brinkley
Sureties; Joseph B. Brinkley, Jr., William H. Curtis

Robert J. Henry & Daniel Benson to view estate of Sarah A., Thomas, Francis L. & Henry F. Brinkley, in care of Elizabeth Brinkley, guardian

Tues., Sept. 22, 1835   All Justices present

Anthony B. Bennett, adm. of Washington Bennett

F. 278   Indenture of 17 July, 1835, binding Levin Blewett apprentice to William Somers, by Elijah C. Johnson & Isaac Leonard, Justices of the Peace, is objected to by said Levin, & his mother, Nelly Blewett, and found illegal & defective

Apprentice; Levin Blewett
Bound to; William W. Handy
Trade; Farmer

Orphan; Thomas J. Handy (of Joseph)
Appointed Guardian; Henry Lankford
Sureties; James Burnett, Theodore G. Dashiell

Robert J. Henry & John H. Cohoon to view estate of Thomas J. Handy, in care of Henry Lankford, guardian

Samuel S.(?) Boggs, adm. of Elizabeth Boggs

Edward Fowler, exe. of William Roberts, to sell negro woman Hannah & child

3 Mar., 1835, Rebecca Nelson, adm. of Tubman Nelson, by her attorneys, William W. Handy & Samuel J. K. Handy, filed petition, marked exhibit 'A'; states that Tubman Nelson borrowed $430.00 from Joshua Hitch,
         giving said Hitch a bill of sale for his eleven negroes to
F. 279   insure repayment. Negroes are now increased to thirteen.

Joshua Hitch, at time of loan, issued Tubman Nelson a back bond, or writing obligatory, explaining said bill of sale. He has since gotten hold of said back bond by fraudulent means, and refuses to deliver it to your petitioner. Tubman Nelson died 1834

F. 280   Joshua Hitch, by Edward Long, his attorney, files answer to petition, marked exhibit 'B'; states bill of sale for nine negroes issued 16 Mar., 1832.. As loan not repaid, Tubman lost all claim to negroes

F. 281   Sworn before Jesse Walter, J. P., 23 June, 1835

Rebecca Nelson files interrogations

F. 282   Miranda Smith testifies

Joshua Hitch files interrogations

F. 283   Rebecca Smith testifies

F. 284   Rebecca Nelson files further interrogations

Capt. John Turner testifies; states original transaction took place in home of Francis D. Nelson

Joshua Hitch files further interrogations

F. 285   John Turner states that Joshua Humphriss was present

Court orders Joshua Hitch to turn over back bond to Rebecca Nelson; 22 Sept., 1835

F. 286   Parker Dickerson, guardian to Emeline Dickerson

William Gunby, guardian to James K. Gunby

Whitty Fontaine, guardian to William Long

George Todd, guardian to Alexander H., Robert S. & Eliza A. Todd

Joseph Leonard, William Gordy & Henry Bacon, temporary guardians to Sarah A., Edwin L. D., George J. & George Parker (of Elisha)

Posthumous account of Thomas Bradley, late temporary guardian to Eli Badley

Isaac M. Adams & John A. Lankford to divide negroes from estate of William Cluff

Tues., 13. Oct., 1835   Daniel Ballard, Peter Bell present

Robert Bell, adm. of Nathaniel Bell

F. 287   Thomas Robertson & John H. Cohoon to view estate of Thomas
          H. Bell (of Nathaniel), in care of Robert Bell, temporary
guardian

Nathan C. Connor, adm. dbn of Mary Connor

James & Isaac Lawson to divide negroes from estate of John Ward

Orphan; Noah Riggin (of Noah)
Appointed Guardian; James Davis
Sureties; John T. Adams, Henry Riggin

Levin Tyler & William Adams to view estate of Noah Riggin (of Noah),
in care of James Davis, guardian

Benjamin Gordy & Henry Dulaney to divide negroes from estate of John
Leatherbury

Tues., Oct. 27, 1835   Daniel Ballard, James Stewart present

James Stewart appointed Justice

F. 288   William T. G. Polk, one of the adms. of George A. Dashiell

Henry Trader & George W. Hitch to view estate of Elizabeth M. Elzey
(of Henrietta), in care of William C. Kellum, temporary guardian

Orphan; John D., Ellen, Drucilla, David Long (of John W.)
Appointed Guardian; Henry Long
Sureties; Levin Wilson, Isaac H. Dryden

John A. Lankford & Thomas A. Dryden to view estate of John D., Ellen,
Drucilla & David Long, in care of Henry Long, guardian

Apprentice; Joshua R. Duer
Bound to; Brodwater & Briding
Trade; Coach making business, in harness making & trimming departments

Orphan: Alcy K., Mary E., Sarah P, Martha J., Isaac J. T. Harriss (of
William)
Guardian; John Hopkins, revoked
Appointed Guardian; William H. Acworth
Sureties; Samuel G. Holbrook, John L. Moore

Robert Stewart & Benjamin J. Dashiell to view estate of Alice K., Mary
E., Sarah P., Martha J. & Isaac J. T. Harris (of William), in care of
William H. Acworth, guardian

F. 289   Tues., Nov. 10, 1835   Daniel Ballard, James Stewart present

George Johnson, exe. of Josiah Johnson

George H, Johnson, exe. of Josiah Johnson

'174'

Priscilla Walker, adm. of William Huffington

William B. Jones, adm. of John H. Anderson

Henry T. Tull, adm. of Caroline Tull

Eliza R. W. Waters, adm. of Levin L. Waters

Orphan; Elizabeth, Mitchell, William Bozman (of David)
Appointed Guardian; James Phoebus
Sureties; Robert Patterson, Arnold H. Ballard

F. 290   Levin Ballard & Ballard Reid to view estate of Elizabeth, Mitchell & William Bozman, in care of James Phoebus, guardian

Tues., Nov. 17, 1835   All Justices present

Orphan; Lecascy A. Hitch (of William A.)
Appointed Guardian; Thomas Hitch
Sureties; Robert Morris, Jesse Leatherbury

George W. Hitch & Henry Trader to view estate of Lecascy A. Hitch, in care of Thomas Hitch, guardian

George W. Hitch, adm. of Robert Hitch

Wed., Nov. 18, 1835   All Justices present

William Costen, adm. cwa of Mary Harris

F. 291   Esther Broughton, adm. of John H. Broughton

Levin Phillips & Jesse Walter to divide negroes from estate of William Phillips

James Wilson, adm. of John C. Wilson

Clement Goslee, adm. of Elias Taylor

Orphan; Rebecca, Richardson D., James, Henry Smith (of Henry C.)
Appointed Guardian; James Donoho
Sureties; Levin C. Smith, James R. W. Conway

John S. Crockett, adm. of Charles Venables

Daniel Ballard & John Curtis to divide negroes from estate of Ann Handy

F. 292   Thurs., Nov. 19, 1835   All Justices present

James Stewart, adm. of Charles W. Harding

Fri., Nov. 20, 1835   All Justices present

William H. Acworth, adm. of Isaac Harris

William H. Acworth, adm. of Alcy Harris

Cadmus Dashiell & John S. Crockett, adms. of Matthias Dashiell

Sarah B. Dashiell & William T. G. Polk, adms. of George A. Dashiell

F. 293 Matthias O. Toadvine, guardian to Elizabeth R. & Esther G. Handy

John Austin, guardian to Eliza James

George Twilley, guardian to Ann M. & Samuel J. Twilley

John T. Fontaine, guardian to John E. & Eleanor A. E. Fontaine

John McDaniel, guardian to Almira Nelson

Daniel Ballard, guardian to Elizabeth Collins

Levin Morris, guardian to Alexander Waller

William Smith, guardian to Theodore T. Gibbons

Harriet Bell, guardian to Leah A. W. Bell

Samson Adams & wife, guardian to Washington & Catherine Miles

Cyrus Nelson, guardian to Horatio Nelson

George M. Willing & John P. Langford to view estate of Jane, Eliza, Thomas & Sarah Blain

Robert J. Henry & Henry Lankford to view estate of John Handy, in care of James Burnett, guardian

Robert J. Henry & Benjamin Lankford to view estate of heirs of Caroline Tull, in care of Henry T. Tull, temporary guardian

John S. Crockett & John S. Evans to view estate of William & Joseph Weatherly, in care of Edmond Weatherly, guardian

James H. Spicer & John Freeny to divide negroes from estate of Hannah Hearn

Robert J. King & Reuben Adams to view estate of Mary W., Littleton & Elizabeth H. S. Landen, in care of Amelia Perkins, temporary guardian

Jehu Parsons & Samuel Leonard to view estate of Edwin L. D., George J. & Sarah A. Parker, in care of William Gordy, guardian

F. 294 William Whayland & Thomas Morris to divide negroes from estate of James Bailey

'176'

James & Isaac Lawson to divide negroes from estate of John Ward

Tues., Nov. 24, 1835   Peter Bell, James Stewart present

John Austin, adm. of John [Samuel in orig.] Green

Robert J. Henry & John H. Cohoon to view estate of Thomas J. Handy, in care of Henry Lankford, guardian

Tues, 8 Dec., 1835   Daniel Ballard, James Stewart present

Negroes Luckey(?) & Hannah erroneously appraised in estate of Levin L. Waters, the former belonging to James C. Hyland, the latter to Arnold E. Waters

Cadmus Dashiell & John S. Crockett, adms. of Matthias Dashiell

John S. Crockett, adm. of Shiles Crockett

F. 295   Tues., Dec. 22, 1835   Daniel Ballard, James Stewart present

Edward Fowler, exe. of William Roberts

Anthony B. Bennett, adm. of Washington Bennett

Thomas Walter, adm. cwa of Peggy Porter

James B. Moore, adm. dbn of James Bailey, revoked. Adm. granted to Henry Pollitt. Sureties; William Hitch, Levin Pollitt

Levin Phillips & Jesse Walter to divide negroes from estate of William Phillips; cannot divide. Elizabeth Phillips & William H. Wailes, adms., to sell

F. 296   Tues., Jan. 12, 1836   Daniel Ballard, James Stewart present

Apprentice; Mitchell D. Bozman
Bound to; William B. Phoebus
Trade; House Carpenter

Apprentice; William Bozman
Bound to; George A. Noble
Trade; House Carpenter

Tues., Jan. 26, 1836   Daniel Ballard, James Stewart present

Orphan; Matilda A. Redden (of Littleton)
Appointed Guardian; Mary H. Redden
Sureties; Margaret Done, James C. Hyland

Tues., 9 Feb., 1836   All Justices present

F. 297   John Cottman, adm. of Margaret B. Chapman

Daniel Ballard, guardian to Elizabeth Collins, to build tenant house on farm called Carsley's

Tues., Feb. 23, 1836   Daniel Ballard, James Stewart present

Exe. of George Parker

John T. Sasser, exe. of Elizabeth Sasser

Orphan; Caleb R., Caroline R. A., Thomas B. F., Mary A., Ariana, John C. Hughes (heirs of Nehemiah Nelson)
Appointed Guardian; Caleb Hughes (father)
Sureties; Marcellus Jones, John S. Crockett

Caleb Hughes, adm dbn cwa of James T. Nelson, to sell negro Levin

19 Jan., 1836, Jane Puzey exhibits paper purporting to be will of William Dorman;

F. 298   1) To wife Jane Puzey, her thirds of real estate
         2) to wife Jane Puzey, half of personal estate
3) To wife Jane Puzey's children; Elizer, Caroline & Thomas Shella(?)

Witnesses; C. W. Harding   19 Aug., 1833
           Littleton P. Dennis   his
                                    William X Dorman
                                            mark

Filed for Jane Puzey, by Samuel J. K. Handy, her attorney

Thomas P. Dorman, by William W. Handy, his attorney, files caveat against will

Jane Puzey declines to further prosecute case

F. 299   After hearing testimony from Arnold H. Ballard, that signatures of two witnesses are not in their handwriting, court declares will a forgery

Tues., Mar 8, 1836   All Justices present

Obediah Riggin, adm. dbn of William Perkins

George H. & Ware Wainright, exes. of Levin Wainright

Susan Horsey, adm. cwa of John Horsey

F. 300   John S. Crockett & John S. Evans to divide negroes from estate of John Horsey

23 Feb., 1836, Levi Howarth & Nancy, his wife, by William W. Handy, their attorney, file petition; ask that certain negroes bequeathed to Nancy by John Ward be delivered by exe.

Thomas Ward, exe. of John Ward, summoned; appears with his attorney, C. C. Carroll

Court orders negroes, Levi & Kessey, delivered to Levi Howarth

Obadiah Riggin, adm. dbn of William Perkins, to sell negro woman Nancy, & her two children

F. 301 Noah Rider, claimant, & James Stewart, adm. of Charles W. Harding, ask court to appoint John Jones & George M. Willing to settle dispute between them

Exe. of George Parker to sell negro woman Phillis to the lowest bidder

Wed., Mar. 16, 1836   Daniel Ballard, James Stewart present

1 Mar., 1836, paper purporting to be will of Henry Crawford exhibited;
1) to four eldest sons; William _.(?), Barney, Beason & James, $1.00 & no more
2) To daughter Maria Twilley, negro man Ben
3) To James Bounds & six children he had by my daughter Elizabeth, $1.00 each & no more
4) To daughter Hester Crawford, negro man John
5) To son Perry, negro man Spencer, $200.00 to be paid to him by my son Horatio Nelson Crawford, when said Horatio shall reach 22 years
       6) To son Henry, negro man David, $200.00...[as above]
F. 302 7) To son Horatio Nelson Crawford, farm to a ditch that leads to Mrs. Water's land, & land on east side of road through woods to Quantico Rd.; negro man Perry, negro woman Tina. All property for use of my wife, Mary K. Crawford, during her life
8) To son Andrew, land, negro boy Richard, negro woman Sarah
9) To two sons Horatio Nelson & Andrew, negro man Joseph, his wife Amelia & their children
10) To sons Horatio & Andrew, residue of estate
11) Wife Mary K. Crawford & son-in-law George Twilley exes.

Witnesses William Bounds (of Richd.)   7 Apr., 1831
         James Bounds
         James Goslee   Henry Crawford

NB., If any claim from John Wiley, Pensylvani, to be paid from bequest to sons Perry & Henry

16 Mar., 1836, came William, James, John, Levin & Marcellus Bounds, & Esther Bounds, by James Bounds, their guardian & next friend, & William W. & Levin Handy, their solicitors, filed caveat against will

F. 303 The petition of William, Esther Anne, James, John, Levin & Marcellus Bounds, infant children of James Bounds, & his dec. wife Elizabeth, who was a daughter of Henry Crawford, dec. Elizabeth died intestate during Henry's lifetime. Henry not of sound mind. He left a widow, Mary K. Crawford, exe. of supposed will, & children; William H., Barney, Beason, James, Hester Anne, Perry, Henry, Horatio N. & Andrew Crawford, & Maria Twilley (wife of George)

F. 304   Came Mary K. Crawford, Henry K. Long, next friend & guardian
         to Horatio N. & Andrew Crawford, infants, by John W.
Crisfield, attorney, file answer; Henry Crawford died 28 Jan., 1836;
         made will voluntarily, and while of a sound mind. I found
F. 305   will in a drawer, carefully filed with other valuable papers
         Sworn before Thos C. Dorsey, J.P.

F. 306   James Bounds, one witness to will state that Henry Crawford
         was of sound mind; saw James Goslee & William Bounds (of
Richard) sign will. Caveat is withdrawn, will admitted to probate

Sally Pollitt, exe. of Nehemiah Pollitt

Tues., Mar. 22, 1836   Daniel Ballard, James Stewart present

Negro Tom, freed by will of Phillis Robertson, granted permission to
stay in county for 12 months

Daniel Boston, exe. of Alexander S. Bird

F. 307   22 Dec., 1835, Levi Howarth, by J. W. Crisfield, his
         attorney, filed petition; says he is entitled to a share of
estate of John Ward, mostly negroes. Division already approved by
court without my knowledge is unjust. Asks that it be set aside,
negroes sold, and proceeds divided

Appeared on the 22 Mar., 1836, Levi Howarth and John B. Stevenson,
Thomas, Elisha, John, William & Noah Ward; agree to reversal of
division of estate. Witnesses; William Roach, Jr., Henry Ward.
Original division made by James & Isaac Lawson; filed 27 Oct., 1835, &
approved 20 Nov., 1835. Thomas Ward, exe., to sell negroes

F. 308   Order of 8 Mar., 1836, for sale of negro woman, Phillis,
         allegedly part of estate of George Parker, rescinded, as exe.
claims no ownership. Peter Bell claims she is part of estate

Mary Anderson, adm. of Peter Anderson

Hannah Miles & Joshua Dougherty, adms. of John Miles

Henry White, adm. of George Sirman, filed petition on 26 Jan., 1836;
adm. granted 19 Jan., 1836. Claims part of estate concealed by
William Kibble

F. 309   William Kibble delivers property to Henry White

Tues., Apr. 5, 1836   Daniel Ballard, James Stewart present

Robert L. Miles, exe. of Matthias Miles

James Wilson, exe. of Sarah Whitney

John H. Adams, adm. of George Robertson

F. 310   William T. Wood & wife, guardian to George W., Mary E. L. &
          Sally A. Johnson

Littleton D. Maddux, guardian to Henry D. Maddux

Joseph S. Cottman, guardian to John A. H. Cottman

James Brittingham, guardian to Ann F. D., Edward J. C. & Rosanna E. M.
J. Wainright

Margaret Hayman, guardian to Theodore & Sarah M. Hayman

Obadiah Riggin & wife, guardian to Littleton, Mary W. & Elizabeth H.
S. Landen

Levin Tyler, guardian to Sally N. & William T. White

Levin Tyler, guardian to Samuel C., Patty A. & Rebecca M. Broughton

Levin Wilson, guardian to Mary E. & Sally A. Cluff

James Brittingham, guardian to Rosanna E. M. J. Wainright

Elzey Foxwell, guardian to Benjamin Foxwell

[original minutes end at this point]

Tues., 12 Apr., 1836   All Justices present

F. 311   Orphan; John H. Anderson (of John H.)
          Appointed Guardian; William B. Jones
          Sureties; William H. Jones, William Adams

Charles Rider, adm. cwa of James R. J. M. C. Fontaine, to sell negro
man Elbert

Eleanor Bounds & Ralph Lowe, adms. of John Bounds, to sell negro man
John

Robert Bell, adm. of Nathaniel Bell

Tues., May 3, 1836   Daniel Ballard, James Stewart present

F. 312   Mary K. Crawford & George Twilley, exes. of Henry Crawford

Orphan; Levin T. Jones (of Thomas)
Appointed Guardian; Samuel B. D. Jones
Sureties; Isaac D. Jones, John L. Moore

William Coston, adm. cwa of Mary Harris

Edward Parks & Thomas Robertson, exes. of William Parks

Handy Burbage, adm. of Cyrus Leonard

Tues., May 17, 1836   Daniel Ballard, James Stewart present

Tubman Bedsworth, adm. of Zipporah Graham

F. 313   Tubman Bedsworth, adm. dbn of Philip Graham

John E. Harris, trustee for Nancy Hopkins, claimant, & William H. Collier & Sarah Graham, adms. of Charles E. M. Collier, ask court to appoint Thomas D. Evans & John S. Evans to settle dispute between them

James F. Kelly, exe. of John Kelly

Thomas H. Dougherty, adm. of Stephen Dougherty, gives counter security to Joshua Brattan & Joseph Walker. Sureties; Alexander S. D. Evans, Whittington Kennerly

Wed., May 18, 1836   All Justices present

Orphan; Azariah W., William D. Donoho (of Philip M.)
Appointed Guardian; Priscilla Donoho
Sureties; Ralph Lowe, John S. Crockett

F. 314   Tubman Bedsworth & John S. Evans to view estate of Azariah W. & William D. Donoho, in care of Priscilla Donoho, guardian

Thomas P. Dorman & James Brittingham, adms. of William Dorman

Thurs., May 19, 1836   Daniel Ballard, James Stewart present

Marcellus Jones & Thomas B. Robertson to view estate of Sarah P., Isaac J. T., Martha J., Mary E. & Alice K. Harris, in care of William H. Acworth, guardian, in place of Robert Stewart & Benjamin Dashiell

Motion of William W. Johnston against Nancy Walls, widow of George, to show cause why she does not adm. estate

Orphan; Jane Evans (of Levin)
Appointed Guardian; Alexander S. D. Evans
Sureties; John N. Bowland, Levin W. Dashiell

Alexander S. D. Evans, adm. of William C. Evans

Nancy Wilson, adm. of Levin Wilson

F. 315   Tues., May 24, 1836   All Justices present

John H. King, adm. of Samuel King

Alice White & Edward Fowler, adms. cwa of Henry White, to sell negro boy William

William Roach, adm. of John J. Davis, to sell negro woman Bridget

Henry T. Tull, temporary guardian to heirs of Samuel Tull, to erect tenant house on farm called Adams' Place

George H. & Ware Wainright, exes. of Levin Wainright, to sell negroes Charlotte, Robert, Mary & Reuben

F. 316   Tues., 14 June, 1836   All Justices present

George Perry Jones, adm. dbn of Levin D. Jones

Elizabeth Phillips & William H. Wailes, adm. of William Phillips

George H. & Ware Wainright, exes. of Levin Wainright

William W. Maddux, adm. of Margaret E. Dashiell

Charlotte Smith, adm. of John J. Smith

William Gordy, guardian to orphans of Daniel Parker & divisees of George Parker, to repair mills

Overpayment on estate of William Harris, by Isaac Harris, acting adm., to be retained by William H. Acworth, adm. of Isaac, dec.

F. 317   Tues., June 28, 1836   All Justices present

George Perry Jones, adm. of Levin D. Jones

Mary K. Crawford & George Twilley, exes. of Henry Crawford

Susan Horsey, exe. of John Horsey

Orphan; Emeline, Sarah A., Joshua P. Dougherty (of Joshua)
Appointed Guardian; Henry Ward
Sureties; Henry S. Handy, Theodore G. Dashiell

Morris H. Adams, exe. of Thomas Adams

Stephen Miles & John W. Handy, adms. of William Miles

Orphan; Sarah E., George McDorman (of Lewis)
Appointed Guardian; Nancy McDorman
Sureties; Robert Patterson, John Smith

Tues., July 12, 1836   James Stewart, Peter Bell present

Edward P. Cluff, exe. of Robert Cluff

F. 318   Orphan; James M. Stone (legatee of Susanna Waters)
         Appointed Guardian; William M. Stone (father)
         Sureties; Robert Stewart, Thomas W. Stone

Benjamin J. Dashiell & George Twilley to view estate of James M. Stone, in care of William M. Stone, guardian

Orphan; Henry Crawford (of Henry)
Appointed Guardian; William H. Crawford
Sureties; James Bounds, George Twilley

Orphan; Noah Riggin
Guardian; James Davis, revoked
Appointed Guardian; Isaac Riggin
Sureties; William Williams, Jr., William H. Curtis

Orphan; William Taylor (of John, Jr.)
Appointed Guardian; Jonathan B. Phillips
Sureties; John W. Taylor, John Taylor

Isaac B. Jackson, exe. of Elihu Jackson

Robert Stewart, adm. of George D. Atkinson

Thomas Walter, adm of Peggy Porter

Stephen Miles & John W. Handy, adms. of William Miles

John W. Nelson & Levin Jones, adms. of Francis D. Nelson, revoked.
Adm. dbn cwa granted to James Bounds. Sureties; John S. Crockett,
Robert Stewart

F. 319   Tues., July 26, 1836   Daniel Ballard, James Stewart present

Orphan; Isaac White (of Beauchamp)
Appointed Guardian; Elijah White
Sureties; Levin W. Disharoon, Jonathan Huffington

William Whayland & Isaac Anderson to view estate of Isaac White, in
care of Elijah White, guardian

Orphan; Nathaniel T. Bell (of Nathaniel)
Appointed Guardian; Amelia Bell
Sureties; Robert Bell, John T. Adams

Thomas Robertson & John H. Cohoon to view estate of Nathaniel T.
Bell, in care of Amelia Bell, guardian

Charlotte Smith, adm. of John J. Smith

Henry Marshall & the children of Elizabeth Marshall, to wit; Henry,
William, George, Reuben & Nancy Marshall, of Somerset Co., MD, are
heirs of Benjamin Marshall, master-at-arms of the Virginia navy in the
Revolutionary War

Robert J. Henry & Levin Tyler to view estate of Elizabeth Collins, in
care of Daniel Ballard

Tues., Aug. 2, 1836   Daniel Ballard, James Stewart present

Orphan; Henry, William, George, Reuben, Nancy Marshall (heirs of John
& Benjamin Marshall)
Appointed Guardian; Isaac Anderson
Sureties; William Whayland, Chesed(?) Purnell

Isaac Anderson, guardian to Henry, William, George, Reuben & Nancy
       Marshall (infant children of Elizabeth Marshall, one of the
F. 320   heirs of Benjamin & John Marshall, warrant officers in the
       Virginia navy in the Revolutionary War), to sell certificates
of land bounty scrip

John Hopkins, guardian to Isaac J. T., Sarah P., Martha J., Elizabeth
& Alice K. Harris

Levin Connor, guardian to Henry C. Connor

William Gunby, guardian to James K. Gunby

Parker Dickerson, guardian to Emeline Dickerson

Matthias O. Toadvine, guardian to Elizabeth G. Handy

John U. Turpin, guardian to Levin Goslee

William Gordy & others, temporary guardians to George J., Edwin L. D.
& Sarah A. Parker

Elizabeth Phillips & William H. Wailes, temporary guardians to Mary B.
Phillips

George Todd, guardian to Alexander H., Robert S. & Eliza A. Todd

Robert Stewart, temporary guardian to George S., Isaac S., William R.,
Mary P. & Eliza A. Atkinson

William W. Johnston, guardian to George K. Wise

Robert J. King & Daniel Benson to view estate of Sarah A., Thomas,
Francis L. & Henry F. Brinkley, in care of Elizabeth Brinkley,
guardian

Robert Jones, guardian to George P. Jones

Whitty Fontaine, guardian to William Long

F. 321   Tues., Aug. 16, 1836   Daniel Ballard, James Stewart present

George H. Johnson, exe. of Josiah Johnson, to give counter security to
Theodore G. Dashiell

Edward P. Cluff, exe. of Robert Cluff

John Cottman, temporary guardian to Sarah A. Chapman, to repair corn
house, & porch of dwelling, & ditch land

Tues., Aug. 30, 1836   Daniel Ballard, James Stewart present

Orphan; Robert T. Smith (of John J.)
Appointed Guardian; John W. Smith
Sureties; Daniel Boston, Lodowick J. Milbourne

Levin Tyler & Robert J. Henry to view estate of Robert T. Smith, in care of John W. Smith, guardian

Susan Horsey, exe. of John Horsey

Orphan; Gilbert S. Milbourne (of Benjamin)
Appointed Guardian; Lazarus Lankford
Sureties; Isaac S. Lankford, John T. Adams

Edward P. Cluff & Daniel Boston to view estate of Gilbert S. Milbourne, in care of Lazarus Lankford, guardian

F. 322   Tues., Sept. 13, 1836   Daniel Ballard, James Stewart present

William W. Johnston, adm. of George Walls

Orphan; Mary W., Littleton, Elizabeth H. S. Landen(?) (of Samuel, & representatives of William Perkins)
Appointed Guardian; Josiah Furniss
Sureties; John U. Turpin, James Gibbons

Isaac M. Adams & Henry Maddux to view estate of Mary W., Littleton J. & Elizabeth H. S. Landen, in care of Josiah Furniss, surety[?]

William Sudler, adm. dbn of Nehemiah Walston

Levin Atkinson, guardian to Sarah E. Atkinson

Lucretia Harris, guardian to Miranda & Eleanor Leatherbury

Charles Rider, guardian to James M. C. Fontaine

Samuel McBryde & Samuel G. Holbrook to divide negroes from estate of William Pollitt

Levin Ballard & Ballard Reid to view estate of Elizabeth, Mitchell & William Bozman, in care of James Phoebus, guardian

F. 323   Tues., Sept. 27, 1836   Daniel Ballard, James Stewart present

William Sudler, adm. of Thomas H. Walston

William Whayland & Isaac Anderson to view estate of Isaac White, in care of Elijah White, guardian

Tues., 11 Oct., 1836   All Justice present

Stephen D. Coulbourn, adm. of Robert H. Coulbourne

Samuel G. Holbrook & Levin Ballard (of Jarvis?) to view estate of heirs of Nehemiah Walston, in care of William Sudler, temporary guardian

Thomas E. Ballard & Tubman L. Hall to view estate of heirs of Thomas H. Walston, in care of William Sudler, temporary guardian

William Sudler, adm. of Nehemiah Walston

F. 324   William Sudler, adm. of Thomas H. Walston

Whitty Fontaine, guardian to William Long, to sell negro man Isaac

Orphan; Benjamin T. Bell (of John H.)
Appointed Guardian; George McElhiney
Sureties; James Steward, William H. Curtis

Tues., Oct. 18, 1836   All Justices present

James S. Anderson, claimant, & Sarah B. Dashiell & William T. G. Polk, adms. of George A. Dashiell, ask court to appoint Thomas Dorsey & William M. Jones to settle dispute between them

William W. Johnston, adm. of George Walls

F. 325   Henry Pollitt, adm. dbn of James Bailey

Tues., Oct. 25, 1836   All Justices present

Joshua Brattan & Marcellus Jones to divide negroes bequeathed in will of Isaac Atkinson, to children of George D. Atkinson

Thomas Robertson & John Miles, Jr., to divide negroes from estate of Caroline Tull

Benjamin Lankford & Henry Thomas to view estate of Kitty, Marcellus, Hambleton & Maria J. Moore, in care of Job Moore, guardian

Robert C. J. Waters, adm. cwa of Esther Broughton

Samuel W. Jones, guardian to Joseph Sudler, to sell negro girl Nancy

F. 326   Orphan; Mary H. E. Robinson (of Charles)
          Appointed Guardian; Hetty Deverix
          Sureties; Bennett L. Fish, John F. Taylor

Henrietta Atkinson & Joseph Nichols, guardian to children of George D. Atkinson, to sell negro Sam

Tues., Nov. 8, 1836   All Justices present

Jane Hitch, adm. of Littleton Hitch

Daniel Benson, adm. of George Dakes

'187'

Adm. of Josiah Cottingham

Orphan; Caroline, Robert Marshall (of William)
Appointed Guardian; Lewis Smith
Sureties; James Smith, Robert Morris

Robert C. J. Waters, adm. cwa of Esther Broughton

Orphan; Joseph B., William T. Cox (of Tubman)
Appointed Guardian; Ann Cox
Sureties; George Cox, John T. Adams

F. 327   Levin Tyler & William Beauchamp to view estate of Joseph B. & William T. Cox, in care of Ann Cox, guardian

Orphan; Isaac White (of Beacham)
Appointed Guardian; Robert Morris
Sureties; James & Lewis Smith

Orphan; Joseph, Clement Gillis (of Josiah)
Appointed Guardian; Thomas Langsdale
Sureties; Jesse Walter, Thomas W. Fletcher

Tues., Nov. 22, 1836   Daniel Ballard, James Stewart present

Samuel W. Jones, exe. of Milcah G. Jones

Samuel W. Jones, adm. dbn cwa of Matthias Jones

Levin Walter, adm. of Mary K. Crawford

James Lawson, adm. of Josiah Cullen

F. 328   Thomas Newman, exe of William Newman, to sell negroes Jesse & Nanny

Edward Parks & Thomas Robertson, exes. of William Parks

Orphan; John, Adrian, Elizabeth Marshall (of Adrian)
Appointed Guardian; Daniel Benson
Sureties; William H. Curtis, Theodore G. Dashiell

On 26 July, 1836, it was ordered that; 'Henry Marshall & the children of Elizabeth Marshall, to wit; Henry, William, George, Reuben & Nancy Marshall, are the only heirs of Benjamin Marshall', & on 23 May, 1833, it was ordered; 'Henry Marshall & Elizabeth Marshall, nephew & niece of John Marshall, are only heirs of John Marshall'. Since then have come forward others who are related to Benjamin & John Marshall, some through the father of Elizabeth Marshall, dec. Former orders null & void

F. 329   Tues., Nov. 29, 1836   All Justices present

James Smith, soldier in the MD Line, 3rd Reg., in the Revolutionary War, died intestate, and had no children; Stoughton & James Smith[?] are nephews & only heirs

James F. Kelly, exe. of John Kelly

Robert J. Henry & Levin Wilson to divide negroes from estate of Robert Cluff

Handy Burbage, adm. of Cyrus Leonard

John Byrd, claimant, & Levin G. Irving, adm. of Levin W. Disharoon, ask court to appoint Purnell Toadvine & John W. Rider to settle dispute between them

F. 330   Wed., Nov. 30, 1836   All Justices present

Benjamin H. Byrd, adm. of Elizabeth Byrd

William Whayland & John Leatherbury to divide negroes from estate of George A. Dashiell

Levin Walter, adm. of Mary K. Crawford

Benjamin H. Byrd, adm. of Elizabeth Byrd, to sell old negroes Jacob & Rose to lowest bidder

Orphan; George L. R. Walter (of George)
Appointed Guardian; Clement Goslee
Sureties; Edwin Dashiell, Samuel Goslee

Jesse Walter & George Kelly to view estate of George L. R. Walter, in care of Clement Goslee, guardian

Benjamin Marshall, Master-at-Arms in state navy of Virginia in the Revolutionary War, & John Marshall, Boatswain in state navy of Virginia in the Revolutionary War, were brothers, died intestate, leaving no children or descendants of a child, or father or mother, but they left two brothers & two sisters, viz.; George,
F. 331   Adrian, Ellis & Elizabeth Marshall, all dec., who left children, & descendants of children, as follows;

    I) George Marshall (brother of Benjamin & John)
      A) John Marshall. died intestate
        1) Samuel Marshall
        2) Elizabeth Marshall, wife of John Hayman
      B) Nancy Marshall, dec., married Robert Morris
        1) Robert Morris
        2) James Morris
        3) Sally Morris, now widow of William Bounds
        4) Betsy Morris, now widow of Thomas Banks
        5) Polly Morris, dec., wife of Beacham White
          a) Isaac White, minor

C) Elizabeth Marshall, died intestate, children all minors
      1) Henry Marshall
      2) William Marshall
      3) George Marshall
      4) Reuben Marshall
      5) Nancy Marshall
   D) William, died intestate
      1) Sarah Marshall, wife of Lewis Smith
      2) Caroline Marshall, minor
      3) Robert Marshall, minor
   E) Henry Marshall, now living
   F) George Marshall, died intestate & childless

II) Adrian Marshall, dec. (brother of Benjamin & John)
   A) Martha Marshall, dec., wife of Risdon Marshall
      1) Adrian Marshall
      2) William Marshall
      3) Peggy Marshall
   B) Ephraim Marshall, dec.
      1) Sally Marshall, now living
      2) Ann Marshall, now Ann Fitzgerald
      3) Elijah Marshall, dec.
         a) Ephraim Marshall
   C) Levina Marshall, died intestate & childless
   D) Sally Marshall, died intestate & childless
   E) Polly Marshall, died intestate & childless
   F) Hetty Marshall, living, widow of [not given] Riggin

III) Ellis Marshall (sister of Benjamin & John)
   A) Risdon Marshall (died intestate), m. Martha Marshall
      1) Adrian Marshall, dec.
         a) John Marshall
         b) Adrian Marshall
         c) Elizabeth Marshall
         d) James Marshall
      2) William Marshall, living
      3) Peggy Marshall, living
   B) Charles Hall, son by marriage to John Hall, died intestate &
      & childless

F. 332 IV) Elizabeth Marshall (sister of Benjamin & John), m. John
            Swift
   A) Nancy Swift, m. George Lankford
      1) Gatty Lankford, living
      2) Polly Lankford, living
      3) Thomas Lankford, living
      4) William Lankford, dec.
   B) John Swift, died intestate
      1) John Swift, living
      2) William Swift, living
      3) Sally Swift, living, m. Thomas Lankford, son of Nancy
         Swift Lankford, above

       4) Peggy, dec., m. Henry(?) Ritcher
         a) Robert Ritcher, minor
         b) Eleanor Ritcher, minor
       5) Nelly Swift, living
     C) Thomas Swift, died intestate
       1) Henry Swift
       2) Stephen Swift
       3) Jane Swift
     D) Betsy, died childless
     E) Milly Swift, living

Thurs., Dec. 1, 1836   All Justices present

Court called by A. H. Ballard

Robert Bell, adm. of Nathaniel Bell

Tues., Dec. 6, 1836   Daniel Ballard, James Stewart present

Benjamin Lankford, crier

F. 333   12 July, 1836, Henry Crawford, by William H. Crawford, his guardian & next friend, & Edward Long, his attorney, filed petition; regarding legacy from father, Henry Crawford, in testamentary paper

Mary K., Barney, Beason Crawford, George Twilley & wife, Hestor A., Horatio N., Andrew Crawford, William, Esther, James, John, Levin, Marcellus Bounds & James Bounds, Sr., summoned

               Appeared same on 13 Sept., 1836, give answer; Mary K.
. F. 334   Crawford & George Twilley are rightful exes. of will, including testamentary paper

Robert Stewart & Marcellus Jones state that testamentary paper is in handwriting of Henry Crawford

F. 335   Testamentary paper admitted as codicil to will

Adm. of Charles E. M. Collier

John H. Adams, adm. of George Robertson

Orphan; John, Henry Silverthorn
Appointed Guardian; Samuel S. Silverthorn (father)
Sureties; John W. B. Parsons, Lambert W. Hyland

Stephen D. Coulbourne, adm. of Jane Coulbourne

F. 336   Tues., 13 Dec., 1836   Daniel Ballard, James Stewart present

Orphan; George W., James F., Esther H. B Dashiell (of George A.)
Appointed Guardian; Sarah B. Dashiell
Sureties; Joseph S. Cottman, Esther H. Cottman

James Wilson & Levin Ballard, Jr., to divide negroes from estate of
Henry White

Orphan; James Chittam (legatee of John Chittam)
Appointed Guardian; John B. Slemons
Sureties; Josiah Ellingsworth, John McDaniel

Orphan; John B. Chittam (legatee of John Chittam)
Appointed Guardian; Josiah Chittam
Sureties; John B. Slemons, Isaac Anderson

William Whayland & Isaac Anderson to view estate of James Chittam, in
care of John B. Slemons, guardian

William Whayland & William R. Byrd to view estate of John B. Chittam,
in care of Josiah Chittam, guardian

Tues., Dec. 27, 1836   Daniel Ballard, James Stewart present

Jeptha Morris, adm. of Francis Disharoon

F. 337   Henry Hyland, adm. of Priscilla Atkinson, to sell negroes
         James & Mary Ann

John Leatherbury & Benjamin J. Dashiell to divide negroes from estate
of Priscilla Atkinson

Obadiah Riggin, adm. dbn of William Perkins, to sell negro Lot

Apprentice; Alexander Course
Bound to; John S. Zieber(?)
Trade; Printer

Tues., Jan. 10, 1837   Daniel Ballard, James Stewart present

William Whayland & John Leatherbury to divide negroes from estate of
George A. Dashiell; give sons' portions to widow, as children too
young

Orphan; Elizabeth M. Elzey (of Henrietta)
Appointed Guardian; William C. Kellam
Sureties; George W. Hitch, William W. Maddux

William Wailes & Richard Waller to view estate of Elizabeth M. Elzey,
in care of William C. Kellam, guardian

F. 338   Estate of Samuel E. Moore sold without court order, but
         confirmed by court

Apprentice; Mary A.(?) Morris, Jr.(?)
Bound to; George W. Humphreys
Trade; Housework

'192'

Apprentice; Samuel Morris, Jr.(?)
Bound to; Jeptha Morris
Trade; Farming

David Vance, adm. of Samuel E. Moore

Wed., Jan. 11, 1837   Daniel Ballard, James Stewart present

Francis D. Nelson, late guardian to Francis, Hamilton & Amelia A. Mitchell

George Twilley, guardian to Samuel J.(?) & Ann M. Twilley

Littleton D. Maddux, guardian to Henry D. Maddux

Posthumous account of Thomas Jones, late guardian to Henrietta E. Jones

William M. Stone, guardian to James M. Stone

Levin Tyler & William Adams to view estate of Noah Riggin, in care of James Davis

Robert J. Henry & Daniel Benson to divide negroes from estate of Joseph B. Brinkley

Benjamin J. Dashiell & George Twilley to view estate of James M. Stone, in care of William M. Stone, guardian

F. 339   Tues., Jan. 24, 1837   Daniel Ballard, James Stewart present

William Harris, adm. of Rachel Newman

Stephen D. Coulbourne, adm. of Robert H. Coulbourne

Whitty Fontaine, guardian to William Long, sold negro man Isaac

Robert Patterson appointed trustee of property left in will of Ballard Reid, to son Robert Reid

William Roach, Jr., exe. of William Roach, Sr., enters into bond with Elisha Gunby, William Miles (of H.), Job Moore, Henry Ward, Henry S. Handy & Henry T. Tull

Samuel W. Jones, adm. dbn cwa of Matthias Jones

Samuel W. Jones, exe. of Milcah G. Jones

F. 340   Feb. 7, 1837   Daniel Ballard, James Stewart present

Orphan; William B. G. C. Calloway (of Isaac, late of Sussex Co., Del.)
Appointed Guardian; Richard Waller
Sureties; Robert Dashiell, Isaac Hastings

William T. Wood & William Wailes to view estate of William B. G. C. Calloway, in care of Richard Waller, guardian

Noah Rider & William W. Maddux, exes. of Peter Bell

Levin G. Irving, adm. of Levin W. Disharoon

William Costen, exe. of Isaac Harris

Levin G. Irving, adm. of Levin W. Disharoon

Thomas P. Dorman & James Brittingham, adms. of William Dorman

Tues., 14 Feb., 1837   Daniel Ballard, James Stewart present

William Roach, exe. of William Roach

F. 341   Thomas Robertson & Robert J. Henry to divide negroes from estate of William Roach, Sen.

William Roach, exe. of William Roach, Sr.

Thomas Newman, exe. of William Newman

Obadiah Riggin, temporary guardian to Littleton, Elizabeth H. S. & Mary W. Landen

Tues., Feb. 28, 1837   Daniel Ballard, James Stewart present

Stephen Riggin, exe. of Isaac Riggin

Orphan; Indiana Coulbourne (of Robert H.)
Appointed Guardian; Stephen D. Coulbourne
Sureties; William H. Curtis, Theodore G. Dashiell

Nathan Gordy, adm. of Hannah Hearn

F. 342   Peter D. Weatherly, adm. of James Weatherly

Tues., Mar. 14, 1837   Daniel Ballard, James Stewart present

Biddy Willin, adm. cwa of Tubman Willin

Noah Rider, adm. of Sampson Parker

Hetty Banks, adm. of Henry Banks

Thomas M. Hargis, exe. of Hancock Shreves

F. 343   Josiah Chittam, temporary guardian to James & John B. Chittam

Elizabeth Simpkins, adm. cwa of Charles Simpkins

Nathan T. Tull, exe. of James C. Coulbourne

William Fowler & Samuel B. D. Jones, adms. of Sarah Fowler

Leah A. W. Beauchamp, adm. cwa of Thomas G. Beauchamp

F. 344   Adm. of George A. Dashiell

Benjamin & John Marshall, said to be in the Virginia Rowgallies in the Revolutionary War, both died subsequently to 1st Jan., 1797

Matthias O. Toadvine, guardian to Esther G. Handy

John U. Turpin, guardian to Levin Goslee

George Hargis & wife, guardian to William Broughton

Levin Tyler & William W. Beauchamp to view estate of Joseph B. & William T. Cox, in care of Ann Cox, guardian

Benjamin Gordy & Henry Dulaney to divide negroes from estate of John W. Leatherbury

Robert J. Henry & Levin Tyler to divide negroes from estate of Robert Cluff

William Whayland & John Leatherbury to divide negroes from estate of George A. Dashiell

Tues., Mar. 28, 1837   Daniel Ballard, James Stewart present

Benjamin Dashiell's appointment to divide negroes from estate of Priscilla Atkinson annulled, at request of Henry Hyland, adm. John Leatherbury & Caleb Hughes to divide negroes

F. 345   Robert Patterson declines to act as trustee for Robert Reid

Henry S. Handy & wife, guardian to John J. & William C. Bell

Orphan; Alexander, William Johnson (of Josiah)
Appointed Guardian; Joshua P. Horsey
Sureties; Edward K. Horsey, Benjamin Lankford, Henry S. Handy

John T.(?) Sasser, exe. of Elizabeth Sasser

Adm. of John Miles

Tues., Apr. 4, 1837   Daniel Ballard, James Stewart present

F. 346   Benjamin J. Dashiell appointed Justice

Daniel Ballard, guardian to Elizabeth Collins, to build house on farm called McCready farm

John T. Sasser, exe. of Elizabeth Sasser

Alexander Donoho & Asa Phillips, adms. of William R. Donoho, to sell store goods

Orphan; Eleanor H. Whitelock (devisee of Esther Broughton)
Appointed Guardian; Elisha E. Whitelock
Sureties; Theodore G. Dashiell, Martin Bowen

Adm. of George A. Dashiell allowed to retain $992.00 due trustees of Washington Academy

F. 347   Tues., 11 Apr., 1837   Daniel Ballard, James Stewart present

Adm. of Edward Coulbourne

Adm. of John C. Wilson

Orphan; Mary J. D. Holland (of James)
Appointed Guardian; William Dryden
Sureties; John & James Dryden

Elizabeth Brinkley, guardian to Thomas, Henry F. & Francis L.(?) Brinkley, to build corn house & enclose garden belonging to heirs of Joseph B. Brinkley

John U. Turpin, guardian to Levin Goslee

George Hargis & wife, guardian to William Broughton

Tues., Apr. 25, 1837   All Justices present

Anthony B. Bennett, adm. of Richard Jenkins

F. 348   [1st lines of folios become hard to read at this point]

Martha B. W. Mitchell, adm. of John H. Mitchell

Thomas Robertson & John H. Miles to divide negroes from estate of Caroline Tull; recommend sale, as there are six heirs & only five negroes. Henry Tull, adm., to sell

Mary F. Porter, adm. of Mary Porter

Elizabeth Hopkins, adm. of William Hopkins

John D. Adams, adm. of Robert James

Orphan; Samuel L.(?) Tull (of Samuel)
Appointed Guardian; Henry T. Tull
Sureties; Theodore G. Dashiell, John S. Handy

F. 349   Tues., May 9, 1837   All Justices present

David & Thomas White, exes. of William White, being sued by adm. of John H. Anderson, to retain balance of estate until case settled. Balance on 21 Sept., 1835, $190.00 & 96 1/2 cents

Henry Milbourn, exe. of Lovitha Milbourn

John Hopkins, adm. of George Dashiell, revoked. Adm. dbn granted to George H. Woolford

William H. Hall, adm. of George Hall

William Miles, guardian to Elizabeth J. C. Stewart

Elizabeth Brinkley, guardian to Francis L., Sally A., Thomas & Henry F. Brinkley

Henry Long, guardian to John D.(?), Drucilla C., Eleanor W. & David H. Long

Matthias O. Toadvine, guardian to Esther G. Handy

William M. Stone, guardian to James M. Stone

Daniel Ballard, guardian to Elizabeth Collins

Levin Connor, guardian to Henry C. Connor

Levin Tyler, guardian to Rebecca M. Broughton

F. 350   Levin Morris, guardian to Alexander Waller

Cyrus Nelson, guardian to Horatio Nelson

George Hargis & wife, guardian to William Broughton

John A. Lankford & Thomas A. Dryden to view estate of John D., Ellen, Drucilla & David Long, in care of Henry Long, guardian

Robert J. Henry & Levin Tyler to view estate of Elizabeth Collins, in care of Daniel Ballard, guardian

James Wilson & Levin Ballard to divide negroes from estate of Henry White

William Miles (of S.) & Joseph Richards to view estate of Sally E. Atkinson, in care of Levin Atkinson, guardian

Jesse Walter & George Kelly to view estate of George R. Walter, in care of Clement Goslee, guardian

Whitty Fontaine, guardian to William Long

Tues., May 16, 1837   All Justices present

Jeptha Morris, adm. of Francis Disharoon

John Leatherbury & William Miles to view estate of George W., James F. & Esther H. B. Dashiell, in care of Sarah B. Dashiell, guardian

F. 351   Orphan; Ann Maria McDorman (of Tubman)
          Appointed Guardian; John W. Carew
          Sureties; Severn Mister, James F. Kelly

Edward Fowler, adm. of William Fowler

William Roach, exe. of William Roach, Sr., bought lot of corn from estate for $178.40, assuming corn to be merchantable. As corn was defective, adm. allowed from estate for loss of $45.60 at sale in Baltimore

Whitty Fontaine, guardian to William Long, sold negro Isaac, belonging to orphan, for $800.00, but spent $44.94 to apprehend and secure said negro

Wed., May 17, 1837   All Justices present

Ralph Lowe, one of the temporary guardians to children of John Bounds

          Orphan; James, Marcellus Owings (of Jesse)
F. 352   Appointed Guardian; Elijah Badley
          Sureties; Levin Phillips, Matthew Mearain(?)

Thomas Boothe, of Somerset Co., MD, is brother & only heir of William Boothe, formerly Master in State Navy of Virginia in the Revolutionary War. William died 1810

Thurs., May 18, 1837   Daniel Ballard, James Stewart present

Henry Thomas, adm. cwa of Aaron Sterling

Lucretia Harris, guardian to Eleanor Leatherbury

Margaret Hayman, guardian to Theodore & Sarah M. Hayman

Isaac M. Adams & Henry Maddux to view estate of Mary W., Littleton J. & Elizabeth H. S. Landen, in care of Josiah Furniss, guardian

Levin Ballard & Samuel G. Holbrook to view estate of heirs of Nehemiah Walston, in care of William Sudler, temporary guardian

William Whayland & William R. Byrd to view estate of John B. Chittam, in care of Josiah Chittam, guardian

George W. Hitch & Henry Trader to view estate of Lecascy A. Hitch, in care of Thomas Hitch, guardian

John Lowe & Robert Twilley to view estate of children of William Phillips, in care of Elizabeth Phillips & William H. Wailes, temporary guardians

William Whayland & Isaac Anderson to view estate of James Chittam, in care of John B. Slemons, guardian

F. 353   Thomas Robertson & John H. Cohoon to view estate of Nathaniel T. Bell, in care of Robert Bell, temporary guardian

Tubman Bedsworth & John S. Evans to view estate of Azariah W. & William D. Donoho, in care of Priscilla Donoho, guardian

Levin Tyler & William Beauchamp to view estate of Joseph B & William T. Cox, in care of Ann Cox, guardian

Levin Tyler & Robert J. Henry to view estate of Robert T. Smith, in care of John W. Smith, guardian

Henry Trader & George W. Hitch to view estate of Elizabeth M. Elzey, in care of William C. Kellam, temporary guardian

George Twilley & George Waller to view estate of Elizabeth A. G. & Sarah E. Moore, in care of Thomas Mitchell, guardian

John S. Crockett & John S.(?) Zieber(?) to divide negroes from estate of Charles E. M. Collier

Thomas Robertson & Robert J. Henry to divide negroes from estate of William Roach

George Waller & Andrew W. Anderson to divide negroes from estate of James Moore

Tues., May 23, 1839 [37]   All Justices present

William Roach, Jr., exe. of William Roach, to give counter security

F. 354   Henrietta B. Haynie, adm. of William Done

William Riggin, adm. of George Riggin

Hiram Gilliss, adm. of Samuel Gilliss

Samuel S. Miles & James Wilson to divide negroes from estate of John J. Davis

William C. Kellam, guardian to Henrietta Elzey

Parker Dickerson, guardian to Emeline Dickerson

Tues., June 6, 1837   All Justices present

John Williams, exe. of Samuel Williams

F. 355   Jane(?) Hitch, adm. of Littleton Hitch

Benjamin H. Byrd, adm. of Elizabeth Byrd

Daniel Ballard, exe. of Nicholas Tull

Orphan; Jane W. Jones (infant)
Appointed Guardian; William H. Jones (father)
Sureties; Samuel K. Handy, John Sanders

William Harris, adm. of Rachel Newman

Tues., June 13, 1837   All Justices present

Case of sureties of William Roach, exe. of William Roach, demanding counter security; said Roach too sick to attend

Orphan; Robert, Eleanor Ritcher (infants of Henry & Peggy, dec.)
Appointed Guardian; John Leatherbury
Sureties; Marcellus Jones, Alexander Donoho

Alexander S. D. Evans, guardian to Jane Evans, gives counter security to John N. Bowland & Levin W. Dashiell. Sureties; Alexander Donoho, Peter W. Langsdale

F. 356   Tues., June 27, 1837   All Justices present

Marcellus Jones, adm. of Gillis Bird

Biddy Willen, adm. cwa of Tubman Willen

Thomas A. Spence, adm. dbn of Robert T. Walker

Exe. of William Pollitt

James Tilghman, adm. of James Bloyd, claimant, & Thomas M. Hargis, exe. of Hancock Shreves, ask court to appoint Isaac M. Adams & John A. Lankford to settle dispute between them

Tues., July 11, 1837   All Justices present

F. 357   Smith Somers, O. S. on board U. S. frigate Brandywine, died 20 Apr., 1837. Adm. granted to father, Jesse Somers, only heir

Isaac T. Marshall, adm. of Josias Marshall

Guardian to James Mc. C. Fontaine (of James R. J. McC.), to build one story house on foundation of old house

Robert Patterson, trustee, from 24 Jan. - 28 Mar., 1837, of estate bequeathed to Robert Reid, by Ballard Reid, is reappointed trustee

Henry Milbourne, exe. of Lovitha Milbourne

John Austin & George Twilley to divide negroes from estate of James R. J. McC. Fontaine

Orphan; Azariah, Shalmanezer, Zerniah, John, Arza(?), Adin Davis (of John J.)
Appointed Guardian; Mary Davis
Sureties; Stephen B. Roach, William Miles (of Henry)

F. 358   William W. Maddux, adm. of Ezekiel Bell

Orphan; Hetty A., Betsy E., George W., Josiah F., Adeline S., Theodore M. Disharoon (of Francis)
Appointed Guardian; Ebenezer Disharoon
Sureties; Arthur Lankford, William H. Lankford

Robert Morris, guardian to Isaac W.(?) White, infant child of Polly Morris (who intermarried with Beauchamp White), one of the heirs of Benjamin & John Marshall, warrant officers in Virginia navy in Revolutionary War, to sell certificates of land bounty scrip

Daniel Benson, guardian to Adrian, John & Elizabeth Marshall, infant children of Adrian Marshall, heir of Benjamin & John Marshall...[as above]

John Leatherbury, guardian to Robert & Eleanor Ritcher, infant children of Peggy Swift (who intermarried with Henry Ritcher), heir of Benjamin & John Marshall...[as above]

Lewis Smith, guardian to Caroline & Robert Marshall, infant children of William Marshall, heir of Benjamin & John Marshall...[as above]

Tues., Aug. 1, 1837   All Justices present

Adm. of William Dorman

Thomas Marshall & Levin Tyler to divide negroes from estate of John J. Smith

F. 359   Exes. of William Parks

Noah Rider & William W. Maddux, exes. of Peter Bell

Isaac S. Cottman, adm. dbn of Margaret B. Chapman

Orphan; Whittington Parks (of William)
Appointed Guardian; Edward Parks
Sureties; John W. King, John T. Adams

Joshua Brattan & Marcellus Jones to divide negroes from estate of Isaac Atkinson

William T. Wood & William Wailes to view estate of William B. G. C. Callaway, in care of Richard Waller, guardian

John Leatherbury & Caleb Hughes to divide negroes from estate of Priscilla Atkinson

Levin Atkinson, guardian to Sarah E. Atkinson

John Dougherty, temporary guardian to Robert, Hetty A., Margaret, Biddy, Mary & Priscilla Walter

Tues., 8 Aug., 1837   All Justices present

William Sudler & Daniel Ballard to view estate of Samuel S. & Isaac F. Gibbons, in care of Theodore T. Gibbons, guardian

F. 360   James Tilghman, adm. of James Bloyd

Award in case of James Tilghman, adm. of James Bloyd, claimant, & Thomas M. Hargis, exe. of Hancock Shreves, made by Isaac M. Adams & John A. Lankford, approved

Samuel S. Miles & James Wilson to divide negroes from estate of John J. Davis

Levin Morris, guardian to Ann M. Morris & Alexander Waller

James Brittingham, guardian to Edward J. C. & Rosanna E. M. J. Wainright

Tues., Aug. 22, 1837   All Justices present

Marcellus Jones, adm. of Gillis Bird

William Sudler, adm. dbn of Nehemiah Walston

Isaac Anderson, adm. of Henry Banks, Jr., to sell negro James, wood at the landing & Schooner Marion

F. 361   Noah Rider, exe. of Wilson Rider

William Wailes & Richard Waller to view estate of Elizabeth M. Elzey, in care of William C. Kellam, guardian

Gabriel Webster & John Kelly to view estate of Ann Maria McDorman, in care of John W. Carew, guardian

Mary H. Redden, guardian to Matilda A. Redden

Theodore T. Gibbons, guardian to Isaac F.(?) & Samuel S. Gibbons

Levin Tyler, guardian to Sally N. White

Tues., Sept. 5, 1837   All Justices present

Negro Tom, freed by will of Phillis Robertson, granted permission to remain in county for 1 year

Daniel Benson, adm. of George Dakes

F. 362   Theodore T. Gibbons, guardian to Isaac F. Gibbons (of Isaac), to repair corn house

Orphan; Elias B., Susan J., James P., Sarah A., Samuel B. Smith (of John J.)
Appointed Guardian; Charlotte Smith
Sureties; Samuel D. Milbourn, John W.(?) Smith

James Wilson & William Miles (of Samuel) to divide negroes from estates of Matthias Jones and Milcah G. Jones

Tues., Sept. 19, 1837   All Justices present

Martha B. W. Mitchell, adm. of John H. Mitchell

Hetty Banks, adm. of Henry Banks

F. 363   James Stewart, adm. of Ware C. Pollitt

Isaac W. Milbourne, adm. of Ralph Milbourne

James Stewart, adm. of Charles W. Harding

Theodore T. Gibbons, guardian to Samuel S. Gibbons

Tues., Sept. 26, 1837   James Stewart, Benjamin J. Dashiell present

James Wilson & William Miles, appointed on 5th instant to divide negroes from estates of Matthias & Milcah G. Jones; whereas James Wilson unable to attend to duties, appointment null & void

William Miles (of Saml.) & William H. Curtis to divide negroes from estates of Matthias & Milcah Gale Jones among children according to will

F. 364   Arnold H. Ballard, adm. of William R. Warwick

Tues., 10 Oct., 1837   Daniel Ballard, James Stewart present

James Benson, adm. of Mary Digner

Thomas M. Hargis & Levin Atkinson, exes. of Levin Pollitt

Exe. of Henry Crawford

William Riggin, adm. of George Riggin

Stephen Riggin, exe. of Isaac Riggin, to sell negro boy George

F. 365   Court approves guardian bonds of Eliza R. W. Waters,
         heretofore appointed guardian to Levin L. & Ann E. E. Waters,
minor legatees of Arnold E. Waters, dec., formerly of the state of MD,
but lastly of the state of Mississippi

Tues., Oct. 24, 1837   All Justices present

James Benson, adm. of Mary Digner

George Twilley, adm. cwa of Robert Twilley

Samuel W. Jones, adm. dbn of Matthias Jones

Samuel W. Jones, exe. of Milcah G. Jones

Jeptha Morris, adm. of Francis Disharoon

Orphan; William W., Thomas L., James F. Coulbourne (of James C.)
Appointed Guardian; Nathan T. Tull
Sureties; William Miles, Levin Connor

F. 366   Thomas Robertson & Henry Ward to view estate of William W.,
         Thomas L. & James F. Coulbourne, in care of Nathan T. Tull,
guardian

Tues., Nov. 7, 1837   All Justices present

George Handy, adm. of Mary S. Wilson

James Tilghman, adm. of James Bloyd

Elizabeth Wilson & Levin Connor, adms. of William Wilson

Henry Lankford & John W. Handy to view estate of heirs of William
Wilson, in care of Elizabeth Wilson & Levin Connor, temporary
guardians

Adm. of Cyrus Leonard

Azariah Davis & John N. Bowland, adms. of Mary Davis

F. 367   Ann White, adm. cwa of Thomas White

Thomas Robertson, adm. of David Walston

James Tilghman, adm. of James Bloyd, to sell negro boy Charles

Tues., Nov. 28, 1837   All Justices present

Isaac M. Adams & William Miles (of Samuel) to divide negroes from
estate of Levin Pollitt

Levin Tyler & Thomas Marshall to divide negroes from estate of Isaac
Riggin

F. 368   Noah Rider & Arthur Lankford to view estate of Hetty A.,
         George W., Josiah F., Betsy E., Adaline S. & Theodore M.
Disharoon, in care of Ebenezer Disharoon, guardian

Apprentice; Alfred James (free negro)
Bound to; James Dryden
Trade; Farming

Wed., Nov. 29, 1837   All Justices present

Apprentice; Sarah Hinton
Bound to; John W. B. Parsons
Trade; Housework & c

Caleb Hughes & Benjamin I. Jones to view estate of heirs of Tubman Willing, in care of Biddy Willing

Levin Ballard, adm. of Samuel S. Miles

George Handy, adm. of Mary S. Wilson

Edward Fowler, adm. of William Fowler

Adm. of John Bounds

F. 369   Tues., Dec. 5, 1837   All Justices present

Benjamin W. Roberts, adm. of Thomas Goddard

John McDaniel & Josephus Humphriss to view estate of Alexander P., John H. & Mary E. Goddard (of Thomas), in care of Benjamin W. Roberts, temporary guardian

John E. Harris, exe. of Lucretia Harris

Covington Cordray & Benjamin I. Jones to divide negroes from estate of Robert Walter

Tues., Dec. 12, 1837   All Justices present

F. 370   Daniel Ballard, guardian to Elizabeth Collins, to sell negro
         man Jeremy

Orphan; Hampden H., Edwin, Amelia Jane, Nathaniel P. Dashiell
(legatees of Lucretia Harris)
Appointed Guardian; Seth Dashiell (father)
Sureties; Edwin Dashiell, Lambert H. Dashiell

George Twilley & Henry Gale to view estate of Hampden H. Dashiell, in care of Seth Dashiell, guardian

Tues., Dec. 26, 1837   All Justices present

Court called by A. H. Ballard

Levin Phillips & John T. Darby, adms. of Jonathan B. Phillips

William Tull, adm. of Ann Handy

Edward P. Cluff, exe. of Robert Cluff

Orphan; Eleanor Leatherbury (of John)
Appointed Guardian; John F. Collier
Sureties; William H. Collier, John Dougherty

Orphan; Levin P., Mary D. H., Margaret A., John R. N., Sidney G., Susan D., Sally L. Bowland (legatees of Levin Pollitt)
   Appointed Guardian; John N. Bowland (father)
F. 371   Sureties; Samuel G. Holbrook, James Powell, Joseph Richards

Ordered that adm. of Cyrus S. Leonard retain dividend in payments directed by will of Elihu Jackson, to be made to Elihu J. & Andrew J.(?) Puzey by said Leonard as condition of divise of land to him & his son John by said Jackson; and pay the same to said Elihu J. & Andrew J. Puzey when they reach 21

Tues., Jan. 16, 1838   Daniel Ballard, Benjamin J. Dashiell present

Isaac Leonard crier pro tem

Isaac H. Johnson, adm. of James Johnson

Thomas M. Hargis & Levin Atkinson, exes. of Levin Pollitt

Isaac H. Johnson, adm. of James Johnson

William H. Whittington & Nathan C. Connor to view estate of George & Henry J. Johnson (of James), in care of Isaac H. Johnson, temporary guardian

F. 372   Allowance of 5% on estate of John J. Davis made to William Roach, late adm., on application of Wm. Roach, his exe.

Levin Tyler & Thomas Marshall to divide negroes from estate of Isaac Riggin; cannot divide. Stephen Riggin, exe., to sell

Edward Fowler, adm. of William Fowler, asks court to strike negro Mary out of inventory

William Harris, adm. of Rachel Newman, to sell negro Aaron

Orphan; George W., Henry J. Johnson (of James)
Appointed Guardian; Nathan J. Lankford
Sureties; Samuel Adams, Benjamin Lankford

William H. Whittington & Nathan C. Connor to view estate of George W. & Henry J. Johnson, in care of Nathan J. Langford, guardian

Matthias O. Toadvine, late guardian to Esther G. Handy

Tues., Jan. 30, 1838   All Justices present

Benjamin Lankford crier

John Williams, exe. of Samuel Williams, to sell negroes Mary, Thomas (son of Mary & infant child) & James

F. 373   James S. Anderson, adm. cwa of Thomas Morris, to sell personal estate, except such property as was put in partnership with James Mallone for cultivating a crop this year on farm rented by said Morris of James Stewart, agent for heirs of William Pollitt, as shall be determined by Marshall McDaniel, a witness to contract

Maria Leatherbury, exe. of John H. Leatherbury

Isaac Anderson, adm. of Henry Banks, Jr.

Hetty Banks, temporary guardian to John Williams, Margaret Hester & Josiah Thomas Banks (of Henry)

Edward Fowler, adm. of William Fowler, allowed credit for negro Mary, property of William Barnes

Maria Leatherbury, exe. of John H. Leatherbury

James Wilson & John Smith to view estate of minor children of John H. Bell, in care of James Stewart, temporary guardian

Leah A. W. Beauchamp, adm. cwa of Thomas G. Beauchamp

F. 374   Wed., Jan. 31, 1838   All Justices present

James Stewart, exe. of John H. Bell

William H. Curtis & William Miles (of Saml.) to divide negroes from estates of Matthias & Milcah G. Jones

Isaac M. Adams & William Miles (of Saml.) to divide negroes from estate of Levin Pollitt

Tues., 13 Feb., 1838   All Justices present

Sarah Matthews, adm. of William Matthews

F. 375   Orphan: Maria T., John H., Sally Elizabeth, Charlotte Emily Cohoon (of John H.)
Appointed Guardian; Thomas Robertson
Sureties; John H. King, Theodore G. Dashiell

William J. L. Willing, adm. of Joseph Hardy

James Tilghman, adm. of Sarah Blaine

Thomas Newman, exe. of William Newman

Tues., Feb. 27, 1838   All Justices present

F. 376   Nathan T. Tull, exe. of James C. Coulbourne

Sale of real estate of John H. Bell, dec., by James Stewart, trustee, ratified

Orphan; Edward T., Rosa J., George W., Emeline P. Riggin (of Isaac)
Appointed Guardian; Mary Riggin
Sureties; Stephen Bounds, John T. W. Riggin

Levin Tyler & Thomas Marshall to view estate of Edward T., Rosa J. & George W. Riggin, in care of Mary Riggin, guardian

George H. Rencher, adm. of Adam E. Rencher

George B. Waller, adm. of Robert Reid

Levin Ballard, adm. of Samuel S. Miles

Ralph Lowe, one of exes. of John Bounds

F. 377   Azariah Davis & John N. Bowland, adms. of Mary Davis

Adm. of Sarah Blaine allowed credit for colt in inventory that actually belongs to Thomas Blaine

Stephen Riggin, exe. of Isaac Riggin

Margaret Hayman, guardian to Theodore Hayman

John H. Adams, temporary guardian to Mary E. Powell

Levin Wilson, guardian to Mary E. & Sally Cluff

George Todd, guardian to Alexander H., Eliza A. & Robert S. Todd

Josiah Furniss, guardian to Elizabeth H. S., Mary W. & Littleton J. Landen

Jeptha Morris, guardian to Elizabeth E., Adeline S., George W., Theodore M., Hetty A. & Josiah F. Disharoon

Tubman DeBonne, guardian to Leah J. Walston

John Leatherbury & William Miles (of S.) to view estate of George W., James F. & Esther H. B. Dashiell, in care of Sarah B. Dashiell, guardian

'208'

Benjamin Lankford & Henry Thomas to view estate of Kitty, Marcellus, Hamilton & Maria J. Moore, in care of Job Moore, guardian

Henry Lankford & John W. Handy to view estate of heirs of William Wilson, in care of Elizabeth Wilson, temporary guardian

Thomas Marshall & Levin Tyler to divide negroes from estate of John J. Smith

F. 378   Wed., Feb. 28, 1838   Daniel Ballard, James Stewart present

Court called by A. H. Ballard

Elisha T. Taylor, guardian to Mary J. Green

William Sudler & Daniel Benson to view estate of Samuel S. & Isaac F. Gibbons, in care of Theodore T. Gibbons, guardian

William H. Whittington & Nathan C. Connor to view estate of George W. & Henry J. Johnson, in care of Nathan J. Langford

Tues., Mar. 13, 1838   All Justices present

Benjamin Lankford crier

Anthony B. Bennett, adm. of Richard Jenkins

Isaac McCready, Jr., adm. of Solomon McCready

James Tilghman, adm. of Sarah Blaine

F. 378b   James Tilghman, adm. of Sarah Blaine, to sell negro man Ishmael

Whitty Fontaine, guardian to William Long

Tues., Mar. 27, 1838   All Justices present

Orphan; John H., William Done (of William)
Appointed Guardian; Henrietta B. Haynie
Sureties; Henry K. Long, John H. Stewart

Thomas W. Stone, exe. of William M. Stone

Levin Walter, adm. cwa of George D. Walter

Thomas Wilson, adm. of Mitchel Wilson

F. 379   Thomas W. Stone, exe. of William M. Stone

Levin Walter, adm. cwa of George D. Walter

George E. Larmore, adm. of John Larmore

William J. Hall, exe. of Richard Hall

Biddy Willin, adm. cwa of Tubman Willin

F. 380   George H. Rencher, adm. of Adam E. Rencher

Orphan; James L., Josiah S. Cullen (of Josiah)
Appointed Guardian; Jacob Cullen
Sureties; Theodore G. Dashiell, William Roach

Adm. cwa of Benjamin Bailey granted to William Anderson & Isaac Covington. Sureties; Marshall McDaniel, James S. Anderson. Justice Stewart dissenting

William T. G. Polk & John Leatherbury to view estate of heirs of Benjamin Bailey, in care of William Anderson & Isaac Covington, temporary guardians

Noah Rider, exe. of Wilson Rider

Ezekiel Haynie, late of Somerset Co., a surgeon in the Army in the Revolutionary War, died intestate, leaving three children; Henrietta B., Charlotte & Hampden (died intestate & childless). Henrietta is now living. Charlotte intermarried with William Done, dec., & died leaving children; John H., William & Henrietta Done. Henrietta B. Haynie & the children of Charlotte Done are only heirs of Ezekiel Haynie

William W. Johnston, adm. of Robert Gibbons

F. 381   Tues., Apr. 3, 1838   James Stewart, Benjamin J. Dashiell

Orphan; John T., Joshua L. Hitch (of Littleton)
Appointed Guardian; Jane Hitch
Sureties; William S. Dashiell, Elisha Owens

William Anderson & Isaac Covington, adms. cwa of Benjamin Bailey

Jane Hitch, adm. of Littleton Hitch

20 Jan., 1838, it was ordered that James S. Anderson, adm. cwa of Thomas Morris, sell estate except property in partnership with James Mallone for purpose of cultivating a crop. James Mallone relinquishes all claim to property. James S. Anderson to sell

3 Jan., last, exe. of James Anderson passed final account, &
          distribution of estate was made. Since Robert Stewart has a
F. 382   claim against estate, distribution is annulled. New
          distribution to be struck after deducting claim. Robert
Stewart to pay expenses.

Tues., 10 Apr., 1838   All Justices present

John S. Crockett & Thomas D. Evans to divide negroes from estate of Levin Wilson

Thomas M. Hargis, exe. of Hancock Shreves

William Roach, late adm. of John J. Davis, didn't complete adm.

Apprentice; Charlotte Trader, 4 year old orphan
Bound to; Samuel J. S. Ker
Trade; House servant

John S. Crockett & Thomas D. Evans to view estate of heirs of Levin Wilson, in care of Nancy Wilson, temporary guardian

Thomas M. Hargis & Levin Atkinson, exes. of Levin Pollitt, claimant, & Thomas M. Hargis, ask court to appoint Littleton Sturgis & William Costen, Sen., to settle dispute between them

Thomas M. Hargis & Levin Atkinson, exes. of Levin Pollitt, claimant, & Isaac Atkins, ask court to appoint Littleton Sturgis &
F. 383   William Costen, Sen., to settle dispute between them

James Wilson, commissioned to view estate of heirs of John H. Bell, revoked. John Smith & Arnold H. Ballard to view estate, in care of James Stewart, temporary guardian

Tues., Apr. 24, 1838   All Justices present

William Williams (of John), adm. cwa of William Williams (of Samuel)

Nathan T. Tull, adm. of Stephen L. Tull

George Handy, exe. of James Wilson

William Sudler, adm. of Nehemiah Walston

F. 384   William Sudler, adm. of Thomas H. Walston

Benjamin I. Jones & John J. Dashiell to divide negroes from estate of George D. Walter

William Anderson & Isaac Covington, adms. of Benjamin Bailey

Thomas Robertson & Daniel Benson to view estate of Robert H. Hall, heir of Richard Hall, in care of William J. Hall, temporary guardian

George Twilley & George L. H. Woolford to divide negroes from estate of Sarah Fowler

Jane Hitch, adm. of Littleton Hitch

John D. Anderson, claimant, & William Anderson & Isaac Covington, adms. of Benjamin Bailey, ask court to appoint Arnold H. Ballard & William T. G. Polk to settle dispute between them

John H. King, exe. of Margaret Done

Tues., May 8, 1838   Daniel Ballard, James Stewart present

F. 385   John S. Evans & Stephen Mills to view estate of Harriet, Matthias, William, Esther Ann & Levin M. Wilson (of Mitchell), in care of Thomas Wilson, temporary guardian

Sarah P. Wilson, adm. of Levin Wilson

Isaac McCready, adm. of Solomon McCready

George Handy, adm. of Mary Wilson

Isaac M. Adams & Thomas M. Hargis, to view estate of heirs of Levin Wilson, in care of Sarah P. Wilson, temporary guardian

William Willing, adm. of Joseph Hardy

On authority of act of General Assembly, passed Dec., 1837, entitled 'Act for benefit of heirs of George A. Dashiell', Joseph S. Cottman appointed trustee

F. 386   County surveyor to survey property of George A. Dashiell

William Roach, exe. of William Roach, to give counter security to William Miles, Henry T. Tull & Henry S. Handy

Theodore T. Gibbons, guardian to Isaac F. Gibbons, to repair barn

Joshua W. Tull, adm. of Mary Harriss

William Gordy, guardian to Edwin L. D., George J. & Sarah A. E. Parker

Thomas Mitchell, guardian to Elizabeth A. G. & Sarah E. Moore

Theodore T. Gibbons, guardian to Isaac F. Gibbons

Tues., May 22, 1838   All Justices present

Joel Cornwell, adm. of William Cornwell

F. 387   Orphan; William T., John P., Elizabeth A. Hargis (devisees of Levin Pollitt]
Appointed Guardian; Thomas M. Hargis (father
Sureties; George Hargis, Peter McGee

William Costen, Sen., & Littleton Sturgis to view estate of John P. & William T. Hargis, in care of Thomas M. Hargis, guardian

George L. H. Woolford & George Twilley to divide negroes from estate of Sarah Fowler, cannot equally divide, as there are only two negroes, one man & one boy; recommend sale

Samuel B. D. Jones & William Fowler, adms. of Sarah Fowler, to sell negroes

William Anderson, adm. of Henry Adams

Henry J. Curtis, adm. of Mary Curtis

William Roach, exe. of William Roach, gives counter security to Job Moore. Sureties; Benjamin McCready, Joshua P. Horsey

Isaac M. Adams & William Miles (of Samuel) to view estate of Levin P. Bowland, in care of John N. Bowland, guardian

F. 388   Wed., May 23, 1838   All Justices present

William Riggin, exe. of George Riggin

Orphan; John Somers
Appointed Guardian; John Wilson
Sureties; Stephen B. Roach, Joshua R. Handy

William Williams (of John), adm. cwa of William Williams (of Saml.)

William W. Johnston, adm. of Robert M. Gibbons

Thomas Robertson, guardian to John H., Maria T., Charlotte E. & Sally E. Cohoon, to sell negro woman Violet & her children

Thurs., May 24, 1838   All Justices present

Nathan T. Tull, adm. of Stephen L. Tull

F. 389   Tues., 12 June, 1838   All Justices present

Joseph Nichols, guardian to Isaac S. Atkinson

Orphan; Alexander S. Adams (of Jesse)
Appointed Guardian; William W. Beauchamp
Sureties; Robert W. Swan, James Adams

Orphan; Thomas G., Napoleon Gilliss (of Thomas)
Appointed Guardian; Robert Langsdale
Sureties; Thomas Langsdale, Levin Phillips

James Bounds, guardian to William & Elizabeth Bounds

Samuel S. Silverthorn, guardian to Henry & John Silverthorn

Henrietta B. Haynie, guardian to John H. & William Done, infant children of William Done, & Charlotte, his wife (one of the daughters of Ezekiel Haynie, surgeon in the Revolutionary War), to sell certificates of bounty land scrip

Orphan; Thomas Cottingham
Guardian; David Cottingham, revoked, because he has left state
Appointed Guardian; Henry T. Tull
Sureties; Henry Milbourne, Nathan C. Conner

Agreement between J. W. Crisfield, attorney for John H. King (exe. of Margaret Done), & Wm. W. Handy, attorney for Mary Judah; Mary Judah & John H. King, exe. of Margaret Done, agree that Isaac D. Jones, Esq., to decide issues between them; 1) the right of property to negro boy Charles, mentioned in will of Margaret Done; 2) if found to be property of Mary Judah, to decide sum due said King, as exe., for raising said negro

F. 390   Nathan C. Conner, adm. dbn of Mary Conner

Alice Broughton, guardian to Isaac & Francis Barnes

Levin Cooper, guardian to Martin, Severn & Elizabeth Cooper

Lazarus Lankford, guardian to Gilbert S. Milbourne

John Taylor, guardian to George, Perry W. & Thomas B. Moore

Josiah Ellingsworth, guardian to Washington & Josephus Brewington

Tues., June 19, 1838   All Justices present

Charlotte Dashiell & John R. Dashiell, adms. cwa of Benjamin Dashiell

Elizabeth Simpkins, adm. cwa of Charles Simpkins

Henry Milbourne, exe. of Lovitha Milbourne

Isaac M. Adams & Thomas M. Hargis to view estate of William Henry, Lemuel D., Sarah A., Edward, Mary A., Margaret E. T. & Levin P. Wilson, in care of Sarah P. Wilson, temporary guardian

William T. G. Polk, adm. of John Done [Dove?]

F. 391   Orphan; Sally A., Mary E. Cluff (of William)
Appointed Guardian; Edward Cluff
Sureties; Levin Tyler, Stephen Coulbourne

Tues., June 26, 1838   All Justices present

Josephus Humphriss, adm. cwa of Levin Taylor

Benjamin W. Roberts, adm. of Thomas Goddard

Orphan; James M. Stone (of William M.)
Appointed Guardian; Thomas W. Stone
Sureties; Benjamin J. Dashiell, Edward Fowler

James Adams, guardian to Peter J. Palmer

William Anderson, adm. of Henry Adams

F. 392   William(?) Gordy, guardian to George J., Edwin L. D. & Sarah A. Parker

James Adams, guardian to Brennas & Peter J. Palmer

Edward Fowler, guardian to Irving Kennerly

27 Feb., 1833, admx. of Tubman Cox passed final account, & distribution was made. Now George A. Cox has claim against estate, distribution is annulled, new distribution to be made. George A. Cox to pay expenses

George Handy, exe. of James Wilson, & Edward Long, exe. of Zadock Long, agree to cancel outstanding claims

INDEX TO BOOK 2, 1829 - 1838

ABBOTT:

Mason..................103,112

ACWORTH:

Elizabeth..............110,123
Kitturah H.............132,149
Samuel.................106,125
Train..............111,124,134
William H.108,123,125,126,129,
              173,175,181,182

ADAMS:

Alexander S................212
Beauchamp D................111
Eleanor N..............129,136
Elizabeth..............129,136
Elizabeth A................129
Henry..107,125,147,161,212,214
Hope...............122,123,131
Isaac M...121,165,172,185,197,
          199,201,203,206,211,212,213
James..........126,212,213,214
Jesse..............124,129,212
John D.................156,195
John H.........116,179,190,207
John T....124,129,166,173,183,
                185,187,200
Maria C................129,136
Martha D...................122
Morris H...........109,132,182
Reuben.................164,175
Ruth.......................109
Sally......................166
Samuel.........136,141,175,205
Sarah E................129,136
Stephen....101,110,129,140,150
Thomas.................132,182
Thomas P...............112,166
William............173,180,192

AIRES:

Thomas.....................150

ANDERSON:

Andrew W...........141,148,198
Gillis.............107,121,141
Isaac..150,183,184,185,191,198,
                201,206
James...107,122,139,152,162,209
James S............186,206,209
John D.107,121,126,139,141,147,
                152,162,210
John H.............174,180,196
Lucinda.....107,125,131,147,161
Mary............163,167,168,179
Peter...........163,167,168,179
Stephen G...107,121,131,149,160
William.107,148,209,210,212,214
Zebedee............104,109,113

ANSLEY:

Asbury (Asberry)....102.105,121
Elizabeth...........102,105,121
George.........................102
Hetty...............102,105,121
William.............102,105,121

ATKINS: (Atkinson?)

Isaac......................210

ATKINSON:

Eliza A....................184
Eliza A.R..............145,151
George D...106,145,153,161,183,
                              186
George S........145,146,150,184
Henrietta.......145,146,151,186
Isaac..............146,186,200
Isaac S.....145,146,150,184,212
Levin..170,185,196,201,202,205,
                              210
Mary E.A...................146
Mary P.............145,151,184
Priscilla..146,163,164,191,194,
                              201

(cont.)

(Atkinson cont.)

Sally E..................170,196
Sarah E..................185,201
Thomas D...121,122,123,168,170
William......................146
William R.........145,151,184

AUSTIN:

Ann M...................108,149
John..105,106,109,110,113,127,
       132,147,168,175,176,200

BACON:

Henry......141,144,149,157,172

BADLEY: (Bradley?)

Eli.........................172
Elijah..............150,159,197
Elizabeth...................144
James K.....................128
James W.....................102
Levin.......................117
Thomas......................144

BAILEY: (Bayly)

Benjamin..107,122,139,151,152,
           160,162,209,210
Betsy..................105,122
Hamilton...............145,152
James.145,152,159,169,175,176,
                            186
Josiah.............102,103,104
Thomas.........102,103,104,105

BALLARD:

A.H........119,130,190,204,208
Arnold H..127,129,174,177,202,
                            210
Daniel....101,102,105,106,108,
   113,114,116,117,118,119,120,
   121,124,125,126,127,128,129,
   130,131,134,135,138,139,140,
   141,142,143,144,145,146,147,
   148,149,150,151,153,154,155,
   156,157,158,159,160,161,162,
   163,164,165,166,167,168,169,
   170,172,173,174,175,176,177,
              (cont.)

(Daniel Ballard cont.)

    178,179,180,181,183,184,185,
    187,190,191,192,193,194,195,
    196,197,199,201,202,204,205,
                        208,211
Henry.......................105
Jarvis..............136,137,186
Levin..116,124,136,137,147,150,
    169,170,174,185,186,191,196,
                        197,204,207
Sarah.......................121
Severn......................143
Thomas E....................186

BANKS:

Betsy.......................188
Henry.......170,193,201,202,206
Hetty...............193,202,206
John T......................170
John W......................206
Josiah T....................206
Margaret H..............170,206
Thomas......................188

BARKLEY: (Barkly)

Abraham.....................111
David..........108,118,126,131
Jonathan....................116
Joseph..111,116,118,136,150,152
Margaret T..................131
Margaret T.W............108,118

BARKLY (See Barkley)

BARNES:

Francis.............135,148,213
Isaac.......................213
Isaac T.................135,148
Margaret................135,148
Parker..............116,119,135
William.....................206

BAYLY (See Bailey)

BEAUCHAMP:

Ann.....................143,144
George......................144
Isaac...................143,144
              (cont.)

'217'

(Beauchamp cont.)

Leah A.W...............194,206
Martha.....................143
Thomas.....................143
Thomas G...........135,194,206
William................187,198
William H..................166
William W..............194,212

BEDSWORTH:

Tubman....131,134,144,153,156,
                        181,198

BELL:

Amelia.....................183
Benjamin T.................186
Elizabeth..................116
Ezekiel....................200
George.....................116
Harriet...101,109,123,141,160,
                           175
Jane W.............109,116,119
John H....126,130,131,134,139,
  151,152,157,162,166,186,206,
                       207,210
John J.........109,119,151,194
Leah A.W..101,109,123,141,160,
                           175
Nathaniel.142,143,147,151,171,
           172,173,180,183,190
Nathaniel T............183,198
Peter.130,135,136,145,148,149,
  161,162,164,167,168,169,170,
       172,176,179,182,193,200
Robert.172,173,180,183,190,198
Thomas......103,113,136,157,158
Thomas H...................173
William............116,119,151
William C......109,119,151,194

BENNETT:

Anthoney B....135,136,139,153,
           156,171,176,195,208
Betsy..................108,167
Ebenezer T.............159,167
Elizabeth..................159
George.................132,143
Hamilton (Hambleton) B.132,143
James......................159

James T....................108
Joshua J...............159,167
Mary D.................159,167
Washington.............171,176
William................148,157

BENSON:

Daniel 103,104,116,140,162,163,
  166,167,171,184,186,187,192,
               200,202,208,210
James..................202,203
Jesse..................117,118
William....................166

BIRD: (Byrd)

Alexander..................166
Alexander S................179
Benjamin H.............188,199
Elizabeth..........104,188,199
Gillis.................199,201
Jacob......................113
John...................104,188
William R..............191,197

BLAIN: (Blaine)

Eliza......................175
Elizabeth..................166
James......103,107,164,166,167
Jane...................166,175
Sarah..........166,175,207,208
Thomas.............166,175,207

BLAND:

Theodorick.............107,117

BLEWETT:

Levin......................171
Nelly......................171

BLOODSWORTH:

Risdon.....................120

BLOYD:

James..............199,201,203

BOGGS:

Elizabeth...............170,171
Samuel S................170,171

BOOTHE:

Thomas..................143,197
William.................143,197

BOSTON:

Daniel.....139,140,143,179,185

BOUNDS:

Douty.......................140
Eleanor.....................180
Elizabeth...............178,212
Elizabeth R.................163
Esther..................178,190
Esther A....................178
George......................138
Isaac J.H...............140,157
James..146,178,179,183,190,212
James H.....................163
John..117,144,145,146,158,178,
         180,190,197,204,207
Levin...................178,190
Marcellus...............178,190
Richard.................178,179
Richard S...................163
Sally.......................188
Stephen.....................207
William...117,140,144,163,178,
               179,188,190,212
William A.D.............140,157
Zipporah................117,144

BOWEN:

Martin..................141,195

BOWLAND:

John N....107,130,157,165,170,
         181,199,203,205,207,212
John R.N....................205
Levin P.................205,212
Margaret A..................205
Mary D.H....................205
Sally L.....................205
Sidney G....................205
Susan D.....................205

BOZMAN:

David.......................174
Elizabeth...............174,185
Mitchell................174,185
Mitchell D..................176
William.............174,176,185

BRADLEY: (Bradly, Badley?)

Elizabeth...............148,156
James K.....................127
Thomas..103,119,148,156,157,172
Wilson..................103,119

BRADLY (See Bradley)

BRADY:

Francis.............101,102,113

BRATTAN:

Bruff.......................133
Joshua.117,130,146,159,162,167,
                   181,186,200

BREWINGTON: (Bruington)

Joseph..............105,120,144
Josephus....................213
Mary........................144
Sarah.......................144
Washington..........144,149,213

BRINKLEY:

Betsy...................126,142
Elizabeth..117,118,119,171,184,
                       195,196
Francis L..142,143,171,184,195,
                           196
Henry F.142,143,171,184,195,196
Joseph..................118,119
Joseph B...107,109,112,117,118,
         119,124,126,130,142,143,171,
                       192,195
Sally A.....................196
Sarah A.........142,143,171,184
Thomas..142,143,171,184,195,196

BRITTINGHAM:

James.122,123,150,152,161,168,
         180,181,193,201

BROADWATER:

Covington..............117,124
James..................117,124
Levin J.M.P............117,124
Mary.......................124
Sally......................124
Thomas J.W.............117,124

BROUGTHON:

Alice..................148,213
Edward.....................110
Elijah.............147,148,149
Esther.103,110,174,186,187,195
Henry......136,139,140,147,148
Isaac M................102,103
John H.................110,174
Josiah.....................110
Mary A.T.......140,143,147,149
Patty A....109,123,125,142,180
Rebecca M.109,123,125,142,180,
                           196
Sally..136,139,140,143,147,151
Samuel C.......109,123,142,180
William...109,120,132,143,153,
               167,194,195,196
William S.101,102,103,108,114,
                           125

BROWN:

David......................127
George.................104,110
Henrietta..................146
John A.....................146
Samuel.........106,112,146,149
Thomas.....................127
William H..................146

BRUINGTON (See Brewington)

BURBAGE:

Handy..................180,188

BURNETT:

James..148,163,165,166,170,171,
                           175
Mary...................165,166

BYRD (See Bird)

CALLOWAY:

Isaac......................192
William B.G.C......192,193,200

CANNON:

Burton.............101,102,103
James......................133
Sally......................103
Winder.................101,102

CANTWELL:

John.......................139
Joseph.........139,163,164,165

CAREW:

John M.....................162
John W.............160,197,201

CARROLL:

C.C........................178
Charles C..........155,165,166
Michael B..............105,122
Thomas K....101,102,105,113,114

CARSLEY:

Peter..................130,138

CARTER:

John.......................108

CATLIN:

Elizabeth..................135
Nehemiah...............135,140

CHAPMAN:

Margaret B....112,122,129,138,
                147,166,176,200
Sarah A...112,122,129,138,147,
                        166,184

CHITTAM:

James..............191,193,198
John...130,131,139,142,144,191
John B............191,193,197
Josiah....130,131,139,142,144,
                191,193,197

CHRISTOPHER:

Belitha................114,117
Elijah.........106,114,117,118

CLUFF:

Edward.....................213
Edward P.......182,184,185,205
Mary E.....165,168,180,207,213
Robert....144,149,183,184,188,
                        194,205
Sally......................207
Sally A........165,168,180,213
William...135,142,165,168,172,
                            213

COHOON:

Charlotte E............206,212
John H....171,173,176,183,198,
                        206,212
Maria T................206,212
Sally E................206,212

COLLIER:

Charles E.M...101,111,152,156,
        157,162,164,181,190,198
Cheney.................107,108
Francis....................111
Helena.............135,136,138
John F.................111,205
Levin D....................106
William H.111,114,133,156,157,
            164,165,166,181,205
William H.D................111

COLLINS:

Ann S......................127
Elizabeth..105,108,114,118,121,
        134,142,144,149,160,175,177,
                183,194,196,204
James..................105,168
Peter..................105,120
Stephen....................105
William....105,107,108,116,160,
                        161,168
William H..............146,150

CONNELLY:

Thomas.....................105

CONNOR:

Elijah.....................140
Henry C....104,121,134,148,149,
                158,184,196
Henry Q....................169
Isaac......................148
Isaac W....................104
Levin..148,149,158,163,166,169,
                184,196,203
Mary...104,121,134,148,151,152,
                169,173,213
Nancy......................140
Nathan C....169,173,205,208,213
Samuel T........148,151,152,169

CONWAY:

James R.W.......123,126,150,174
William.....123,126,142,150,169

COOPER:

Eleanor............113,114,125
Elizabeth..................213
Elizabeth E................154
Levin..................154,213
Martin.................154,213
Polly..................107,154
Samuel.................107,154
Severn.................154,213

CORDRAY:

Covington..108,128,134,151,155,
                157,161,162,204

CORNWELL:

Joel........................212
William....................212

COSTEN:

George B.R.................103
William...103,115,152,168,174,
           180,193,210,211

COTTINGHAM:

Abraham W..................112
David..................140,213
John T.....................112
Josiah.............158,166,187
Samuel.....................140
Thomas.............139,140,213

COTTMAN:

Esther H...................190
Henry......................133
Isaac S....................200
John...............133,176,184
John A.H.........101,115,180
Joseph B.............101,115
Joseph S..101,102,115,180,190,
                            211
Margaret B.................200
Priscilla..................133

COULBOURN:

Alexander..............103,104
Edward.....104,127,129,135,195
Emeline....................101
Henry W....................118
Indiana....................193
Isaac..................129,130
Isaac H....................123
James C...101,113,122,193,203,
                            207
James F....................203
Jane.......................190
Nancy..................129,130
Peggy..................117,118
Robert H...........185,192,193
Stephen........135,143,166,213
Stephen D......185,190,192,193
Thomas L...................203
Thomas W...................123

William K...........127,129,135
William W...................203

COURSE:

Alexander...................191

COVINGTON:

Isaac..107,121,131,149,159,209,
                            210
Philip..............115,123,133

COX:

Ann.........135,143,187,194.198
George......................187
George A...........135,143,214
Joseph B....135,143,187,194,198
Mary E..................135,143
Tubman..121,135,148,150,187,214
William T...135,143,187,194,198

CRAWFORD:

Andrew..............178,179,190
Barney..................178,190
Beason..................178,190
Elizabeth...................178
Henry..102,109,123,178,179,180,
             182,183,190,202
Hester......................178
Hester A................178,190
Horatio N...........178,179,190
James.......................178
Maria.......................178
Mary K.178,179,180,182,187,188,
                            190
Perry.......................178
William.....................178
William H...........178,183,190

CRISFIELD:

J.W.....................179,213
John W..................164,179

CRISP:

John S......................166

CROCKETT:

Eleanor H..................122
Hetty......................122
John S....124,128,132,134,135,
  143,150,153,156,157,162,174,
  175,176,177,181,183,198,210
Josiah.....................122
Levin......113,114,120,123,125
Shiles....102,105,111,120,123,
          124,125,128,132,176
William B..................122

CROSWELL:

John..............110,122,132
Mary..............110,122,132
Severn............110,122,132

CULLEN:

Isaac W...............146,156
Jacob.113,146,148,150,153,156,
                       158,209
James L...................209
John............101,120,153,158
Josiah................187,209
Josiah S..................209
Nancy.......146,148,150,153,158
Sally.....................137
Samuel S..............146,156

CURTIS:

Henry J...................212
John..............108,113,174
Mary......................212
William H.127,129,135,147,149,
  156,158,161,164,165,166,167,
  171,183,186,187,193,202,206

DAKES:

Daniel............108,152,158
George................186,202

DARBY:

Benjamin T........128,130,162
John T......128,130,140,162,205
Richard B.........128,130,162
Thomas............128,130,140

DASHIELL:

Amanda E.J.................154
Amelia J...................204
Amelia P...................125
Benjamin.............181,194,213
Benjamin J.154,155,156,173,182,
  191,192,194,202,205,209,213
Cadmus.................175,176
Chapman................104,105
Charlotte..................213
Edwin..............170,188,204
Eliza A.C..................104
Elizabeth R................104
Esther H.B.........190,197,207
George..118,125,153,154,166,196
George A...131,134,152,173,175,
  186,188,190,191,194,195,211
George W.........154,190,197,207
Hampden H..................204
Henry J.........106,120,126,141
Henry W....................104
Ichabod................161,165
James F............190,197,207
James W................139,141
John..............141,153,154
John C.....................154
John J.................139,210
John R.....................213
Lambert H..................204
Leah.......................133
Levin J.E..................125
Levin W............170,181,199
Margaret...................133
Margaret C.................161
Margaret E.............146,182
Matthias...126,130,136,138,142,
  145,150,151,169,170,175,176
Messen.....................119
Nathaniel P................204
Nelly......................154
Peter......................106
Priscilla..........108,113,114
Robert.............120,134,192
Sarah B......175,186,190,197,207
Seth.......................204
Susan J....................154
Susan U.P..................165
Theodore G.104,135,156,171,182,
  184,187,193,195,206,209
William................118,125
          (cont.)

(Dashiell cont.)

William F......101,125,161,165
William J...............130,132
William S..................209

DAVIS:

Adin.......................200
Arza.......................200
Azariah............200,203,207
Benjamin..105,116,128,129,134,
                   163,164,167
James..............173,183,192
John.......................200
John J....144,163,181,198,200,
                   201,205,210
Mary...............200,203,207
Peter B....................109
Shalmanezer................200
Thomas.................126,130
Zerniah....................200

DeBONNE:

Tubman.........163,164,167,207

DENNIS:

John...........120,124,130,153
John U.............104,144,147
L.P........................119
Littleton......105,107,122,137
Littleton J............120,124
Littleton P...104,112,117,130,
               153,156,158,159,177
Littleton T................133
Littleton U...104,129,136,144,
                           147

DENSON:

Isaac.105,106,107,108,120,126,
                           141
James..........151,159,161,167

DEVERIX:

Hetty......................186

DICKERSON:

Elizabeth..................136
Emeline....115,132,147,160,172,
                       184,198
Parker.115,132,147,160,172,184,
                           198

DIGNER:

Mary...................202,203

DISHAROON:

Adeline S..........200,204,207
Amelia L...................115
Betsy E................200,204
Betsy E.J..........154,158,163
Betsy W....................154
Caleb......................137
Ebenezer.......134,137,200,204
Elizabeth E................207
Francis........191,197,200,203
George W...........200,204,207
Hetty...134,135,137,138,146,161
Hetty A............200,204,207
James..134,135,137,138,146,153,
                       156,161
John...............134,137,161
Josiah F...........200,204,207
Leah.......................146
Levin W....115,120,150,158,183,
                       188,193
Susan J................102,154
Theodore M.........200,204,207
Thomas.....................137
Thomas L...................115
William.....135,137,138,151,161
William S..........102,158,163

DIX:

Patty.......152,153,156,161,162
William....................147

DIXON:

Betty.......117,118,119,124,130
Elizabeth..............117,118
William....................119

DONE: (Dove?)

Charlotte..............209,212
Henrietta..................209
John...................138,213
John H.............208,209,212
Margaret...........176,211,213
Sarah M....................124
William...102,103,105,115,118,
    124,127,161,198,208,209,212

DONOHO:

Alexander.120,122,123,125,161,
                        195,199
Azariah W..............181,198
James..........120,122,136,174
Philip M...................181
Priscilla..............181,198
Sophia R...........120,123,125
William D..............181,198
William R......120,123,125,195

DORMAN:

Leah M.....................162
Leah R.....................151
Levin......102,145,148,151,162
Mary...............130,133,152
Matthias...................145
Thomas P...........177,181,193
William........177,181,193,200

DORSEY:

Thomas.....126,127,134,136,186
Thomas C...................179

DOUGHERTY:

Emeline....................182
Esther.....................128
James......................149
John..104,106,119,120,128,131,
            135,143,149,201,205
Joshua.....117,128,129,179,182
Joshua P...................182
Levi...................104,106
Rachel.....................135
Robert.............131,143,149
Sarah A....................182
Stephen............127,131,181
Thomas H...........127,131,181

DOVE: (Done?)

John.......................213

DRURA:

George.................110,168

DRYDEN:

Harriet....................153
Isaac H....................173
James.......124,129,166,195,204
John...101,110,115,124,129,135,
                152,160,167,195
Littleton..115,124,135,152,160,
                            167
Mary W.....................124
Sally......................124
Thomas A...............173,196
William................124,195

DUER:

Joshua R...................173

DULANEY:

Henry..................173,194

DUNN:

Priscilla..................113

ELLINGSWORTH:

Josiah.........144,149,191,213

ELZEY:

Elizabeth M.....173,191,198,201
Henrietta.......170,173,191,198

ENGLISH:

Levin......................154

EVANS:

Alexander S.D..142,147,159,164,
                    167,181,199
Elizabeth..........147,159,167
            (cont.)

(Evans cont.)

Hamilton...................102
Jane.......147,159,167,181,199
John S....131,143,149,153,162,
          175,177,181,198,211
Levin......142,147,159,164,181
Peter.....................122
Thomas D...........102,181,210
William............147,159,167
William C.................181

FISH:

Bennett L.................186

FITZGERALD:

Ann.......................189

FLETCHER:

Hester A.......112,120,140,153
John W.........112,120,140,153
Mary A....................112
Samuel............120,136,140
Sarah R........112,120,140,153
Thomas....................112
Thomas W...........140,157,187
Zipporah..................112

FONTAIN: (Fontaine)

Eleanor A.E...........116,175
Elizabeth.................153
Elizabeth M...............114
Henry.................114,156
James M.......157,162,185,199
James R.J.M...157,164,180,199,
                              200
John E................116,175
John T................116,175
Sally A...................156
Sally A.E.................153
Whitty....106,114,153,156,168,
    172,184,186,192,196,197,208
William H.................156

FOWLER:

Edward....115,124,130,138,145,
    147,150,152,153,171,176,181,
          197,204,205,206,213,214

Eleanor...................169
Sarah..........194,210,211,212
William.194,197,204,205,206,212

FOXWELL:

Benjamin..................180
Elzey.................107,180
William E.................107

FREENY:

John..................162,175
William...................119

FURNISS:

Henry J.C.................106
Josiah..106,152,162,185,197,207

GALE:

Henry...112,128,131,140,141,204
Sarah H...........102,103,118

GARRETTSON:

Sarah.....................120

GERMAN:

William...................166

GIBBONS:

Francis........114,116,146,162
Isaac......114,129,133,167,202
Issac F....127,150,167,201,202,
                          208,211
James.................166,185
John..................129,133
Robert....................209
Robert M..................212
Samuel.........114,116,146,162
Samuel S...127,150,167,201,202,
                              208
Theodore T.105,116,150,167,175,
               201,202,208,211

GILES:

Isaac.....................105
John P....................121
Mary A....................121

GILLIS:

Clement....................187
George.....................131
Hiram..................128,198
Joseph.....................187
Josiah.....................187
Levin......................131
Napoleon...................212
Samuel.........127,128,129,198
Thomas.........127,129,131,212
Thomas G...................212

GLADDEN:

Susan......................165

GODDARD:

Alexander P................204
John H.....................204
Mary E.....................204
Thomas.................204,213

GORDON:

Samuel....106,108,115,116,159,
                       167,170

GORDY:

Benjamin.......151,162,173,194
Nathan.............105,162,193
William...141,144,149,157,169,
          172,175,182,184,211,214

GOSLEE:

Clement........165,174,188,196
Elizabeth......115,132,157,164
James.109,126,128,140,141,150,
                       178,179
John.......................109
Levin..115,132,157,184,194,195
Mary A.....................169
Samuel.....................188
Sarah L................140,150
Thomas.........119,125,128,134

GRAHAM:

James..............111,112,150
Philip.........111,115,168,181

Sarah..........150,159,164,181
Thomas.....................150
Zipporah...............168,181

GRAVNER:

Benjamin.......111,112,150,159

GREEN:

John...................109,176
Mary J.104,109,113,122,131,147,
                       167,208
Sally A....................113
Samuel.................127,176
Susan E................104,113

GUILLETT:

Peter......................106

GUNBY:

Caroline...................139
Caroline L.................135
David.......122,123,124,126,135
Elisha.....................192
Francis A..............135,142
James K.107,121,152,160,172,184
John W.................135,168
Kirk.......................107
Mary...................122,123
Mary A.....................121
Mary J.................135,139
Mary S.....................126
Stephen D..............135,168
William........152,160,172,184
William H.S................135

HALL:

Charles................119,189
Ellis......................189
George.................168,196
John.......................189
John M.................112,160
M.S........................119
Richard................209,210
Robert H...................210
Tubman L...................186
William H..............168,196
William J..............209,210

HANDY:

Alexander H....115,121,129,142
Ann...130,144,145,150,165,169,
174,205
Betsy K.....................114
Elizabeth G.................184
Elizabeth R...115,121,129,142,
175
Esther G..115,121,129,142,175,
194,196,206
George....115,139,156,162,203,
204,210,211,214
Gordon M.C.115,121,124,129,142
Henry S...151,160,182,192,194,
211
Hope........................115
James.101,102,103,110,112,121,
122,149
John....................165,175
John S.....121,135,139,142,195
John T..................163,170
John W........182,183,203,208
Joseph....130,136,141,144,145,
150,163,170,171
Joshua R................102,212
Levin.......................178
Meriah......................166
Noah....................165,166
Richard H......105,106,109,115
Samuel J.K........165,171,177
Samuel K....................199
Sarah.......................102
Sarah A.....................165
Thomas..................102,165
Thomas J................171,176
W.W.........................119
William.............114,128,131
William W.108,113,114,116,118,
120,128,133,137,155,171,177,
178,213

HARCUM:

Henry L...........103,106,120
Lee P.........103,106,116,120

HARDING:

C.W.........................177
Charles W.158,162,174,177,178,
202

HARDY:

Joseph..................206,211

HARGIS:

Elizabeth A.................211
George.109,120,132,143,153,167,
194,195,196,211
John P......................211
Thomas M...121,193,199,201,202,
205,210,211,213
William T...................211

HARRIS: (Harriss)

Alcy................126,129,175
Alcy (Alce) K..109,126,130,136,
173
Alice K.............173,181,184
Elizabeth...................184
Ephraim K...............139,141
Isaac..103,108,123,125,126,128,
129,134,140,162,163,164,175,
182,193
Isaac J.T..109,126,130,136,173,
181,184
Isaac W.....................167
John........................111
John E..........128,144,181,204
Joseph......................139
Joseph C....................141
Lucretia...111,144,153,156,185,
197,204
Martha J...109,126,130,136,173,
181,184
Mary....................174,211
Mary E.109,126,130,136,173,180,
181
Sarah P....109,126,130,136,173,
181,184
William....126,131,136,139,141,
173,182,192,194,205
William J...............109,131

HARTMAN:

Jonas...................152,162

HASTINGS:

Isaac.......................192

HAYMAN:

Elizabeth...................188
Hezekiah...............132,138
Isaiah.................127,158
John.......................188
John H.....................139
Josiah.....................168
Margaret..127,139,158,167,180,
                     197,207
Rebecca S..................168
Sarah M........158,167,180,197
Theodore...158,167,180,197,207

HAYNIE:

Charlotte..............209,212
Ezekiel................209,212
Hampden....................209
Henrietta B...115,118,124,127,
           161,198,208,209,212

HAYWARD:

Sarah......................102

HEARN:

Henrietta......157,162,175,193

HEATH:

John M.................151,164
Josiah W...................111
Parthena M.................111
Rebecca....................111
Samuel.............102,109,111
Sarah M.A..................111

HENRY:

Robert J..105,106,107,108,114,
    116,118,140,150,164,170,171,
    175,176,183,185,188,192,193,
                   194,196,198

HICKMN:

Jonathan...................116

HILMAN:

William....................126

HINTON:

Sarah......................204

HITCH:

George W...158,173,174,191,197,
                          198
Jane...........186,199,209,210
John T.....................209
Joshua.........144,149,171,172
Joshua L...................209
Lecascy A..............174,197
Littleton......186,199,209,210
Robert..116,120,144,149,158,174
Thomas.................174,197
William....................176
William A..........119,120,174

HOLBROOK:

Anne R.........111,124,136,137
Edward H.......104,122,169,170
Henry......................152
Samuel G...104,108,118,119,122,
       137,143,152,159,165,166,169,
              170,173,185,186,197,205
Sarah J....................111
Thomas.............143,145,152

HOLLAND:

Ann............103,106,129,148
Caroline J.................129
James..........103,106,129,195
Martha J...................129
Mary J. D..................195
Noah...............108,118,129
Samuel.....................108
Smith..............108,118,129
Thomas.....................119

HOPKINS:

Betsy..........111,112,119,135
Elizabeth..................195
George.............103,104,133
George M...................133
Isaac......................133
Isaac S....................133
John...106,108,118,125,126,128,
       130,132,134,136,149,173,184,
                                196
(cont.)

(Hopkins cont.)

Nancy....................181
Samuel M................158
Stephen.............148,158
William...101,111,112,119,128,
           135,142,195

HORSEY:

Anda................162,163
Edward K................194
John............177,182,185
Joshua P....162,163,194,212
Josiah..................166
Polly...................117
Stephen.............119,151
Susan...........177,182,185

HOWARD:

Asbury C........120,151,162
Ebenezer D..........103,115
Edward..................119
John........101,102,103,106
Joseph......103,106,111,116
Rachel..............103,111
Sally.......103,108,114,125
William.................166

HOWARTH:

Levi............177,178,179
Nancy...................177
William.........110,122,132

HUFFINGTON:

Jonathan.......107,108,113,183
William...........102,160,174

HUGHES:

Ann M.........103,113,157,158
Ariana..................177
Caleb.109,121,149,162,177,194,
                       201,204
Caleb R.................177
Caroline R. A...........177
James...............103,158
Jesse.105,108,126,130,136,157,
                   159,162,167
John C..................177

John S............103,157,158
John W.S................113
Mary A..................177
Thomas B.F..............177

HUMPHREYS: (Humphriss)

Elijah.................. 103
Elizabeth M.......113,121,133
Frances...........113,121,133
George W............110,191
Humphrey................110
John U..........103,123,125
Joseph..................140
Josephus........139,204.213
Joshua........103,139,140,172
Leah M..........113,121,133
Mary A..................110
Sarah...............123,125

HUMPHRISS (See Humphreys)

HURST:

James...............130,131
John....................163

HYLAND:

Henry..106,111,116,117,122,127,
       128,129,130,131,135,136,138,
       139,140,141,142,143,144,145,
       146,147,148,150,151,153,154,
       155,156,157,158,159,160,162,
                   163,164,191,194
James C.................176
Lambert W...........157,190

INSLEY:

Betsy...................155
Elizabeth...155,160,161,167,169
John...113,155,160,161,164,167,
                           169

IRVING:

Handy H.................122
Leah....................118
Levin G.............188,193
Levin J.................118
Peggy K.................122

JACKSON:

Elihu......163,164,168,183,205
Isaac B........163,164,168,183

JAMES:

Eliza......106,110,113,147,175
Mary.......106,110,113,124,147
Robert....................195

JENKINS:

George....................110
Richard........134,137,195,208

JOHNSON: (Johnston?)

Alexander.................194
Ann...............106,115,125
Benjamin.D 124,129,134,145,157
Elijah C...105,106,115,138,171
Francis M.................115
George..........110,121,173,205
George H............173,184
George W..........180,205,208
Henry J.............205,208
Isaac H....104,107,109,112,205
Isaac M...................104
James.............109,140,205
Jesse..............104,107,109
John W.............134,150
Josiah.............173,184,194
Julia A............134,150
Mary E.............134,150
Mary E.L..................180
Purnell............106,115,125
Sally A............134,150,180
Thomas.............124,129,157
William...................194

JOHNSTON: (Johnson?)

William W.117,124,132,141,181,
184,185,186,209,212

JONES:

Alexander............110,118
Alfred................104,115
Arnold E..104,106,107,108,110,
111,112,114,116,125,136,137
Benjamin..152,154,155,157,160,
163

Benjamin I.136,138,154,155,156,
157,160,163,169,204,210
Betsy D...................154
Betsy W...................154
Betty.....................154
Catherine T...............113
Charles.....104,105,112,115,116
Cotter....................126
Elizabeth..........104,112,115
Emily H...................113
George.101,105,106,109,114,116,
120,125,159
George H............104,115
George P...........116,182,184
George W..................154
Henrietta......116,117,125,149
Henrietta E........133,139,192
Isaac D.144,154,155,156,180,213
J.D.......................153
James.................110,123
Jane W....................199
John...106,147,150,152,154,155,
157,160,163,178
John P....................113
John Q.A..................154
John W....................136
Joshua....................113
Juliana M.J...............147
Juliet S..................113
Levin..103,105,108,127,128,131,
132,135,138,143,146,157,158,
183
Levin D.....117,120,125,149,182
Levin T...................180
Marcellus..102,105,107,108,109,
110,131,133,135,136,141,145,
146,149,150,151,177,181,186,
190,199,200,201
Maria.....................116
Matthias....187,192,202,203,206
Milcah G....187,192,202,203,206
Robert.101,105,106,109,114,116,
119,120,125,131,159,184
Samuel B.D......155,180,194,212
Samuel D..................154
Samuel W...117,118,119,120,121,
123,124,125,126,130,157,158,
162,186,187,192,203
Susan J...................121
Thomas.102,109,114,115,117,123,
125,128,131,133,146,147,149,
157,180,192
Thomas D..................147
(cont.)

(Jones cont.)

William...104,108,111,114,124,
125,136,147
William B..............174,180
William G.H...............147
William H.........113,180,199
William M.................186

JUDAH:

Mary.....................213

KELLAM (See Kellum)

KELLUM: (Kellam)

John.....................115
William C..170,173,191,198,201

KELLY:

George................188,196
James F...103,115,116,124,181,
188,197
John..............181,188,201
Margaret..................133
Obadiah...................133

KENNERLY:

Bayard................145,157
Caleb......128,132,144,153,156
Caroline..................145
Henry.................145,157
Irving................145,214
Louisa....................145
Orrell................145,151
Whittington...............181

KER:

Cassan....................147
Samuel J.S................210

KIBBLE:

Alexander.............130,133
William...................179

KING:

Jesse.....................128
John.............102,127,138
John H........181,206,211,213
John U....................148
John W........127,138,145,200
Planner H.............145,148
Robert J......170,171,175,184
Robert J.H.......135,152,153
Samuel....................181
William...............128,132

KIRWAN:

Elliott...................120
Jacob.............112,113,130
John.......112,113,120,130,140

LANDEN:

Elizabeth H.S..164,175,180,185,
193,197,207
Littleton...164,175,180,185,193
Littleton J........185,197,207
Mary W.164,175,180,185,193,197,
207
Samuel................164,185

LANDRETH:

John..................112,113
Sarah.................112,113

LANGFORD (See Lankford)

LANGSDALE:

Huet..............118,122,145
John......................104
Mary..............118,122,145
Peter W...................199
Robert....................212
Thomas......128,129,131,187,212

LANKFORD: (Langford)

Aaron C...................148
Abraham...................156
Abram.................127,131
Arthur................200,204
Benjamin...112,119,124,151,170,
175,186,190,194,205,206,208
(cont.)

(Lankford cont.)

David..................101,103
Gatty......................189
George.....................189
Henry.102,103,104,106,109,124,
    144,147,149,152,158,166,170,
        171,175,176,203,208
Isaac S....................185
John A....121,122,123,129,136,
    140,150,165,168,170,172,173,
              196,199,201
John P....107,112,114,117,164,
              166,167,175
Lazarus................185,213
Nancy......................189
Nathan J...............205,208
Polly......................189
Sally......................189
Thomas.....................189
Tubman.....................152
William....................189
William H..............152,200

LARMORE:

George E...................208
James..................142,148
John.......................208
Louisa.................142,148

LAWSON:

Elijah.110,115,120,121,129,147
Emeline....110,115,120,129,147
Grace..........101,115,121,129
Harriet............101,111,121
Isaac..101,111,121,173,176,179
James.146,153,156,158,173,176,
                 179,187
John...............101,111,121
Travers................101,121
William............101,111,121

LAYFIELD:

Elizabeth..............104,116
George.................104,116
John...................104,116
Levin..................104,116
Mary...................104,116

LEARY:

Charles................106,116

LEATHERBURY:

Ebenezer...................125
Eleanor....128,131,144,153,156,
              157,185,197,205
Jesse......................174
John...109,114,116,117,118,120,
    139,159,164,165,173,188,191,
    194,197,199,200,201,205,207,
                         209
John H.....................206
John M.....................128
John N.....................144
John W......126,128,139,141,194
Levin K....................107
Maria......................206
Miranda....128,131,144,153,156,
                  157,185
Robert.................110,141

LEMMON:

Dr.........................137
Richard....................168

LEONARD:

Cyrus..............180,188,203
Cyrus S....................205
Isaac..................171,205
John.......................205
Joseph......141,144,149,157,172
Samuel.................169,175

LONG:

David.......121,152,162,173,196
David H....................196
Drucilla...............173,196
Drucilla C.................196
Edward.134,137,143,163,172,190,
                         214
Eleanor W..................196
Ellen..................173,196
Henrietta..........159,160,168
Henry..............164,173,196
Henry K.....118,151,158,179,208
John D.................173,196
John W............158,164,173
            (cont.)

(Long cont.)

Littleton..........101,102,103
Sally A.E...................106
William...106,153,168,172,184,
          186,192,196,197,208
William H...................151
Zadock........102,130,151,214
Zadock J....................151

LORD:

John..............117,120,129

LOWE:

John..................170,198
Ralph.131,134,140,145,153,156,
        158,180,181,197,207

MADDUX:

Daniel................127,129
George....................166
Henry............108,185,197
Henry D...104,116,125,127,129,
          141,149,160,180,192
Joe.......................166
Littleton.................160
Littleton D...104,116,125,141,
              149,166,180,192
Sarah S....104,116,125,127,129
William...................167
William W.133,146,182,191,193,
                          200

MALLONE:

James.............168,206,209
Robert.................105,168
Thomas.....................163

MARSHALL:

Adrian.........187,188,189,200
Ann........................189
Benjamin..183,184,187,188,189,
                      194,200
Caroline..........187,189,200
Elijah.....................189
Elizabeth.143,183,184,187,188,
                      189,200
Ellis..................188,189

Ephraim....................189
George......183,184,187,188,189
Harvey.....................161
Henry........143,183,184,187,189
Hetty......................189
Isaac T................161,199
James......................189
John...143,183,184,187,188,189,
                      194,200
Josias.....................199
Levina.....................189
Martha.....................189
Nancy.......183,184,187,188,189
Patty......................161
Peggy......................189
Polly......................189
Reuben..........183,184,187,189
Risdon.....................189
Robert.............187,189,200
Sally......................189
Samuel.....................188
Sarah......................189
Thomas......200,203,205,207,208
William.....183,184,187,189,200

MARTIN:

Daniel.....................117

MASON:

John.......................102

MATTHEWS:

John..................148,150
Sarah......................206
William....................206

MEARAIN:

Matthew....................197

MERRILL:

William H..................166

MEZICK:

Littleton..................109

MILAWAY:

Mary.......................111

MILBOURNE:

Benjamin............132,138,185
Charles................110,129
Gilbert S..............185,213
Henry..............196,199,213
Isaac W....................202
John...................129,149
John W.................110,129
Lodowick...........110,129,153
Lodowick J.........102,156,185
Lovitha (Levitha).110,121,122,
                   196,199,213
Lovitha A..............112,149
Mary A.................158,166
Ralph......................202
Samuel.....................162
Samuel D...................202
Sophia.....................161

MILES: (Mills?)

Catherine..107,108,112,113,175
George.....................167
H..........................192
Hannah.....................179
Henry......................200
Isaac..................107,112
Isaac J.T..................112
Isaac T.W..................107
Jane..........107,108,112,113
John...110,121,151,179,186,194
John H.....................195
Mary.......................167
Matthias...................179
Robert L...................179
S......................196,207
Samuel....126,130,131,202,203,
                     206,212
Samuel S.......198,201,204,207
Stephen........120,123,182,183
Washington.....108,112,113,175
William...101,102,107,121,126,
    130,131,139,147,153,167,170,
    182,183,192,196,197,200,202,
             203,206,207,211,212

MILLICAN: (Milligan)

Eli................124,128,131
Isaac..............124,128,131

MILLIGAN (See Millican)

MILLS: (Miles?)

Stephen............104,124,211

MISTER:

Severn.....................197

MITCHELL:

Amelia A...................192
Ebenezer...........119,131,134
Francis....................192
Hamilton...................192
John.......................119
John H.................195,202
Martha B.W.............195,202
Thomas.........159,170,198,211

MOORE:

Aaron..................112,113
Benjamin....140,141,165,166,169
Elizabeth A.G...141,170,198,211
George.................169,213
Hamilton (Hambleton)...112,113,
                      125,186,208
James...138,141,148,159,170,198
James B.140,141,159,166,169,176
Job....112,113,125,146,150,186,
                    192,208,212
John L..110,123,140,167,173,180
Kitty.......112,113,125,186,208
Levi...................128,131
Marcella...........112,113,125
Marcellus..............186,208
Maria J....112,113,125,186,208
Perry W................169,213
Samuel E...............191,192
Sarah..................138,141
Sarah E........141,170,198,211
Thomas B...............169,213

MORRIS:

Albert N...............143,152
Amelia A...................141
Ann M......................201
Betsy......................188
James......................188
Jeptha......191,192,197,203,207
John...................125,141
        (cont.)

(Morris cont.)

John P.J...................141
John Q................143,152
Joseph................143,145
Levin.108,121,132,149,157,175,
                        196,201
Maria.................143,152
Mary A....................191
Nancy.....................188
Polly.................188,200
Robert....105,107,108,116,127,
       160,161,168,174,187,188,200
Sally.....................188
Samuel....................192
Thomas....105,134,137,162,164,
                    169,175,206,209
William...................132
William Q.............143,152

MORTON:

Ann.......................133

McBRYDE:

Samuel.102,109,118,159,160,185

McCALLAHAN:

Elijah....................133

McCLESTER:

Elizabeth.............108,119
John......................106

McCREADY:

Benjamin..................212
Isaac.................208,211
Solomon...............208,211

McDANIEL:

John...146,150,161,175,191,204
Marshall...161,164,167,206,209

McDORMAN:

Ann M.................197,201
George....................182
Lewis.........126,128,139,182
Matilda...................160
Nancy.........126,128,139,182

Sarah E...................182
Tubman............160,162,197

McELHINEY:

George....................186

McGEE:

Peter.....................211

McINTIRE:

Jesse.....................120
John W....................120

McKENZIE:

John......................160

NELSON:

Almira..127,132,146,150,161,175
Charlotte J...........109,121
Cyrus.........146,150,175,196
Eleanor...........127,132,167
Elizabeth E...........109,123
Esther A.U............109,121
Francis D..127,128,132,146,172,
                        183,192
Horatio....127,132,143,146,150,
                        175,196
James T...............162,177
John W.127,128,132,147,152,167,
                            183
Nehemiah..................177
Rebecca.........164,168,171,172
Sarah H.........147,152,167
Tubman........164,168,171,172

NEWMAN:

Rachel............192,199,205
Thomas............187,193,207
William...........187,193,207

NICHOLS: (Nicols)

Isaac..........103,147,150,170
Joseph......145,146,150,186,212

NICHOLSON:

Amelia W..............101,115

NICOLS (See Nichols)

NOBLE:

George A...............114,176
John..........107,113,152,160

OUTTEN:

Ephraim...................166

OWENS: (Owings?)

Elisha....................209
Jesse.................127,128

OWINGS: (Owens?)

James.....................197
Jesse.....................197
Marcellus.................197

PALMER:

Brennas...............141,214
Brennas N.................126
Charles...............126,131
Elizabeth.................141
Mary......................141
Peter J...105,108,126,131,141,
                        213,214

PARKER:

Daniel............144,169,182
E.........................157
Edwin L.D.144,149,157,169,172,
                175,184,211,214
Elisha....................172
Emeline B.............113,122
George....141,144,149,157,169,
            172,177,178,179,182
George J..144,149,157,169,172,
                175,184,211,214
Sampson...................193
Sarah A...157,169,172,175,184,
                            214
Sarah A.E.........144,149,211
William...................166

PARKS:

Charles...............162,163
Edward............180,187,200
Whittington...............200
William...........180,187,200

PARSONS: (Pasons)

Ben...................134,137
Benjamin..........134,137,157
Elijah....................106
George................145,148
J.........................145
Jehu...109,134,135,136,145,148,
                150,157,169,175
John W.B....115,161,164,190,204

PASONS (See Parsons)

PATRICK:

Levin H.....144,148,149,151,162

PATTERSON:

Robert.117,139,174,182,192,194,
                            199

PEARCE:

Gideon....................106

PERKINS:

Amelia............151,164,175
William.151,164,177,178,185,191

PHILLIPS:

Asa.......................195
Elijah....................104
Elizabeth..154,170,176,182,184,
                            198
Handy.................127,128
Jonathan B............183,205
Levin...150,174,176,197,205,212
Mary B....................184
Mrs.......................118
Peregrine.................104
Samuel................103,111
Thomas....................119

(cont.)

(Phillips cont.)

William...104,130,131,154,158,
170,174,176,182,198
William A.R................104

PHOEBUS:

James.144,145,152,169,170,174,
185
William B.................176

POLK:

James.101,102,103,110,116,120,
124,130,135,137,138,153,156,
158,159,166
Margaret W.................130
Samuel............105,130,148
William T.G...105,130,148,162,
164,165,173,175,186,209,210,
213

POOL:

John W....................166

POLLITT:

Edward................120,150
Elizabeth R...........108,109
George........141,143,151,156
Henry.................176,186
James.................120,150
James S...................150
John......................158
Letitia...................165
Levin.105,122,170,176,202,203,
205,206,210,211
Nehemiah..............169,179
Robert................141,156
Robert C..............143,151
Sally.................169,179
Samuel....................159
Thomas................119,125
Ware C............159,165,202
William....159,165,185,199,206
William K.............108,109

PORTER:

Mary......147,153,168,170,195
Mary F........147,153,168,195

Peggy.............168,176,183
William.................116,119

POWELL:

James..............101,113,205
John.......................166
Levin......................170
Mary E.....................207
William....................133
Zadock.....................141

PRICE:

George.........105,108,116,170
Joseph.................105,108
Robert.................105,108

PURNELL:

Chesed.....................184

PUZEY: (See Shella)

Andrew J...................205
Caroline...................177
Elihu J....................205
Elizer.....................177
Jane.......................177
John.......123,139,142,145,163
Joseph M...........123,139,142
Peter..............139,142,145
Thomas.....................177

QUINN:

William....................110

REDEEN:

Littleton..........164,166,176
Mary H.................176,201
Matilda A..............176,201

REID:

Ballard........174,185,192,199
Robert.........192,194,199,207

RENCHER:

Adam E.................207,209
George H....102,103,169,207,209

RHODES: (Roads)

Beauchamp....................104
James.......................104
Sarah A.....................104
William.....................114

RICHARDS:

Joseph............170,196,205

RIDER:

Charles...120,140,157,162,164,
                        180,185
John W......................188
Noah..120,139,140,153,156,178,
              193,200,201,204,209
Susan.......................119
Wilson..................201,209

RIGGIN:

Edward T....................207
Emeline P...................207
George............198,202,212
George W....................207
Henry.............126,130,173
Hetty.......................189
Isaac..183,193,202,203,205,207
John T......................141
John T.W....................207
Mary........................207
Noah..............173,183,192
Obed........................129
Obediah....177,178,180,191,193
Robert......................101
Rosa J......................207
Stephen........193,202,205,207
William.............198,202,212

RITCHER:

Eleanor...........190,199,200
Henry.............190,199,200
Peggy.............190,199,200
Robert............190,199,200

RITCHIE:

Thomas............163,164,165

ROACH:

Stephen B...............200,212
William....101,116,117,146,150,
    152,156,158,161,162,163,166,
    179,181,192,193,197,198,199,
              205,209,210,211,212

ROADS (See Rhodes)

ROBERTS:

Benjamin....................118
Benjamin W..............204,213
Elizabeth...................118
Thomas......................163
Thomas G.R..................118
Underwood.........130,138,147
William.....152,153,163,171,176

ROBERTSON:

Andrew..................151,161
Eli.....................124,138
Elias...........132,149,159,168
Elijah..................148,157
Elizabeth...............124,138
Frances.........132,149,159,168
Francis.............159,167,168
George.........104,111,179,190
George W....141,151,159,167,168
Henry C.............159,167,168
James...............111,136,138
John...111,124,134,138,151,159,
                    160,161,167
John Q..............159,167,168
Mary J..............159,167,168
Phillis.............163,179,201
Robert D...111,124,132,136,145,
                            160
Samuel.111,136,141,151,159,167,
                            168
Sarah J.....................111
Thomas.101,111,114,116,126,136,
    139,140,141,142,143,145,150,
    163,165,166,167,171,173,180,
    183,186,187,193,195,198,203,
              206,210,212
Thomas B............126,131,181
Washington..............151,161
William S...................117

ROBINSON:

Charles..................186
Henrietta B............144,145
Mary H.E..................186

RUSSELL:

James..............127,131,156

RUSSUM:

Robert C..................103
William P.................103

SANDERS:

John..........116,146,158,199

SASSER:

Elizabeth..............177,194
John T.................177,194

SHELLA: (See Puzey)

Carolina..................177
Elizer....................177
Thomas....................177

SHREVES:

Hancock........193,199,201,210

SILVERTHORNE:

Henry..................190,212
John...................190,212
Samuel....................120
Samuel S..........150,190,212

SIMPKINS:

Charles...105,106,160,163,167,
                        193,213
Elizabeth..............193,213
Major.................105,106

SIMPSON: (Simson)

Benjamin...151,158,159,160,166

SIMSON (See Simpson)

SIRMAN:

George....................179

SLEMONS:

John B 127,128,136,138,144,161,
                        191,198

SMITH:

Charlotte..........182,183,202
Elias B...................202
Henry.....................174
Henry C...................174
James..............174,187,188
James P...................202
John...........167,182,206,210
John J..182,183,185,200,202,208
John W.............185,198,202
Levin C...................174
Lewis..............187,189,200
Miranda...................172
Rebecca...............172,174
Richardson D..............174
Robert M..................115
Robert T..............185,198
S.........................167
Samuel....................114
Samuel B..................202
Sarah.....................189
Sarah A...................202
Stoughton.................188
Susan J...................202
William....105,114,116,127,146,
                150,162,167,175

SMULLING:

Nathaniel H.J..........101,113
Zorobabel.................130

SOMERS: (Summers)

Jesse.....................199
John......................212
Louisa....................110
Smith.....................199
William...................171

SPENCE:

Asa.......................156
Thomas A....135,145,155,163,199

SPICER:

James H...............162,175

STANFORD:

Isaac H.W.............118,167
Levin J.M.W...........118,167
William S.H...............118

STAYTON:

Leolin....................117

STERLING:

Aaron.................171,197

STEVENS:

William W.............144,151

STEVENSON:

John B....................179

STEWART:

Elizabeth.............153,167
Elizabeth J...............101
Elizabeth J.C.....121,139,196
Elizabeth J.H.............147
James.111,134,150,158,159,160,
    161,162,165,166,173,174,176,
    177,178,179,180,181,182,183,
    184,185,186,187,190,191,192,
    193,194,195,197,202,206,207,
              208,209,210,211
John H....................208
Mary A.101,121,139,147,153,167
Robert....101,102,105,106,113,
    114,117,126,131,142,145,146,
    147,149,150,153,158,161,173,
        181,182,183,184,190,209

STONE:

James M...134,182,192,196,213
Thomas W.......134,182,208,213
William M.124,134,139,182,192,
                  196,208,213

STURGIS:

Littleton.............210,211

SUDLER:

Emory S...................136
Henrietta M.W.....122,124,157
Joseph..122,124,157,158,162,186
Matthias J........157,158,162
William....105,116,132,136,139,
    141,143,145,150,159,160,162,
    167,185,186,191,201,208,210

SUMMERS (See Somers)

SWAN:

Betsy.....................190
Elizabeth.................189
Henry.....................190
Jane......................190
John......................189
Milly.....................190
Nancy.....................189
Nelly.....................190
Peggy.................190,200
Robert W..............153,212
Sally.....................189
Stephen...................190
Thomas....................190
William...................189

TAYLOR:

Elias.................165,174
Elisha........109,122,131,147
Elisha T..............167,208
George W..............115,152
Isaac.....................159
John..................169,183,213
John B....................159
John F....................186
John W................169,183
Levin.....................213
Maria.................115,152
Samuel................115,152
Stephen...................141
William...................183

THOMAS:

Henry.........171,186,197,208

TILGHMAN:

Elizabeth E.W..............102
James.103,107,126,135,140,166,
    167,199,201,203,207,208

TINGLE:

William....................156

TOADVINE:

Matthias O....106,109,115,121,
    124,129,142,175,184,194,196,
    206
Purnell............115,169,188

TODD:

Alexander H...110,121,132,135,
    136,147,160,172,184,207
Eliza A...110,121,132,135,136,
    147,160,172,184,207
George....110,121,132,135,136,
    147,160,172,184,207
Robert J...................121
Robert S..110,132,135,136,147,
    160,172,184,207
Spencer....................135

TOWNSEND:

Teagle.................134,136

TRADER:

Charlotte..................210
Henry.........173,174,197,198

TRAVERS:

Edward.....................110
Jabez (Jabuz)..127,132,146,150
John.......................110

TREHEARN:

Leah.......................136
Teagle.....................136

TULL:

Caroline..117,168,170,174,175,
    186,195

Eliza A....................133
Emily S....................133
Henry......................195
Henry T....117,168,170,174,175,
    182,192,195,211,213
Hester.....................133
John E.....................133
Joshua W...................211
Julia A....................117
Mary F.....................117
Nathan.....................166
Nathan T....193,203,207,210,212
Nicholas...................199
Samuel......114,116,117,182,195
Samuel L...............117,195
Sarah A....................165
Stephen L..............210,212
Thomas J...................133
Wesley S...................133
William.108,113,133,139,143,205
William H.......133,165,166,169

TURNER:

John...........161,164,167,172

TURPIN:

Elizabeth..................108
John.......................118
John U.115,132,157,164,184,185,
    194,195

TWILLEY:

Ann M...122,132,147,157,175,192
George.122,132,146,147,150,157,
    170,175,178,180,182,183,190,
    192,198,200,203,204,210,211
Maria......................178
Maria A....................132
Robert.............170,198,203
Samuel J...122,132,147,157,175,
    192

TYLER:

Jacob......................146
Levin..105,107,109,118,122,123,
    125,130,135,138,142,143,148,
    150,153,156,161,162,173,180,
    183,185,187,192,194,196,198,
    200,201,203,205,207,208,213
    (cont.)

(Tyler Cont.)

Littleton..........101,111,121

VANCE:

David......................192

VENABLES:

Bridgett................124,132
Charles........102,105,135,174
Robert.............111,124,132

VINCENT: (Vinson?)

George.....................169

VINSON: (Vincent?)

Isaac......................120

WAILES:

William........191,193,200,201
William H.150,154,158,159,167,
              170,176,182,184,198

WAINRIGHT:

Ann F.D....111,150,152,161,180
Edward J.C....111,117,133,150,
              152,161,180,201
George H...............177,182
Jesse H............150,159,160
Levin..............111,177,182
Nancy F.D..........117,133,152
Rosanna....................161
Rosanna A.W....111,117,122,133
Rosanna E.M.J.111,117,133,150,
              152,161,180,201
Ware...................177,182

WALKER:

John.......................125
Joseph.................125,181
Priscilla..102,105,121,160,174
Robert T...............148,199
Thomas.................128,130

WALLACE:

Betsy......................122
Milcah A...................122

WALLER:

Alexander..108,121,132,149,157,
              175,196,201
Ebenezer M.........124,135,143
Elizabeth......105,124,135,143
George.102,104,105,124,135,141,
              148,170,198
George B...........114,147,207
James G....................105
James L....................106
Mary E.............124,135,143
Nelson.....................169
Richard.102,191,192,193,200,201
Wilhelmina..108,121,132,149,157
William............124,135,143
William L..............102.103

WALLS:

George.............181,185,186
Nancy......................181

WALSTON:

David......................203
Leah.......................163
Leah J.........136,164,167,207
Leah J.W...................134
Nehemiah....185,186,197,201,210
Thomas H...........185,186,210
William........126,127,134,164
William E..................136

WALTER:

Ann M.D............108,120,129
Biddy..........138,142,157,201
George..110,138,142,157,161,188
George A C.................161
George D.......133,155,208,210
George L.R.....108,120,129,188
George R...................196
Hetty A....................201
James..............108,128,134
Jesse..115,127,138,142,145,151,
        157,172,174,176,187,188,196
John..................106,122
              (cont.)

(Walter Cont.)

Levin......112,136,187,188,208
Margaret....................201
Mary........................201
Olivia......................157
Priscilla...................201
Robert.119,120,128,131,201,204
Samuel......................111
Sarah.............108,120,129
Thomas.136,155,161,168,176,183

WARD:

Benjamin...............101,120
Elisha......................179
George F...101,111,123,165,166
Henry.156,160,168,179,182,192,
                             203
John...170,173,176,177,178,179
Noah........................179
Stephen............101,111,123
Thomas.............170,178,179
William.....................179

WARWICK:

Josiah......................163
William R...................202

WATERS:

Ann E.E...........157,171,203
Arnold E..........113,176,203
Eliza R.W.141,142,144,151,157,
                 171,174,203
Elizabeth A.................110
Elizabeth A.W...............147
James.......................110
John..........114,132,159,160
Levin L...113,141,142,151,157,
                 171,174,176,203
Louisa......................110
Mrs.........................178
Robert C.J............186,187
Susanna.......124,134,139,182
William E.............110,147
William H...................118
William M...................109

WEATHERLY:

Edmond............ 153,169,175

Edward......................140
Jacob J................153,156
James.............164,170,193
Joseph.140,147,153,159,164,167,
                     169,175
Lee P.................114,140
Peregrine..108,115,121,124,140,
                     149,168
Peter D............164,170,193
Sarah E.....................168
Susan L.....................168
William...............114,175
William H.........140,153,169

WEBSTER:

Berry T.T...................108
Elizabeth...................108
Gabriel.....................201
Henry A.P...................108
Sophia A.M..................108

WHAYLAND:

William....105,107,108,128,134,
      136,140,152,163,169,175,183,
      184,185,188,191,194,197,198

WHITE:

Alce (Alcy).........115,116,124
Alice.......................181
Ann.........................203
Beauchamp (Beaucham)...133,183,
                 187,188,200
Biddy.............133,135,136
David..........115,138,162,196
Elijah............133,183,185
Gowan..........133,135,136,146
Henry..109,115,116,123,124,126,
                 142,179,181,191,196
Henry A.....................148
Isaac..........183,185,187,188

Isaac W.....................200
John........................133
Polly..................188,200
Sally N.....109,123,142,180,201
Samuel......................159
Sarah.................117,118
Thomas........115,162,196,203
William........115,138,162,196
William T......109,123,142,180

WHITELOCK:

Eleanor H...................195
Elisha E................116,195

WHITNEY:

Daniel......................102
Sarah.......................179

WHITTINGTON:

John N..................129,149
Southy..................151,152
William C...............151,152
William H...........121,205,208

WILEY:

John........................178

WILKINS:

Martha......................143
Seth................107,143,144

WILLIAMS:

Arietta.................120,122
Elijah..................147,169
John...........198,206,210,212
Levin......120,122,136,141,160
Nathaniel...................161
Samuel....106,115,125,126,198,
                    106,210,212
Sarah A.....................160
Thomas......................101
Underwood...............147,150
William...101,103,104,107,109,
    110,111,112,116,117,118,119,
                    183,210,212

WILLIN (See Willing)

WILLING:

Biddy..........193,199,204,209
George M..104,107,109,110,127,
    129,134,136,152,157,158,160,
    162,164,165,166,167,171,175,
                            178
Matthias E..................152
Tubman.........193,199,204,209

Ware....................108,110
William.....................211
William J.L.................206

WILSON:

E.K.....................119,148
Edward......................213
Elizabeth...............203,208
Ephraim K.......101,103,112,117
Esther A....................211
George..............105,123,132
Harriet.....................211
Henry P.C...113,114,125,139,162
James..105,106,110,111,112,113,
    123,132,135,140,143,145,149,
    151,163,164,174,179,191,196,
    198,201,202,206,210,214
John................127,168,212
John C.113,114,125,139,140,151,
                    162,174,195
Lemuel D....................213
Levin..135,142,158,164,165,168,
    169,173,180,181,188,207,210,
                            211
Levin M.....................211
Levin P.....................213
Margaret E.T................213
Mary........................211
Mary A......................213
Mary S..................203,204
Matthias....................211
Mitchell................208,211
Nancy..........139,169,181,210
Sally.......................113
Sarah A.....................213
Sarah P.................211,213
Thomas..................208,211
William....104,140,166,169,203,
                        208,211
William H...................213

WINDSOR:

Joseph......142,157,159,164,167

WISE:

Edward M................117,132
George K................117,184
William W...........117,124,141

WOOD:

William T.114,119,121,131,139,
        157,159,169,180,193,200

WOOLFORD:

George H....................196
George L.H.....126,158,210,211
Levin H....................148

WRIGHT:

Willing.............128,130,162

ZIEBER:

John S..................191,198

FREE NEGROES WITH SURNAMES

GUNBY:

John......................168

JAMES:

Alfred....................204

FREE NEGROES WITHOUT SURNAMES

Durham......................166
Steve.......................166

SLAVES WITH SURNAMES

CHASE:

Sam.....................154,163

JAMES:

William....................153

INDEX TO SLAVES

Aaron...205	Levin...106,177
Abraham...168	Littleton...154,163
Adam...125,139	Lot...191
Amelia...114,178	Luckey...176
Ann...154	Lucretia...154
Banda...125	Lydda...154
Ben...178	Major...119
Betsy...142	Mary...182,205,206
Biddy...123	Mary A...191
Bridgett...181	Meda...152
Candis...110	Messen (Messer)...154
Charles...203,213	Metilda...154
Charlotte...168,182	Milly...124
Cipio...168	Nancy...178,186
Cloe...154	Nanny...187
Cyrus...161	Nathan...124
Daniel...113,114	Nehemiah...147
David...153,154,169,178	Nelly...119
Denwood...116	Parmen...113
Eben...137	Peggy...142
Edmund...137	Perry...178
Elbert...180	Philip...154
Elijah...110	Phillis...178,179
Frank...146	Polly...142
George...112,169,202	Priscilla...140,154
Gideon...154	Rachel...154
Hannah...171,176	Reuben...182
Harriet...125,165	Richard...178
Henny...119	Robert...182
Henry...139,162	Rose...188
Isaac.130,143,152,161,186,192, 197	Sally...121,147
	Sam...103,119,149,186
Ishmael...208	Sandy...102,161
Jack...143	Sarah...112,131,137,142,165,178
Jacob...188	Sarah A...154
James..119,123,137,191,201,206	Shadrach...123
Jeremy...204	Sophia...119
Jesse...187	Spencer...178
Jim...104	Stephen...125,137
Joe...154	Tamar...161
John...109,110,167,178,180	Thomas...206
Joseph...178	Tina...178
Joshua...135	Titus...130
Kessey...178	Tom...137,163,179,201
Lazarus...161	Tubman...166
Leah...110	Violet...212
Levi...178	Washington...154
	Whitty...119
	William...152,181

www.ingramcontent.com/pod-product-compliance
Lightning Source LLC
Chambersburg PA
CBHW071707160426
43195CB00012B/1601